Community Engagement after Christendom

AFTER CHRISTENDOM *Series*

Christendom was a historical era, a geographical region, a political arrangement, a sacral culture, and an ideology. For many centuries Europeans have lived in a society that was nominally Christian. Church and state have been the pillars of a remarkable civilization that can be traced back to the decision of the Emperor Constantine I early in the fourth century to replace paganism with Christianity as the imperial religion.

Christendom, a brilliant but brutal culture, flourished in the Middle Ages, fragmented in the Reformation of the sixteenth century, but persisted despite the onslaught of modernity. While exporting its values and practices to other parts of the world, however, it has been slowly declining during the past three centuries. In the twenty-first century Christendom is unravelling.

What will emerge from the demise of Christendom is not yet clear, but we can now describe much of Western culture as "post-Christendom." *Post-Christendom is the culture that emerges as the Christian faith loses coherence within a society that has been definitively shaped by the Christian story and as the institutions that have been developed to express Christian convictions decline in influence.*

This definition, proposed and unpacked in *Post-Christendom*, the first book in the After Christendom series, has gained widespread acceptance. *Post-Christendom* investigated the Christendom legacy and raised numerous issues that are explored in the rest of the series. The authors of this series, who write from within the Anabaptist tradition, see the current challenges facing the church not as the loss of a golden age but as opportunities to recover a more biblical and more Christian way of being God's people in God's world.

The series addresses a wide range of issues, including theology, social and political engagement, how we read Scripture, youth work, mission, worship, relationships, and the shape and ethos of the church after Christendom.

Eleven books were published by Paternoster between 2004 and 2016:

Stuart Murray, *Post-Christendom*

Stuart Murray, *Church after Christendom*

Jonathan Bartley, *Faith and Politics after Christendom*

Jo Pimlott and Nigel Pimlott, *Youth Work after Christendom*

Alan Kreider and Eleanor Kreider, *Worship and Mission after Christendom*

Lloyd Pietersen, *Reading the Bible after Christendom*

Andrew Francis, *Hospitality and Community after Christendom*

Fran Porter, *Women and Men after Christendom*

Simon Perry, *Atheism after Christendom*

Brian Haymes and Kyle Gingerich Hiebert, *God after Christendom?*

Jeremy Thomson, *Relationships and Emotions after Christendom*

Two of these (*Worship and Mission after Christendom* and *Reading the Bible after Christendom*) were also published by Herald Press.

The series is now in the hands of Cascade Books, which is republishing some of the existing titles, including *Post-Christendom*, and commissioning further titles, including:

Joshua Searle, *Theology after Christendom*

Andy Hardy and Dan Yarnell, *Missional Discipleship after Christendom*

John Heathershaw, *Security after Christendom*

Jeremy Thomson, *Interpreting the Old Testament after Christendom*

These books are not intended to be the last word on the subjects they address, but an invitation to discussion and further exploration. Additional material, including extracts from published books and information about future volumes, can be found at www.anabaptistnetwork.com/AfterChristendom.

Series Editor, Stuart Murray

Community Engagement after Christendom

Douglas G. Hynd

CASCADE *Books* • Eugene, Oregon

COMMUNITY ENGAGEMENT AFTER CHRISTENDOM

After Christendom Series

Copyright © 2022 Douglas G. Hynd. All rights reserved. Except for brief quotations in critical publications or reviews, no part of this book may be reproduced in any manner without prior written permission from the publisher. Write: Permissions, Wipf and Stock Publishers, 199 W. 8th Ave., Suite 3, Eugene, OR 97401.

Cascade Books
An Imprint of Wipf and Stock Publishers
199 W. 8th Ave., Suite 3
Eugene, OR 97401

www.wipfandstock.com

PAPERBACK ISBN: 978-1-7252-5737-5
HARDCOVER ISBN: 978-1-7252-5738-2
EBOOK ISBN: 978-1-7252-5739-9

Cataloguing-in-Publication data:

Names: Hynd, Douglas G., author.

Title: Community engagement after Christendom / Douglas G. Hynd.

Description: Eugene, OR: Cascade Books, 2022 | Series: After Christendom | Includes bibliographical references.

Identifiers: ISBN 978-1-7252-5737-5 (paperback) | ISBN 978-1-7252-5738-2 (hardcover) | ISBN 978-1-7252-5739-9 (ebook)

Subjects: LCSH: Church and the world. | Christianity and culture. | Missions—History—21st century.

Classification: BR481 .H37 2022 (print) | BR481 (ebook)

Scripture quotations are from New Revised Standard Version Bible, copyright © 1989 National Council of the Churches of Christ in the United States of America. Used by permission. All rights reserved worldwide.

DEDICATION

To *Love Makes a Way* as a nonviolent,
prayerful uprising against injustice

The fact that the Bible is still read in our churches makes it at least possible for them to be places where we, who are members of the dominant culture, can find the courage to face our illusions of noble innocence ... places where the Dream can be unmasked, and the vision reclaimed.[1]

—CHED MYERS

[T]he church is called to embody the integration of justice and love (agape) in ever-expanding networks of relationship across national and cultural traditions, caring for those in need whether they are inside or outside the Christian tradition. This understanding of the church maintains a healthy separation from the state, yet goes to the heart of public sociality by giving attention especially to the most vulnerable.[2]

—MARK BRETT

---

1. Myers, *Who Will Roll Away the Stone?*, xxi.
2. Brett, *Political Trauma and Healing*, 5.

Contents

Preface xi
Acknowledgments xiii
Abbreviations xv
Prologue: A Perfect Storm xvii

PART I: *Reading Scripture "Again"*

1: Implicated in the Exercise of Power, While No Longer "In Control" 3

2: Stories Read "Otherwise" 23

3: Teaching and Performing a Different Kingdom 51

4: Exile: Community Engagement in a Shifting Location 69

PART II: *"Anticipating" Community Engagement after Christendom*

5: Pilgram Marpeck:
A Biographical Approach to Community Engagement 85

6: Theologically "Anticipating" Post-Christendom 98

7: Community Engagement after Marpeck 111

PART III: *Community Engagement on the Way Out of Christendom*

8: The Risks of Contracting 127

CONTENTS

9: Advocacy: Challenging Government while Exiting Christendom 154

10: Practicing Hospitality Toward Refugees and Asylum Seekers 180

11: Presence on the Margins 202

Epilogue: Lingering with the Beatitudes 225

Bibliography 243

Preface

My interest in the issues that I explore in this book goes back decades. I was involved in editorial and research work with what was then the Zadok Institute in Canberra on the changing place of Christian churches in Australian society in the 1980s. I subsequently taught as a sessional lecturer in a variety of courses on church and society at St Mark's Theological Institute in Canberra. At this stage the breakdown of the previous privileged, though unestablished, relationship between the Christian churches with government was under way, though the full implications were not yet clear. My encounter with Stuart Murray-Williams's *Post-Christendom: Church and Mission in a Strange New World*, with its Anabaptist perspective, helped me to grasp the significance of what was happening and raised fresh questions about the future of community engagement by the Christian churches.

I also worked for several decades in the Australian Public Service (APS) on issues related to social and indigenous policy, and public sector accountability. While witnessing the policy shift to contracting in Australia in the late 1990s, I began to wonder about the impact on church welfare agencies in the longer term. Would theological and mission commitments be eroded by neoliberal policy, and its accompanying bureaucratic processes? Would agencies be prevented from advocating for the marginal, and the poor? In 2011 after leaving the public service I undertook interview-driven research shaped by these questions. It was a good time to do so. Many church-related agencies and their sponsoring denominations were beginning to critically reflect on questions of identity, and mission under the pressure of contracting. It was clear that they could no longer rely on their previously privileged relationship to government. That research provided the basis for the case studies in Part III.

So much by way of background. I wrote this book against the background of a rolling series of ecological, health, and economic crises. Barely had Australia recovered from an extended period of bushfires and floods, the one usually follows the other in short order, than we were hit by the COVID-19 pandemic. In the middle of supporting communities in crisis arising from the fire and floods, churches and church-related agencies were faced with the task of reinventing themselves as communities of worship and service, while working out how to operate under lockdown. In the background was the longer-term challenge of post-Christendom manifested for the churches in declining political power and reduced moral influence, amplified by the fallout from sexual abuse scandals and cover-ups.

How will the churches respond to this multilayered crisis? Will they hunker down, tighten up on theological creeds, patrol ecclesial boundaries more rigorously, reach for large doses of nostalgia, and devote substantial resources to the attempt to recreate Christendom? Or will they respond to the perfect storm in which they find themselves as a *kairos* moment, an occasion for conversion and transformation, a moment of grace in which they reimagine community engagement as a compassionate presence with those on the margins?

I have written this book to encourage and assist churches, church-related agencies, and community movements for justice to take the path of transformation rather than retrenchment. In pursuing that goal, I have sought to make the theological arguments in the book accessible to those living out their discipleship, not in the academy, but in the tense spaces between church, community, and government.

Acknowledgments

While I may have my name as the sole author on the title page, this has not been a solitary enterprise. Friends, and the networks that they are part of, have been critical in shaping the discussion at varying points.

The idea for this book came out of conversations with my friend Phil Fountain, who suggested that I should look "sideways" at some of the research I had undertaken on the relationship between church-related agencies and government. Could the material be presented in more interesting and relevant ways than would be the case in an academic publication? That was at the heart of the conversation as I remember it. It proved a fruitful question. I also want to thank Phil for encouragement as the book took shape, and for a friendship that has included vigorous discussions on theological issues over the years. I also want to thank Simon Barrow for encouragement, good advice about the structure and contents of the book, as well as for continuing friendship.

I am greatly indebted to Stuart Murray-Williams for looking at a draft of the proposal for this book, gathering comments from the Anabaptist Network in the UK, and recommending it to Cascade Books for inclusion in the After Christendom series. I want to thank Stuart too for the opportunity to share some of the key themes with a meeting of the Anabaptist Theology Forum in the UK, via Zoom, of course. Thanks too to Jeremy Thomson from the forum, who generously made his manuscript on *Interpreting the Old Testament after Christendom* available to me.

In an ecumenical spirit, the Australian Catholic University Higher Degree Research Seminar in Canberra gave me the opportunity to present a paper on the context and contents of the book. The members of the forum, from a wide variety of backgrounds both Christian and non-Christian, engaged in an encouraging way with questions about my proposals for reading Scripture "again." Thanks go to James Cox and Richard Donnelly for friendship, for reading early drafts of some chapters, and for commenting helpfully on them.

Acknowledgments

I have been talking about Pilgram Marpeck at every opportunity that came my way over the past two decades. The material on Marpeck in chapters 5 and 6 substantially draws on my paper *A life of conscientious dissent*, published by Ethos, EA Centre for Christianity and Society, Zadok Papers, S194 Summer 2012.

The case studies in Part III are based in varying degrees on interviews I undertook with managers and board members from church-related agencies in Australia during 2013 and 2014. The interviewees generously gave me permission to publicly attribute to them quotations from the interviews. I thank them for participating reflectively and candidly in interviews that unpacked their agencies' experience of engaging with government in contracting and advocacy in recent years. The interviews were conducted under clearance from the Australian Catholic University Human Research Ethics Committee (Approval 82N 2013). The case study of Doveton Baptist Church in chapter 11 is a rewritten and expanded version of an article originally published in the *Australian Journal of Mission Studies*, 13, no.1, June 2019, "Church Community Engagement in a Struggle Town," 25–31. I want to thank the editor of the AJMS for his permission to use the substantially revised material in this context.

Heartfelt thanks go to my wife, Jillian, for regularly checking that I was staying focused and actually getting on with writing the book, during a strange year when distractions abounded.

Douglas Hynd

Adjunct Research Fellow
Australian Centre for Christianity and Culture, Charles Sturt University
Canberra

Abbreviations

AAANZ	Anabaptist Association of Australia and New Zealand
AAT	Administrative Appeals Tribunal
ABC	Australian Broadcasting Corporation
ACT	Australian Capital Territory
ACRTF	Australian Churches Refugee Task Force
ACOSS	Australian Council of Social Service
AD	Anno Domini
ALP	Australian Labor Party
APESAA	Advisory Panel on Employment Services Administration and Accountability
APS	Australian Public Service
BCE	Before Common Era
BUV	Baptist Union of Victoria
CEO	Chief Executive Officer
CSC	Community Service Centre
CSSA	Catholic Social Services Australia
DBBS	Doveton Baptist Benevolent Society
DBC	Doveton Baptist Church
DETA	Doveton Eumemmerring Township Association
DOGS	Defence of Government Schools

Abbreviations

GFC	Global Financial Crisis
IT	Information Technology
JRSA	Jesuit Refugee Service Australia
JSS	Jesuit Social Services
LMAW	Love Makes a Way
LNP	Liberal National Party
MCP	Major Church Providers
NSW	New South Wales
PNG	Papua New Guinea
SBS	Special Broadcasting Service
SHEV	Safe Haven Enterprise Visa
SRSS	Status Resolution Support Services
TPV	Temporary Protection Visa
UCA	Uniting Church of Australia
UK	United Kingdom
UNHCR	United Nations High Commissioner for Refugees
US	United States

Prologue: A Perfect Storm

The early church's teaching on charity, David Bentley Hart reminds us, "raised the care of widows, orphans, the sick, the imprisoned, and the poor to the level of the highest religious obligation."[1] The duties of the bishop in the third century included taking responsibility for the education of orphans, providing aid to poor widows, and purchasing food and firewood for the destitute. Community engagement in the early church resulted in sacrificial commitment by laity as well as clergy. During the plague in North Africa in the third century Christians cared for the ill and buried the dead, frequently at the expense of their own lives, demonstrating an ethos at odds with the prevailing culture. From the other side of Christendom, Terry Eagleton picks up this theological commitment, suggesting that God is present when the hungry are filled with good things and the rich are sent away empty. Salvation does not come through religion with its apparatus of cult, law, and ritual, and compliance with a moral code. It comes rather through "feeding the hungry, welcoming the immigrants, visiting the sick and protecting the poor, orphaned and widowed from the violence of the rich."[2]

Post-Christendom

With the unwinding of Christendom, churches in the United Kingdom (UK) and its settler colonies no longer have access to political power to the extent that they used to.[3] They are now only one among many groups involved in advocacy, making a claim to speak on behalf of, and for the benefit of, the

---

1. Hart, *Atheist Delusions*, 164.
2. Eagleton, *Reason, Faith and Revolution*, 18–19.
3. Stuart Murray, in *Post-Christendom*, has provided a good historical summary and theological reading of the far-reaching nature of this change.

Prologue: A Perfect Storm

community.⁴ Many Christians, though, are not yet ready to face the reality of this shift. Somehow, they feel the churches' position of privilege and entitlement was taken away while they weren't looking. Resentment and angst about the loss of privilege, targeted at those deemed to be responsible for this outcome, are widespread in the churches.

The shift beyond Christendom is not finished yet. That's an important reality whose consequences need to be faced, both by those who are in grief at this process, and for those who are enthusiastic about getting beyond Christendom. For those grieving, there is more grief still to come. For those enthusiastic at the prospect of reshaping the churches' community engagement, the enthusiasm needs to be tempered by the reality of what policy analysts call "path dependency." We carry our history with us, and don't get to start with a clean slate. That's why in addition to the terminology of "after Christendom" and "post-Christendom," I will use phrases such as "emerging from Christendom," "on the way out of Christendom," and "the transition from Christendom." The terminology of transition signals that while we can work toward new forms and patterns of engagement, many of the assumptions and images that we will be working with are themselves a legacy of Christendom. If we don't recognize that we are carrying that mental baggage with us we risk subtly reinscribing new forms of Christendom, at the same time as we suppose we are exiting from that historical pattern of engagement.

We are not going to escape from the historical legacy of Christendom quickly or easily. As we have found in recent years, there always seems to be something more emerging from that entangled history that needs to be exposed to the light of the gospel. The role that the settler churches in the colonies played in the European invasion and the dispossession of the First Nations peoples in Australia still awaits a substantive reckoning. Christian churches have yet to fully acknowledge the consequences of that invasion, and the extent to which they have benefited economically and politically from the colonial project over the past two centuries. The inheritance of the churches from the invasion in terms of land and wealth remains, even though the historical Christendom relationship is unwinding. Colonialism is an example of how the historical legacy of Christendom remains to be dealt with even though the structural underpinning of Christendom is being dismantled. I leave this paragraph as a discomforting reminder of a further important agenda awaiting our attention.⁵

4. Murray, *Post-Christendom*, 132–60.

5. For a guide to the literature, and a sketch of the theological issues awaiting attention from an Anabaptist perspective, see Murray-Williams, "Post-Christendom and Post-Colonialism."

Prologue: A Perfect Storm
Why secularization is not quite relevant

Much of the recent debate of the Christian churches and their future has been framed in sociological terms under the heading of secularization. What is the relationship of post-Christendom to secularization, de-secularization, and the suggestion that societies are becoming post-Christian? Through much of the twentieth century advocates of secularization suggested that the Christian churches were in a state of decline under the pressures of modernity. They were confident that the churches would become increasingly irrelevant to politics and public policy. Christianity would survive as an individual consumer choice, "spirituality to go." The trajectory of secularization as a sociological process turned out to be much more complicated and the outcomes equivocal. The conclusion of many sociologists is that we need to avoid reaching into our intellectual toolbox for one-directional, historically inevitable sociological processes when we come to analyzing the impact of modernity on Christian identity and mission.

There are other ways we can visualize the movement of the sacred and the secular, and how they relate to the social and political changes that are going on. The political theologian William Cavanaugh for example has used the metaphor of the migration of the sacred from the sphere of church across to the realm of the state.[6] The historian Eugene McCarraher has identified the continuing presence of the sacred in his narration of the continuing re-emergence of enchantment in the supposedly secular world of business in the US over the past few centuries.[7] The work of both Cavanaugh and McCarraher suggests that we should work with the possibility that the sacred may become secular, and the secular transmogrify into the sacred. Similarly, we should imagine institutional and social boundaries as being porous rather than a rigid channel through which the secular rushes down in full flood to sweep the sacred away.

I have also avoided the use of the terminology of "post-Christian." I regard the term as problematic as a way of viewing the relationship between the church and contemporary society. This is not least the case because Christianity is still present in the "unthought," those taken for granted assumptions we bring to bear in framing our ethical and political debates, shared by both Christians and non-Christians alike. The historian Tom Holland has recently documented how the Christian church and its Scriptures have shaped European culture, and how that influence has remained operative in public debate even if its presence is not always recognized, and this

---

6. McCarraher, *The Enchantments of Mammon*.
7. Cavanaugh, *Migrations of the Holy*.

despite the move beyond Christendom. Secularist critiques of Christianity's public failures, in Holland's view, are driven by moral assumptions that when examined prove to be deeply rooted in Christianity. "[I]n a West that is often doubtful of religion's claims, so many of its instincts remain—for good or ill—thoroughly Christian."[8] The notion that we live in a secularized world that is free of myth and the sacred either misses or misreads a good deal of what is going on.

The deconstruction of Christendom has a long history. Protestant sects in both the UK and the US, from the seventeenth century onward, had sought to undermine Christendom as expressed in the structure of establishment in the UK through their respective struggles for religious freedom. The missionary movement of the nineteenth century, in its periodically tense relationship with the colonial powers, exposed the limitations of Christendom as an exportable model. The questions that began to be raised then about the injustice and dispossession resulting from invasion, are only now receiving some serious attention by the churches in the former colonies. Western Christianity, Jason Goroncy observes, "has not heeded the words of the Hebrew prophets to be a sanctuary unescorted by borders or bullets. Nor has it placed much store in the warning carried in the words 'crucified under Pontius Pilate.' Instead, it has been made inebriated by quaffing from the same wells of imperialism that created the empires of Egypt, Assyria and the United States."[9]

The scope of the book

The past century has seen the United Kingdom (UK), New Zealand, Australia, and Canada transitioning, on varied trajectories, away from the Christendom framework. Whether the United States (US) is most helpfully analyzed using the post-Christendom framework is a matter of some controversy. In some regions of the US, particularly the Midwest and the South, the perceived decline of Christian cultural and political hegemony in the nation is generating patterns of angst clearly tied in important ways to issues of racial identity among white evangelicals. White evangelical efforts to sustain their political and cultural power was manifested in the intense support this group gave to Donald Trump in the 2016 and 2020 elections, though the roots of this development go back to the switch of evangelicals to support for Republicans as far back as Ronald Reagan. Many evangelicals are afraid that a deep-rooted historical settlement is breaking up and have

8. Holland, *Dominion*, xxix.
9. Goroncy, "Race and Christianity in Australia," 52.

PROLOGUE: A PERFECT STORM

seen Trump as the key to resisting that break-up through control over appointments to the judicial system. White evangelicals were prepared to lock in their support for Trump despite his notorious disregard for ethical norms and patterns of personal morality that had previously been issues of first-order moral concern for them.

How do we interpret these developments in the US? Does the current conflict point to a struggle to ensure the continuing survival of Christendom in the US, or does it confirm that the conflict is about a transition to post-Christendom that is already well underway? I am inclined to agree with Jason Mahn when he argues that Christians in the US are still living "in a dominant culture that presumes to be Christian or where Christianity still remains the cultural norm."[10] In his view, the culture of the US idealizes and privileges the Christian tradition while simultaneously relativizing it, making it redundant and innocuous. Qualifying and complicating this assessment is the parallel reality that the Black prophetic church has always been in great tension with government in the US.[11]

A postcolonial world

While I have limited my discussion of community engagement in post-Christendom in this book to the UK and its settler colonies, hopefully future discussion will be able to draw on contributions from Christians in countries such as China, India, Vietnam, and Indonesia. Christian communities in these nations currently face pressing issues about the shape of their community engagement. Facing as they do varying degrees of government hostility, Christendom with its assumptions of a closely connected relationship of the church to the state and of Christian cultural hegemony is not going to provide them with much help either theologically or pastorally. Though the political circumstances in these nations are much more difficult than in the settler colonies that are the focus of my discussion, I hope that my suggestions for reading Scripture and my account of the Anabaptist approach to community engagement may be helpful.

The situation in Oceania, and much of Africa south of the Sahara for that matter, is quite different again. Here Christianity, while transmitted as part of the colonial project, became detached from that heritage during the drive for independence. Christianity is now inextricably intertwined with the achievement of independence, national identity, and a relatively stable political order. Across Oceania "Christianity is the ground and starting

10. Mahn, *Becoming a Christian in Christendom*, x.
11. Goza, *America's Unholy Ghosts*, 153–82.

point of political action. . . . Across the region Christianity and politics have redefined each other in ways that make the two categories inseparable at any level of analysis."[12]

Sexual abuse, institutional self-preservation, and exiting Christendom

Lament by Christians in response to the emerging reality of post-Christendom in Australia has extended along a spectrum from doom-laden invocations of the imminent arrival of the four horsemen of the apocalypse, to a grouchy, stoic muttering of "we'll all be ruined." Then came the flood of public revelations of child sexual abuse by clergy, and of cover-ups by churches. Much of the churches' moral standing and authority previously taken for granted despite the post-Christendom shift was suddenly and irrevocably shredded.[13]

The stories of sexual abuse were shocking. What was more shocking, if that were possible, were the accounts of the lack of regard for victims displayed by church leadership, and institutional management when the abuse was reported to them. Compassion by churches for victims of abuse proved to have been in very short supply, with advice from lawyers to church leadership focusing solely on institutional survival and the management of reputational preservation. Paradoxically, attempts to manage reputational damage almost uniformly only increased that damage when news of it became public.

I can remember listening in a state of deep distress to the daily current affairs account of testimony at the Royal Commission hearings. The yawning gap between the practice and teaching of Jesus, and the behavior of church leaders in putting institutional interests ahead of the claims for justice of the victims of abuse, didn't need to be spelled out to those outside the church. The public were quick to comment publicly and vocally on this contradiction. Churches and their leadership are now facing a loss of trust across the community for reasons that will be long remembered. The pain of betrayal by the churches during this episode has been felt not only by the victims and their families, but also by many of the church's most deeply committed members.

Against the charge of hypocrisy arising from the wide gap between their teaching and practice, the churches have no defense. It is of no use to

12. Tomlinson and McDougall, *Christian Politics in Oceania*, 2.

13. For a comprehensive account of child sexual abuse in Australia and the failure of institutions including the churches, see Royal Commission, *Final Report*.

Prologue: A Perfect Storm

have church leaders pointing out that other significant community institutions, whether they be schools, police, child protection departments of state governments, the Scouts, and other organizations were also involved in egregious cover-ups, driven by motives of institutional and reputational self-preservation. That other agencies performed just as badly as the churches does not cut any ice. Churches more than ever before are being judged against the standards announced and lived out by Jesus in the Gospels.[14]

The shaming circumstances under which the social status and inherited moral prestige of the Christian churches was stripped away has supercharged their difficulties in their attempt to re-envision their life and mission after Christendom. The difficulties that the churches are having with this seismic shift is evident in the public commentary of church leaders on just about any issue. Almost without exception, they manifest an undertone of defensiveness and resentment, modulated through an unacknowledged grief at the loss of power and status. If they cannot get beyond this soon, there is a real risk that they will remain stuck in a self-reinforcing spiral, leading to cultural and social isolation. A toxic mixture of nostalgia, anger, and fear driving church engagement with the community is precisely what we don't need in a context in which the settings for economic, social, and environmental change are all being dialed up to maximum levels. That's the situation in Australia. Nothing that I have read and heard suggests that the situation of the churches in the other English-speaking nations is radically different.

The Anglican lawyer and theologian William Stringfellow identified the demonic character of the drive for institutional self-preservation by the church with a theological clarity that is hard to evade.[15] The churches seem to have rarely engaged with the theological dynamics that he identified. On this Dietrich Bonhoeffer has something important to say to us. Writing from a prison cell in Berlin in 1943, having already surrendered his own reputation, both within and outside the church, being labeled an enemy of the state, he observed that the church in Germany under the Nazi regime had not stood up for the victims of oppression and violence.

> Our church has been fighting during these years only for its self-preservation, as if that were an end in itself. It has become incapable of taking the word of reconciliation and redemption to humankind and to the world. So, the words we have used before must lose their power, be silenced and we can be Christians today in only two ways, through prayer and in doing justice

14. Sullivan, "Margin Call."
15. Stringfellow, *Free in Obedience*, 95–99.

among human beings. All Christian thinking, talking and organizing must be born anew out of that prayer and action.[16]

In response to a church that had given priority to its self-preservation, ahead of concern for the vulnerable, Bonhoeffer called for a time of public silence, accompanied by prayer, and faithful action for justice. In the spirit of Bonhoeffer's advice, I advance a "modest" proposal: that for the next decade Christian churches refrain from public advocacy on any policy issue directly related to their own institutional interests. This disciplined and deliberate silence should be accompanied by careful, patient listening to those who are without a voice, to those whom the church has damaged and abused. This listening should inform communal reflection by the churches on what they hear, and what it means for their life and community engagement.

This self-denying ordinance is not meant to apply to the church's participation in public debate on issues of social policy and community well-being. Far from it. The churches should continue to advocate for those in greatest need, those who do not have a voice, giving priority to the empowerment of those who are on the margins. Even better would be to provide them with the support and resources to enable them to speak for themselves. The church's contribution to public debate on behalf of others will need to carry an acknowledgment in the tone of our contribution, as well as the content, of our shared complicity in the brokenness of the world that we are seeking to repair.

Choosing terms

Finding a phrase to signal the scope of the book wasn't easy. After changing my mind several times, I ended up sticking with the term "community engagement," largely because it is loose and sprawling in its resonance and reference, and for that reason may be less misleading than any of the alternatives. But what do I mean by "community engagement"? For Christians community engagement starts with the call to love our neighbor and extends outward from there. Love for neighbor, directed at human and community flourishing, can include political involvement, advocacy, working in the public or civil service, exercising social responsibility through the voluntary sector, and church-related agencies, and even perhaps (?) contracting with government in providing human services and social welfare.[17]

---

16. Bonhoeffer, *Letters and Papers from Prison*, 389.
17. Bartley, *Faith and Politics after Christendom*, 5–7.

Prologue: A Perfect Storm

In countries that are undergoing the shift beyond Christendom there are still extensive and diverse forms of community engagement being undertaken by the churches. Beyond activities sponsored by individual congregations and denominations, there is the contribution of organizations with a Christian affiliation but without a connection to a congregation or denomination. There are also groups involved in community service that do not label themselves as having a Christian identity but have significant Christian connections and involvement.

The legal, institutional, and denominational differences even between countries that share a common political and religious heritage make it difficult to find a consistent and shared terminology. I have used the terminology of "church-related agencies" to refer to agencies that claim some connection to Christianity and its traditions, whether or not they are directly affiliated to a specific congregation or denomination. The diversity of governance structures for community service agencies between denominations, even within a single nation, let alone across national boundaries, makes a catchall term such as this necessary. On those occasions when I am discussing agencies, at a sector level, that are not structured by either market incentives or under the direct control of government, I have chosen to use the term "nonprofit."

Those readers who are familiar with the literature on this topic may wonder why I have not used the terminology of "faith-based," "religious," and "secular" in referring to community engagement by churches. Though this terminology is by now endemic, I have resisted using it for a variety of reasons. The first is theological. To talk of "faith-based" agencies smuggles into the discussion substantive Protestant theological and ecclesial commitments. The second reason is sociological. Questions of identity and mission are central to all nonprofit social welfare agencies, whether related to the church or not. Attempting to distinguish between agencies using the "secular" and "religious" binary obscures this common element. The literature of organizational sociology suggests the need to pay attention to an agency's identity, as shaped by its founding vision, ethical basis and governance, and its evolving relationship to its founding vision.

On language relating ecclesiology, I have used the term "Christian movement" when I referred to Christianity in its most comprehensive and ecumenical form, including churches, their agencies, related institutions, and grassroots social movements. I have limited my use of the term "church" in the singular to where I am making a theological claim or reference. I use the term "churches" in the plural to refer to the church in its actual diversity and empirical reality.

PROLOGUE: A PERFECT STORM

The structure of the book

Having laid out the historical and sociological context against which the book has been written, I now turn to a sketch of the journey that lies in front of you. I have not attempted to provide a comprehensive guide to community engagement after Christendom. I have rather taken three different approaches to community engagement after Christendom that will help us take our ambiguous context seriously and free up our imagination from the heritage of Christendom.

Part I: On reading Scripture "again"

In Part I, I explore the task of reading Scripture "again." Our reading of Scripture after Christendom is taking place in a new context. Churches and church-related agencies are no longer "in control," but are still implicated in various ways and to varying degrees in the exercise of political and social power. They are carrying a theological and scriptural imagination still shaped by Christendom. So, I begin in chapter 1 with the theme "Implicated in the Exercise of power, While No Longer 'In Control'" as the context for reading Scripture "again."

But what do I mean by the term "in control"? Churches in their Christendom-shaped relationship with government had access to diverse levels of power and influence. In referring to a location of being "in control," I am not suggesting that their access to power was always at the upper end of the spectrum. The terminology of "in control" is a shorthand for this historical connection. I also use it to refer to a Christendom mindset that is still being carried forward by many churches.

In discussing the question of reading Scripture in the context, I start with the Anabaptist movement. The interruption by the Anabaptists of the relationship between the church and the political order in the sixteenth century as a result of reading Scripture "again" provides insight into some of the issues at stake in such reading. I then draw attention to a tradition of Christian radicalism and provide examples of reading the Scripture against the grain of Christendom, suggesting an imaginative engagement with Scripture, rather than looking for biblical principles, or theological models.

In chapter 2, "Stories Read 'Otherwise,'" I turn to the First Testament (Old Testament).[18] I revisit the stories of Joseph, Esther, and Daniel, read as

---

18. Throughout the book I use the terminology of "First Testament (Old Testament)" and "Second Testament (New Testament)." While the traditional terminology of Old Testament and New Testament is unsatisfactory in its supersessionist framing

narratives and provocations that offer opportunities for challenging readings shaped by Christendom and offer interpretations that are "otherwise" to the ones that have often been taught to us. These are accounts of people who were in positions of power without being "in control." What can we learn from these stories about the risks and possibilities of faithfulness in such contexts, the nature and desirability of political success, and the limits of what can be achieved in exercising power in imperial contexts? As a bridge to the next chapter I conclude by exploring the critical stance towards the monarchy in Israel's approach to kingship, informed by the prophet Samuel's critical response to Israel's call for a king.

The Second Testament (New Testament) was also written in a time of empire and bears the marks of that context, though we have often not stopped to think about the implications of that location for the way we read it. In chapter 3, "Teaching and Performing a Different Kingdom," I draw attention to accounts by the Gospel writers of Jesus' ministry, teaching, and performance of the "kingdom of God."

In chapter 4, "Exile: Community Engagement in a Shifting Location," I take up the theme of exile as a location that shifted its meaning and significance for community engagement over time. I start with Jeremiah's letter to the exiles in Babylon and explore the development and nuancing of that theme through the Second Testament (New Testament) and the early church. Thinking about this shifting location in the scriptural accounts of exile helps us pay attention to the tensions of community engagement in undertaking prophetic critique of political power, seeking the flourishing of the city, caring for strangers, and undertaking the administration of the empire, all this in finding our identity as resident aliens and sojourners.

Part II: "Anticipating" a post-Christendom community engagement

I turn in Part II to Anabaptist history and theology. Here I narrate the biography and discuss the theology of Pilgram Marpeck, an Anabaptist public servant, and t explore their relevance to engagement in a pluralist political order. In chapter 5, "Pilgram Marpeck: A Biographical Account of Anabaptist Community Engagement," I trace the life and ministry of Marpeck, a sixteenth-century Anabaptist whose work as a public servant and theology challenges the stereotype of Anabaptism as a stance of withdrawal from the

---

of their relationship, there is not widespread agreement in the Christian community on an alternative terminology. I have chosen this somewhat laborious labeling to assist those reading the book who are not familiar with the theological debates on this topic.

community. In chapter 6, "Theologically 'Anticipating' Post-Christendom," I explore Marpeck's theological arguments on community engagement, and suggest that he anticipates in an interesting way a post-Christendom context. I take up Marpeck's critique of Christendom in chapter 7, "Community Engagement after Marpeck," and explore how his theological argument relates to current Mennonite theology on the relationship between the Christian church and government, while noting its contemporary relevance for Christian churches and church-related agencies in Australia.

Part III: Community engagement on the way out of Christendom

In Part III, I provide some accounts of church and church-related agencies' experience in community engagement in Australia over recent decades, for insights into how these agencies are negotiating post-Christendom, shaped as it is by a neoliberal contracting policy environment. The Australian context may be strange to readers in other Anglophone countries. The provocation of bringing the transition beyond Christendom in Australia to the attention of readers in different national contexts may help them to look at their own experience of post-Christendom in a fresh light, and think about the possibility that a relationship that you have taken for granted as being necessarily the way things are turns out to be quite contingent.

In presenting these stories of community engagement, I have organized them using the themes of risk, advocacy, hospitality, and presence. Nearly half of the stories I tell in this section of the book are about involvement by churches, and church-related agencies, with refugees and asylum seekers. This focus wasn't part of my original plan for the book. As I progressed with the writing a couple of factors worked in tandem to bring about this result. The first was my own involvement over the past two decades in community support and policy advocacy for refugees and asylum seekers. The second was that as governments were taking an increasingly hostile approach to refugees, churches and their agencies because of their transnational connections and theological commitments were finding themselves at odds with government policy.

The role of neoliberalism in driving the shift to contracting has had an important influence in shaping community engagement by churches and their agencies in recent decades.[19] I explore the risks that contracting raises for church-related agencies in chapter 8. I show how contracting with

19. On neoliberalism and the church, see Hargaden, *Theological Ethics in a Neoliberal Age*, and Hynd, "The Impact of Neo-liberalism."

Prologue: A Perfect Storm

government, in both its sacral and bureaucratic modes of operation, can lead church-related agencies into becoming an extension of the state, losing their fundamental theological and ecclesial identity. I draw attention to the value of theological reflection in decision-making processes by agencies on whether and how to engage in community service.

In the remaining three chapters I present approaches to community engagement as forms of practice that can contribute to human flourishing. I start in chapter 9, "Advocacy: Challenging Government while Exiting Christendom," exploring how a particular form of advocacy became possible in an unexpected way following the introduction by government of contracting with church-related agencies. My account illustrates how relationships of trust, friendship, and shared commitments across church-related national coordinating agencies worked to support advocacy against the grain of a neoliberal-contracting environment. In contrast, the story of Love Makes a Way (LMAW) documents a confrontational form of advocacy shaped by a commitment to patient nonviolence and Christian worship, that led to church leaders being arrested in advocating for the claims of the most vulnerable—children of asylum seekers.

In chapter 10, "Practicing Hospitality Toward Refugees and Asylum Seekers," I direct our attention to the exercise of hospitality by church agencies undertaken against the grain of a government policy based on creating fear of refugees and asylum seekers. Here community engagement has been undertaken in conscious opposition to government policy that has demonized asylum seekers. I explore various ways hospitality towards refugees has been provided by church-related agencies in Australia independent of government funding.

I illustrate the theme of chapter 11, "Presence on the Margins," with two case studies of agencies closely connected to local church communities. The Wayside Chapel, a parish mission of the Uniting Church in the inner city of Sydney, is committed to developing a community in which there is no division between "us and them," expressed in a vision of love over hate. Doveton Baptist Church is a small, struggling Baptist congregation located on the economic and social margins of Melbourne. Its congregation is comprised of residents who make their limited resources available to provide space and support to sustain the flourishing of the life of those they live with. I conclude with an Epilogue, "Lingering with the Beatitudes," that reads the Beatitudes as a call to shape our community engagement as a patient presence in the transition beyond Christendom.

Throughout the book I have directed my attention to the Christian movement's approach to community engagement. I have not attempted to

Prologue: A Perfect Storm

provide detailed guidance, but rather have sought to free up the imagination of Christians in approaching this critical dimension of their discipleship.

Part I

Reading Scripture "Again"

1

Implicated in the Exercise of Power, While No Longer "In Control"

Liberation and feminist theologians have been forcefully drawing our attention to the impact of our social and political location on our reading of Scripture, in shaping the presumptions we bring to the reading, and the questions we ask. The more reflective reading of Scripture they are calling for takes account of contexts of vulnerability whether they be sexual, social, or political. The temptation in appropriating this insight for the purposes at hand is to lean into an unqualified binary approach in which you are, for example, either in a position of power, or you're not. This approach to acknowledging our social and political location lacks nuance. Many who are reading this book are likely to be, along with the author, because of our education and employment experience, in a position to exercise some degree of power and influence, even if it is limited.

This idea of a gradient in access to power is relevant to mapping the location of the churches after Christendom. Though churches are no longer able to command power and influence in the way they used to, and while sliding further down the slope because of the sexual abuse scandals, they are not completely powerless. They are in an "in-between" location, not "in control" but still implicated to some degree in the exercise of political and social power, and its outcomes. That's the location from which I am suggesting those of us connected with and committed to the church should be reading Scripture.

I start this chapter by discussing what is involved in reading Scripture "again" from this location, exploring examples of reading Scripture outside of a location of power, over against Christendom. I begin with the Anabaptists, followed by examples of other readers of Scripture from outside

Christendom. In my account of reading Scripture "again," I highlight the importance of undertaking a dialogical and reflective approach that works toward helping the Christian movement to reimagine community engagement beyond Christendom.

What are we doing when we read scripture "again"?

In suggesting that we read Scripture "again," I am not proposing something strange or novel. As individuals and congregations we are constantly, though not always consciously, involved in rereading and reinterpreting Scripture. In paying attention to the preaching of the Word week by week we are offered insights by the preacher hopefully derived from their rereading of Scripture. New commentaries on Scripture, shaped by questions about colonial power and racist politics, show up regularly in Christian bookshops.

Such a rereading acknowledges the possibility of hearing a fresh word from God addressed to us in our contemporary location.[1] Paul the Apostle resisted any absolutist controlling approach to Scripture. "The letter kills but the Spirit gives life" (2 Cor 3:6). Nobody's reading can be final, as the "Character," as Brueggemann puts it, with whom we are engaging in reading Scripture "again" is always beyond us, and beyond our control.[2] Each reading is inescapably provisional, and we need to be ready to be surprised by what we learn.

We should expect that any reading undertaken in the cause of faithful discipleship will call for a response from us. Samuel Wells reminds us that the "test of which readings prove fruitful simply emerges through the experience, wisdom and grace of the Spirit working in the church over time. There is no short cut to a single 'correct' reading, nor any guarantee that there can be a reading that has found everything the text offers to every person in every culture in every time."[3] We are called to read Scripture afresh, as our historical, geographical, and social location, that is, as the culture and politics, as well as the time and place in which we live out our discipleship, changes.

Reading the Scriptures "again" in our current disorienting context is not an artifact of modernity and contemporary culture, and so not a surrender to popular culture. It is an activity with a long history, stretching

---

1. On this topic I acknowledge my debt to Gingerich and Zimmermann, eds., *Telling Our Stories*; Rowland and Roberts, *The Bible for Sinners*; and Brueggemann, *Redescribing Reality*.

2. Brueggemann, "Biblical Authority," 262.

3. Wells, *Power and Passion*, 18.

back through the life of communities that were shaped by wrestling with the Scripture. Brueggemann points to an example of this in the Mosaic teaching in Deuteronomy 23:1–18, that bans from the community those who were identified as being of distorted sexuality and all those who were foreigners. Isaiah 53 in its account of the suffering servant, in a wrestling with God's future for Israel, overturns this judgment. Similarly, Deuteronomy 24:1 teaches that marriage broken by infidelity cannot be restored even if both parties want to do so. Then we come to Jeremiah 3, on which Brueggemann comments:

> God's own voice indicates a readiness to violate Torah teaching for the sake of restored marriage to Israel. . . . The God of Jeremiah's poem willfully overrides the old text. . . . The final form of the text is profoundly polyvalent [and] yields no single exegetical outcome but [allows] layers and layers of fresh reading in which God's own life and character are deeply engaged and put at risk.[4]

Our willingness to read Scripture "again" in new contexts assumes a surplus of meaning in the text, offering the prospect that our existing interpretations will be challenged and new insights emerge. My conviction is that Scripture is able to engage us under the guidance and movement of the Holy Spirit in changing circumstances, enabling us to discern new responses.

The assumptions and images about the relationship of the church to the structures of power inherited from Christendom that we bring with us to our reading of Scripture will continue to shape our reading until we are able to step back, identify them, and reflect critically on their appropriateness for our context. To proceed unreflectively, ignoring changes in our context, closes us off from fresh guidance from the Spirit, and condemns us to ineffectiveness in our engagement in the wider world. In the transition from Christendom, we need to keep in mind that reading "again" will occur primarily, though not exclusively, in the life and activity of a community of disciples. The story of the disciples meeting Jesus on the road to Emmaus is an important reminder of this.[5]

A dialogical approach

Contemporary situations throw up opportunities to interpret experience and conduct through the lens of Scripture and,

---

4. Brueggemann, "Biblical Authority," 264.
5. Lash, *Theology on the Way to Emmaus*, 42.

most importantly, vice versa, to discern the meaning of Scripture through the lens of experience. Scriptural texts when read analogically illuminate everyday life. In this action and commitment are the necessary contexts for discerning God in the midst of human existence.[6]

What I have so far said about reading Scripture "again" in changing contexts has pointed implicitly to the dialogical character of this process. The French theologian and social philosopher Jacques Ellul illustrates the dialogical character of reading Scripture "again." Ellul reminds us that there is a tension in reading Scripture in a way that continually questions and critiques the social theories and realities that he is working with, that is followed by a turning the questions arising from sociology back on the reading of Scripture being undertaken by theologians and clergy.[7]

Ellul suggests that in interrogating contemporary life with biblical revelation we will be challenged to give a response that is shaped by a free dialogue with the God revealed in Jesus Christ. Though influenced by the two Karls, Karl Marx and Karl Barth, and under the overriding influence of Kierkegaard, Ellul did not deploy a general philosophical theory, or systematic theology, but practiced dialectic as an ongoing dialogue with a range of interlocutors. David Neville points out that such a dialogue "carries the sense of distance or contradiction . . . dialogue entails both presence (being with, so as to be able to talk together) and distance, being apart, so as to be able to contribute something different)."[8] The dialogue suggested by Ellul works with the tension between presence as public engagement, and distance as a critical faithfulness to Scripture and Christian tradition. In Ellul's reading of Scripture, there is an inquiry into "the kind of mental images, values and commitments we inevitably bring to the reading of these texts, as people of our time place and culture." We cannot avoid these influences, but we can take responsibility for them by critically examining the cultural glasses "through which we are about to begin reading these texts."[9] These lenses, I suggest, remain powerfully shaped within the church by images and assumptions that we continue to carry with us from Christendom.

In talking about community engagement after Christendom the context still bears the imprint of Christendom in the working assumptions that shape the way churches and their agencies try to relate to government. Our

---

6. Rowland and Roberts, *The Bible for Sinners*, 44.

7. Greenman et al., *Understanding Jacques Ellul*, 98–120, and Neville, "Dialectic as Method in Public Theology."

8. Neville, "Dialectic as a Method in Public Theology," 180.

9. Ellul, *On Being Rich and Poor*, xi.

habits of thought, shaped as they are by a Christendom reading of Scripture, have become deeply engrained, hard to recognize, and hard to change. Critical self-awareness in our interpretation of Scripture requires paying attention to the assumptions that we bring to our reading. If we are reading the First Testament (Old Testament), for example, with an implicit concern with social order and stability as desirable social goals, we are unlikely to pay much attention to the stories of the prophets and their interventions to critique and transform the political order.

Christopher Rowland places an emphasis on openness in our approach to reading Scripture "again" that I think gets things about right. Such a reading does not "presuppose the application of a set of principles, or a theological programme, or pattern to modern situations. We do not need to look for formulas to 'copy' or techniques to 'apply' from Scripture. What scripture offers us is rather something like orientations, models, types, directives, principles, aspirations, elements permitting us to acquire, on our own initiative a 'hermeneutic competency' and thus the capacity to judge—on our own initiative, in our own right—'according to the mind of Christ,' or 'according to the Spirit,' the new unpredictable situations with which we are continually confronted."[10]

In the account that follows I begin with accounts of reading Scripture "again" that emerged in situations where Christendom was still in full swing, those of the Anabaptists and William Blake. I then draw attention to examples of rereading Scripture beyond Christendom that were undertaken from a position where the readers were not "in control," but had some possibility of agency. My brief sample of this tradition introduces William Stringfellow, Fannie Lou Hamer, and Ched Myers.

Anabaptists reading Scripture

The Reformation initially did not represent in important ways a substantial break with Christendom. The mainstream reformers were happy to retain the entanglement of the church and the political order, though replacing the location of entanglement in the imperial order with princely and municipal forms of entanglement. Controversies between local rulers and the reformers were about the exact nature of their ongoing relationship, not about Christendom itself. The Anabaptists by contrast represented, in both their theology and practice, a much more radical challenge, though it achieved only an "interruption," rather than a disruption, to the status quo.

---

10. Rowland and Roberts, *The Bible for Sinners*, 59.

Even though their approach to reading Scripture was pushed aside by the established churches and governments, and survived only on the margins of Christendom, the Anabaptist interruption provides us with an example of an early attempt to read Scripture "again" beyond Christendom. Stuart Murray's historical account of the main practices and themes in the Anabaptist tradition of reading Scripture identifies the tradition as a helpful conversation partner with both contemporary liberation theology and charismatic hermeneutics.[11] With their ethical concern and attention to questions of how life was to be lived, the Anabaptists made the point that Scripture needed to be interpreted by those who were committed to walking in the way of discipleship.

Murray identified six core convictions concerning the Anabaptist reading of Scripture that, though they were expressed in different ways and with varying emphases, were at the center of debate and practice within the early years of the Anabaptist movement. The Anabaptists did not develop a single coherent hermeneutic as their practice of interpretation was worked out by different groups working for most of the period under pressure of persecution. Those early leaders who had academic training and identified with the movement mostly did not live long. Later generations of leaders and teachers in the movement rarely had the opportunity for leisurely scholarship and were largely self-taught.

The key Anabaptist themes bearing on the reading of Scripture identified by Murray were:

- Scripture is self-interpreting in its nature, and not depending on reliance on tradition and theological commentators, and is accessible to the ordinary people.
- Scripture is Christocentric in character.
- The First Testament (Old Testament) should be read in the light of the Second Testament (New Testament).
- There was a stronger emphasis on the role of the Spirit than was the case for the mainstream reformers.
- The congregation functions as a hermeneutical or interpretative community.
- There was a focus on the practical consequences of scriptural interpretation in discipleship, that can be appropriately summarized as a "hermeneutics of obedience."[12]

---

11. Murray, *Biblical Interpretation in the Anabaptist Tradition*.

12. Murray, *Biblical Interpretation in the Anabaptist Tradition*, 15–35. See also Pietersen, *Reading the Bible after Christendom*, 40–66.

These themes are probably better understood as six areas of theology and practice, where competing tendencies or imperatives were held in competing and necessary tension. For example, there is the tension between adherence to the letter of Scriptures and openness to the leading of the Spirit, and similarly a tension between the enfranchisement of the people and attention to trusted teachers. There were limitations in the Anabaptists' overall approach in their tendency to disparage scholarship in interpreting Scripture. Two of these themes are of particular importance for the argument of this book, the hermeneutics of discipleship and the Christocentric focus.

Hans Denck (1500–1527), who was associated with the Anabaptists in the early years of the Reformation, summarized this focus on the connection between discipleship and knowing Christ: "[J]ust as the disciples left all for Christ's sake and yet did not understand who he was until they had accompanied him on the Way, so the life of obedience is the way in which one knows him."[13] This opened the door to a critical approach to the close relationship of church and state in Christendom. Anabaptists, in opening up the reading and interpretation of Scripture, enfranchised the laity in a way that led to questioning of social, political, and ecclesiastical structures. In southern Germany many of the Anabaptists had connections with the Peasant's Revolt, in which manifestoes showed a debt to scriptural themes that addressed issues of justice. There was a rejection of the Reformers' preference for deferring reform to match the political requirements of the princes and city governments. Political conflict was an essential consequence of the Anabaptist reading of Scripture, with its criticism of the lack of recognition of space for dissent and liberty of conscience.

Attention to the teaching and ministry of Jesus was also important to the Anabaptist reading of Scripture. In following this path, the Anabaptists believed we are warranted in shifting our attention away from the traditional systematic accounts of Jesus' roles as priest and king to accounts that pay attention to the images of Jesus as prophet, pastor, and poet. These images are particularly relevant for in reimagining community engagement after Christendom. The activities that fit within the role of the prophet include consciousness raising and critique. These activities go to practices of advocacy that implicitly involve degrees of community disruption in their critique of the status quo, in contrast to the Reformers' attention to maintaining social stability.[14]

---

13. Rowland and Roberts, *The Bible for Sinners*, 65.
14. Pietersen, *Reading the Bible after Christendom*, 70–84.

Reading Scripture against Christendom

The Anabaptists' reading of Scripture in their emergence against Christendom was followed over the centuries by further rereadings of Scripture in a loose tradition of Christian radicalism that positioned itself implicitly, if not always explicitly, against the established churches' comfortable and compromised relationship with structures of political and institutional power. Such radical Christianity has "been less concerned with abstract reflection, and more with active engagement to see another kind of order at work in the world: God's kingdom on earth and the discernment of God in the context of seeking God's kingdom and God's justice."[15]

Throughout history, many Christians in reading Scripture "again" have appealed to the guidance of the Spirit to enable them to penetrate to the heart of the text in empowering their social critique. In choosing examples of reading Scripture "again," I have followed a recurring strand of Christian radicalism. My concern has been to point to the existence of the tradition, rather than comprehensively map it. In the brief discussion that follows, I will highlight some of their theological emphases and their diverse rhetorical approaches. In these accounts I gesture towards reading Scripture as a "lived theology," an approach in which the narrating of faith-filled lives makes a contribution to theological knowledge and analysis.[16]

William Blake

The Civil Wars in England in the seventeenth century produced a range of groups who undertook a radical reading of Scripture in response to a changing social and political context and articulated a commitment to the kingdom preached and lived by Jesus. Religious and political dissent were deeply intertwined. Some groups were still reaching for political control, expressing a commitment to Christendom in a new form, while others looked for a new post-Christendom political and religious order.[17] That ferment continued after the Commonwealth period, despite the return of the monarchy.

---

15. Rowland and Roberts, *The Bible for Sinners*, 62.
16. Marsh et al., *Lived Theology*, 1–20.
17. For a survey of the radical movements and their theology during this period, see Bradstock, *Radical Religion in Cromwell's England*, and Hill, *The World Turned Upside Down*. Hill, *A Turbulent, Seditious and Factious People,* highlights the significance of John Bunyan and radical dissent.

Implicated in the Exercise of Power

William Blake (1757–1827)[18] is perhaps best known for his popular hymn "Jerusalem," a poem that expresses the author's radical critique of industrialization, a critique that that remains opaque to many of those who belt out the words at sporting events, or more reverently intone it at church services. Blake expressed in his art and poetry a deep and continuing critique of the social order, imaginatively grounded in his reading of Scripture. "Blake presents the 'Christianity' of his culture not as a social movement enacting the Spirit-oriented life advocated in the Gospels but as an institutionally oriented tyranny that co-opts the Bible to sustain its own ends."[19] The political and religious order of Christendom to which he attached a range of diverse and mysterious titles, is in Blake's view concerned primarily with the maintenance of power structures and hierarchies. His critique makes visible the gap that he discerns between Jesus and the "Christianity" of his time.

For Blake the Bible, when read in the light of the Spirit, has a meaningful role in shaping his critique. Curtis Freeman is clear that the principal source of inspiration for Blake can be traced to his reading of the Bible, "which Blake described as 'fill'd with Imagination & Visions from End to End.'"[20] Blake's poems and paintings are saturated with biblical imagery, especially from the prophets of the First Testament (Old Testament). Scripture was the generative source of Blake's imagination and prophetic vision. It provided images that enabled him to think outside the dominant ideology of his day.

Blake regarded Scripture as being read by many in a way that provided justification for the oppression and inequality that he saw all around him. He saw the national church in his time colluding with the state and sanctifying itself by reference to Scripture while remaining oblivious to the multiple miseries of the poor. "In Blake's vision church and state were no longer instruments of God's justice but servants of the beast 'among these dark Satanic mills' and Jerusalem would have to be built anew 'in England's green and pleasant land.'"[21] He was also a dreamer whose vision of empire is hard to distinguish from what we term as Christendom, since it was characterized by state and church being united as one. This is a situation "where the evil powers of king and priest ruled society. He refused to abide a religion where the pious 'praise God & his Priest & King' while poor children are clothed 'in the clothes of death.' . . . His was a prophecy against empire. His was a

---

18. My account of Blake's reading of Scripture draws on Freeman, *Undomesticated Dissent*, 133–90; Rowland and Roberts, *The Bible for Sinners*, 73–81; Rowland, "Blake and the Bible"; and Rowland, *Radical Prophet*, 99–127.

19. Rowland and Roberts, *The Bible for Sinners*, 75.

20. Freeman, *Undomesticated Dissent*, 155.

21. Freeman, *Undomesticated Dissent*, 136.

hope for a Christianity after Christendom."[22] Instead of reading Scripture as a book of moral law, Blake offers us a reading of the Gospels that highlighted the centrality of compassion in the life and ministry of Jesus, exercised in his extension of a forgiveness that was always particular to each individual situation. Theologically speaking, forgiveness of sins requires that we remain open to the Spirit, negotiating our way forward through our expressions of mutuality.

Blake talks about "imagination" as an open-ended way of relating to the Bible that was qualitatively different from legalistic approaches. According to Freeman, we can understand Blake's prophetic imagination as having something in common with John Bunyan, whose conviction was that "dreams and visions are a liminal space between time and eternity, a spiritual world. And because Blake's Jerusalem is a vision it is first and foremost an image to be seen through the eye of the mind rather than a poem whose meaning emerges by being studiously analyzed. . . . [H]e sees the world not as others see it but as he imagines it through the eye of prophetic vision."[23] Blake's imagination here is not an arbitrary and unloosed mysticism. It is informed by a scripturally grounded prophetic vision that took poetic form that, in its dreams and imagery, has much in common with the First Testament (Old Testament).

William Stringfellow

My next example of reading Scripture "again" in the radical tradition brings us a good deal closer to our own time. William Stringfellow (1929–1985) was an Episcopalian layperson, a lawyer, and a theologian, though without formal theological training.[24] He was active in the ecumenical movement, and ecumenical in his activism. He was a close friend of the Jesuit activist Daniel Berrigan, whom he harbored while Berrigan was on the run from the FBI as a result of Berrigan's protests against the Vietnam War. Despite his continuing and pungent critique of the failings of the institutional church, particularly in its Episcopal form, Stringfellow remained active in that church, proving a thorn in the flesh to various bishops through his legal and theological support of women's ordination, while remaining a close

---

22. Freeman, *Undomesticated Dissent*, 142–43.

23. Freeman, *Undomesticated Dissent*, 155.

24. For a brief account of Stringfellow's life, see Stevens, "Living into the Prophetic Voice." For Stringfellow's autobiographical, theologically informed reflections, see particularly *My People Is the Enemy*, and *A Second Birthday*.

Implicated in the Exercise of Power

friend of other church leaders, resisting furiously all attempts to pigeonhole him theologically.[25]

Stringfellow's theological critique of America took the form of a life lived against Christendom that found expression in a series of brief, pungent discussions of Scripture.[26] He suffered from a range of significant health issues, to which he paid theological attention, and imaginatively connected this experience to his overall critique of US society and politics. Central to his reading of Scripture was the reality of death and the Pauline themes of the "principalities and powers." He sought to understand America biblically, not the other way around. To be informed by Scripture, he thought, was to gain an enhanced vision of the political and social reality that we are living in. Stringfellow was particularly concerned with action at the limits of decision, situations where principles can break down and turn into an unhelpful legalism that then worked to reinforce the status quo. For Stringfellow the text of Scripture becomes the catalyst for interpretation, and the gateway to a new understanding of experience and politics that is not confined to narrowly religious or ecclesial issues. The Word of God is relevant to all the dimensions of our life.

What Stringfellow demands of the reader is imaginative attention in order to explore the ambiguities, tensions, and problems, and the biographical connections that the text of Scripture offers. For example, Stringfellow allows the imagery of the Apocalypse to be juxtaposed with his own circumstances, whether personal or social, so as to allow the images from Scripture to inform his understanding of contemporary persons and events, and to serve as a guide for action. This would certainly fall under the rubric of the renewal of the mind of which Paul speaks in Romans 12:1–2: "I appeal to you therefore, brothers and sisters by the mercies of God, to present your bodies as a living sacrifice, holy and acceptable to God, which is your spiritual worship. Do not be conformed to this world but be transformed by the renewing of your minds, so that you may discern what is the will of God—what is good and acceptable and perfect."

In reading Scripture, Stringfellow employs anecdote and analogy as strategies for the pursuit of truth, and as a guide to faithful action. Most of his writings bring together Scripture with both personal experience and political engagement that generates a richly textured theological reflection touching the heart and moving the imagination to reflect on the possible shape of Christian action and responsibility. His reflection on the powers

---

25. On Stringfellow's theology, see Campbell and Saunders, *The Word on the Street*, 63–82; Rowland and Roberts, *The Bible for Sinners*, 81–87; and Dancer, *An Alien in a Strange Land*.

26. Stringfellow, *Free in Obedience*; and Stringfellow, *An Ethic for Christians*.

of death and the exercise of Christian freedom drew on his experiences of illness, as well as political engagement in opposition to the Vietnam War. His account of the church's call to live beyond Christendom was stringent. "The Church is summoned by the word of God, now as then, to a vocation of poverty as an institution and now as then it means the radical dissociation of the Church from the prevailing order, from the status quo, from the ruling powers, from the established institutions of politics and finance."[27]

There are connections between the multiple meanings that Stringfellow discerns in this approach to Scripture with the parables of Jesus. A parable has "consistently refused to be tied down to one particular meaning. It offers a mode of moral reasoning that prompts and tantalizes in ways that are unpredictable in their effects and may offer those who persevere a means of understanding reality and thereby illuminate the action and commitment on which they have already embarked."[28] As Stringfellow remarks in a nod to Karl Barth's hermeneutic principle, Christian preachers should "read the Bible more avidly and the daily newspapers more discerningly because both of these testaments witness that the scene of God's presence and vitality is this history with all its ambiguity, alienation, strife, controversy and scandal."[29]

Having returned to Stringfellow's writings recently in the light of the Black Lives Matter movement and the Trump presidency in the US, I have found them prescient in their naming of the destructive powers that have been manifest in the US over the past few years. Their autobiographical character, and the fact that they are written from the streets, from the front line of struggle, make Stringfellow's writings an accessible and engaging example of reading Scripture "again."

Fannie Lou Hamer

The next practitioner of reading Scripture "again" that I want to draw to your attention stands in a long tradition of preaching in the Black church in the United States. This preaching was shaped by the experience of slavery, and the subsequent economic and political oppression. Fannie Lou Hamer's reading of Scripture "again" was delivered orally in the 1960s, in the context of the civil rights movement.

Fannie Lou Hamer was a field hand on a Mississippi cotton plantation, who in 1962 left the cotton fields of the Delta to register to vote and

---

27. Stringfellow, *Instead of Death*, 84.
28. Rowland, *The Bible for Sinners*, 86.
29. Rowland, *The Bible for Sinners*, 87.

Implicated in the Exercise of Power

subsequently, after being evicted from her home by the plantation owner, became active in the civil rights movement.[30] Mrs. Hamer in her voter registration activity and grassroots political organizing gave testimony to a liberating, reconciling faith expressed through African American hymnody, spirituals, and prophetic religion following Jesus as the friend and deliverer of the poor. Charles Marsh in his short but moving account of her life and witness has drawn attention to the depth of her theological insight, and how it drew on a reading and recitation of Scripture. I am indebted to Marsh's account for examples of the reading of Scripture occurring in her appearances in churches and community gatherings, documented by eyewitnesses.

The first account of preaching I want to draw to your attention comes from Mrs. Hamer's attempt to gain support for voter registration from the Black church in the backwoods of rural Mississippi. She attended a worship service at a church whose minister had not yet committed himself to support the program. A volunteer accompanying Mrs. Hamer reported that they entered the church just as the pastor was finishing reading a passage from Exodus 29, a reading that reminded the Israelites that God had brought them out of the land of Egypt in an act of liberation. At the conclusion of the Bible reading, the pastor invited Mrs. Hamer to say a few words to the congregation.

> Her magnificent voice rolled through the chapel as she enlisted the Biblical ranks of martyrs and heroes to summon these folk in the church that Sunday morning to the Freedom banner. Her mounting and rolling battery of quotations and allusions from the Old and New Testaments stunned the audience with its thunder. "Pharaoh was in Sunflower county! Israel's children were building bricks without straw—at three dollars a day!" Her voice broke and tears stood in her eyes. "They're tired! And I am tired of being tired!" . . . [A]s she pointed to the shaken minister . . . Fannie Lou's voice was commanding . . . "And you Reverend Tyler, must be Moses! Leadin' your flock out of the chains and fetters of Egypt—takin' them yourself to register tomorra in Indianola."[31]

The effect on the congregation of the narrated engagement and the action of God and Moses, then, and the struggle for voting rights in Mississippi, now, was striking, even though the gap in time and space was in many ways immeasurable. Mrs. Hamer combined praise and prophetic provocation in her call to an oppressed people to join the journey to freedom land.

---

30. Marsh, *God's Long Summer*, 10–48; and Chappell, *A Stone of Hope*, 71–75.
31. Marsh, *God's Long Summer*, 32.

Marsh also points to the way Mrs. Hamer drew together in her performance at these meetings the slave spirituals in connecting Easter and Passover and drawing a close connection between personal salvation and the liberation of the people of Israel from the bondage of Egypt. In bringing together in her proclamation the spirituals "Go Tell It on the Mountain" and "Go Down Moses," she provided a retelling of the gospel story that brought into clear focus a call to discipleship that was engaged in the struggle for freedom. In Marsh's analysis, Fannie Lou Hamer's reading of Scripture ran something like this:

> My sins are forgiven; my life is made new; the angel of death has passed over me; I have been rescued from an eternal perishing. Still much more is at stake than the fate of my individual soul. For since the good news is proclaimed, I can stand up to Pharaoh, look him in the eye and say, "Let my people go." There is a land beyond Egypt. The song builds momentum until the final verse repeats the phrase, but now no longer as a plea but as a demand of the Gospel—"Let my people go." The Gospel "go tell it" becomes the theological framework for the liberation of the people from oppression.[32]

The reading and interpretation of Scripture as an invocation of liberation, and a call to struggle against oppression, was a prophetic announcement, and a performance of scripture grounded in the life and worship of the black church that called for potentially costly community engagement. Mrs. Hamer faithfully maintained her reading of Scripture as the call to join the struggle for freedom through years of harassment, arrest, and violence. This was a reading that sustained a hard and costly journey, in the course of disrupting Southern racist oppression.

Ched Myers

The last of the examples of reading Scripture "again" that I want to bring to your attention is that undertaken by a contemporary activist Ched Myers, who in recent decades has lived along the boundary lines of church, community activism, and scholarship, allowing his involvement in each dimension to inform the other dimensions. Myers has done much of his work of reading Scripture "again" in Mark's Gospel.[33] Central to Myers's

---

32. Marsh, *God's Long Summer*, 47.

33. Myers in *Who Will Roll Away the Stone?* offers an example of reading Scripture "again."

reading of Scripture is the role of the question in Jesus' teaching and ministry. Myers notes that Jesus' frequent response to questions was to ask a question of his interlocutors. If we want to understand what Jesus stands for, Myers observes, we had better be prepared for a questioning by him of our own allegiance and location.

Myers in the course of his reading draws our attention to the disturbing reality that the more the church is aligned with the social order in a relationship that can fairly be termed Christendom-like, the more its theological discourse has taken on an abstract, defensive, and apologetic character. Once we frankly acknowledge that we are now in a much more marginal context, our reading of Scripture can be more critical of the social order, and more reflective and uneasy about our relationship to that order, as well as more grounded in social reality. Myers's judgment is that it will take courage "to follow Jesus in questioning the public order. It takes just as much courage to turn our criticism of the world back on ourselves. There is no room for self-righteousness, for Jesus is also the questioner of the church."[34] The shift to a prophetic reading of Scripture will require us to focus in a critical prophetic mode inward on the church, as much as outward to the world. This dual focus, as we have just seen, was also at the heart of Fannie Lou Hamer's preaching.

Myers also draws our attention to the need to take account of the stories that shape us in a neoliberal consumer society. We need to bring these stories of consumerism into critical conversation with the stories of Scripture. Jesus' teaching method of asking questions, and the complexity of the situation in which we find ourselves, makes it "far more appropriate to try to present the reader with questions than answers . . . [T]hus, I offer partly a controversy with dominant culture theology, partly what Catholic Workers call an exercise in 'clarification of thought,' and partly a debate with my own community of conviction about where we go from here."[35]

Myers's reading of Mark is self-involving in character, not a detached academic exercise. He guides us through a discussion that brings together a critical reading of Mark that attends to the contemporary social context, and the reality of the church's implication in a consumer society. Whenever "we respond to the invitation to discipleship we join Jesus where he already is, on the Way. This is Jesus, *acompanante*—the one who accompanies us."[36] The exercise of imagination in a radical Christian reading of Scripture, according to Myers, is best understood as one in which the practice of

---

34. Myers, "'I Will Ask You a Question,'" 109.
35. Myers, *Who Will Roll Away the Stone?*, xxv.
36. Myers, *Who Will Roll Away the Stone?*, 415.

discipleship opens up fresh responses to the challenges of the prevailing context.

Reading Scripture imaginatively

I have covered a good deal of ground in this chapter in pointing to some examples of people who have undertaken readings of Scripture beyond Christendom, critiquing our continuing messy involvement in structures of power. What we are committed to in following Jesus, these examples suggest, is a continuing assessment of the integrity and faithfulness of churches, in their community engagement, through a contextual rereading of Scripture. In talking about reading Scripture imaginatively I am not talking about imagination as making something up, but rather as an exercise in being open the possibility of discerning realities that are different to those we take for granted. Walter Brueggemann reminds us that interpretation "is never objective but is always mediated through the voice, hopes, fears, interests and hurts of the interpreter and the context of interpretation. Because interpretation is not objective it is always partial and provisional" and "it must be open to the review of the whole church."[37]

The blind spots in our reading of Scripture are likely to fall under what Charles Taylor calls the "un-thought," our taken-for-granted assumptions inherited from worship, church practice, and the prevailing culture more broadly.[38]

Ray Gingerich helpfully suggests that the hermeneutical guide for reading the First Testament (Old Testament) is to read it as Jesus read it, which was through the eyes of the prophets rather than the kings.[39] This is an important shift as the character of the royal imagination in the First Testament (Old Testament) stands in stark contrast to the prophetic imagination in the way it perceived the world. Even to articulate that perception as a possibility is to subvert the royal imagination. That is to say, "to perceive differently for the rulers of this age is to be delegitimized,"[40] for it requires the surrender of their carefully devised ideology that resists the possibility of an account of the world and action from below. Those operating from below, such as the prophets, were not considered to be serious social actors.[41] The temple and monarchy attempted to maintain a monopoly on the

---

37. Brueggemann, *Redescribing Reality*, 13.
38. Taylor, *A Secular Age*, 428–29; Smith, *How (Not) to Be Secular*, 143.
39. Gingerich, "Reading the Bible in Search of Jesus," 87.
40. Brueggemann, *Interpretation and Obedience*, 37.
41. Brueggemann, *Interpretation and Obedience*, 28–40.

imagination of those who were ruled, providing the official account of what was possible. Despite this the First Testament (Old Testament) recorded a continuing challenge to the royal monopoly of imagination. The Torah as a source of power and wonder functioned as a source of contestation over what was possible, and made images and metaphors available as resources of tradition and memory. The exodus narrative is a recital that comes from the underside of social reality and would not have found its origin in the royal court or temple. The tension between the monopoly of imagination, and the expression of imagination at the margins, is one that Brueggemann insists on.[42]

Reading Scripture "again" after Christendom, understood in this light, involves a hermeneutics of retrieval, an exercise in accessing resources that help us get a fresh theological perspective on our changing context. Sylvia Keesmaat and Brian Walsh suggest that we ask the following questions of the text we are rereading: "What meaning or meanings might this text have carried when it was first written heard or interpreted? And given the range of meanings that might justifiably be attributed to this text in its original composition and reception, what meanings might it bear today and what are the criteria for evaluating any such contemporary interpretation?"[43] The breadth of the task of reading "again" refers not only to what is read, but to who is allowed to do the reading. The task of reading, to pick up the Anabaptist approach, is not confined to the theological scholar or the ordained clergy.

> [A]nyone can at least in principle offer insight as to what the text is really about . . . [is] something that Liberation Theologians have always maintained about the peculiar insight of the poor and the marginalized. This method enables a space to open up for an imaginative relationship with one's own time and place and for the work of the Spirit in a complex process of engagement with the text in which the subjectivity of the interpreter has a part to play.[44]

The imagination of the poet, the rhetoric of the preacher, and the vision of a prophet are all possible means by which we can read Scripture "again." A great example can be found in many of the poems by Kristin Jack in his collection *Poetry and Prophecy*.[45] These reflections, drawing on sixteen years working with Servants of the Poor in Asia, contain a substantial number

---

42. Brueggemann, *Interpretation and Obedience*, 184–204.
43. Keesmaat and Walsh, *Romans Disarmed*, 32.
44. Rowland and Roberts, *The Bible for Sinners*, 38–39.
45. Jack, *Poetry and Prophecy*.

of poems that are a reflection on, as well as a response to specific passages of the First Testament (Old Testament) and the Second Testament (New Testament). His poems provoke fresh insights into the call of discipleship imagined in a context in which to be a Christian is to be truly marginal. The importance of imagination should not come as a surprise to us. James K. A. Smith highlights the reality that we human beings are imaginative creatures "who live off the stuff of imagination, stories, pictures, images, metaphors [that] are the poetry of our embodied existence."[46] We live through and with social imaginaries, the imaginative frameworks about society that we carry around that both tell us about "how things usually go" and "how things ought to go," and that we work with in our interpretation of reality and ethical response on a daily basis.[47]

Walter Brueggemann has paid particular attention to the role of imagination in the way we read Scripture. He highlights the importance of imagination, which he understands as the capacity to entertain images of meaning and reality that are beyond the givens of observable or commonly taken-for-granted experience. Nevertheless, such imagination will, against the practices of Christendom, be local in its reference, not overarching in its claims and scope, remaining fragmentary and open to contestation.[48]

Imagination is the visualizing of alternative accounts of the way things should be. Imagination opens up the possibility of a movement beyond the text that is still informed by the text. Jesus' parables provide us with multiple examples of how the certainties of the Hebrew Scriptures are challenged and other, often disturbing, possibilities are brought into the conversation. There is nothing of fantasy in grounding our imagination in the stories of Jesus and his life, death, and resurrection.

Am I placing too much emphasis on the role of imagination? A quick reflection on everyday life suggests not. The world of advertising is there to train our imagination as to what we should desire, and what is real.[49] But how do we train our imagination to recognize the presence of Jesus as opposed to the desirability of an infinite range of goods and services offered to us through the media? The story by Luke of what happened when two disciples met Jesus on the road to Emmaus is relevant here. The turning point for discernment by the followers of Jesus in this story was in the physical practice of table fellowship, in which Jesus was recognized in the breaking of the bread as they sat down and shared a meal. "Then their eyes

---

46. Smith, *Imagining the Kingdom*, 126.
47. Taylor, *A Secular Age*, 172–73.
48. Brueggemann, *The Word Militant*, 122–25.
49. Campbell and Saunders, *The Word on the Street*, 30.

were opened, and they recognized him; and he vanished from their sight. They said to each other, 'Were not our hearts burning within us while he was talking to us on the road, while he was opening the scriptures to us?'" (Luke 24:31–32).[50]

In conclusion

Our current location is one in which the deep failure by churches and their institutions is tearing apart people's lives. We have been reminded by episodes of sexual abuse and the accompanying institutional cover-up of the damage that follows when we turn institutions into idols, and the lives of vulnerable people are sacrificed on the altar of institutional survival. Reading Scripture "again" is not about deriving rules or models that we can use to ward off such failures in the future, but having our imagination, our vision reshaped by stories and practices that subvert our assumptions about the place of the church in the world. It is about visualizing how things might be "otherwise," in a response which always has an element of improvisation rather than a law or creed. Much, for example, as an actor working with the same script of a play in the same role can give that role a different intonation and meaning in response to changes in the way other members of the cast interpret the script. Faithful and imaginative reading of Scripture if it is to mean anything must function in a dialectical relationship with faithful performance, faithful practice in our everyday life. We need to pay "careful attention to the script but not in such a way that repeats it verbatim but rather works imaginatively with it, sensitive to the leading of the spirit."[51] Brian Walsh and Sylvia Keesmaat helpfully unpack the issue of improvisation.

> If we are called to faithful improvisation, how can we read a text . . . in such a way that its ancient character and historical distance from us is honored and not erased, yet it is as fresh and current as if it had been written this morning? Can the text have that kind of currency for us? How do we read the text and make it integral to our lives so that it can continue to speak to us? . . . [T]he improvisatory discipleship to which we are called requires something of a double immersion. We must be immersed in the biblical text . . . and we must be immersed in the world.[52]

---

50. Campbell and Saunders, *The Word on the Street*, 29–37.
51. Pietersen, *Reading the Bible after Christendom*, 87.
52. Walsh and Keesmaat, *Colossians Remixed*, 136.

We bring all of who we are to the task of reading, that is to say our past, our commitments, our context, our anticipations of the future—and that includes our failures. To acknowledge this requirement is to lay bare the tension that we confront in moving beyond Christendom, acknowledging both our past complicity and our current implication in the exercise of power by the state. The reading of Scripture in Christendom that we relied on has borne bitter fruit, yet our hope in the activity and presence of God means that we cannot do otherwise than return to read Scripture "again," if we are to continue on the path of discipleship.

> Our behaviour as Christians and the performance of the institutions of Christianity have been such as to deprive us of the right to be Christians or to expect credibility for what Christianity stands for.... Real Christianity is quite clearly what Christians actually do and together with the institutions which they actually have.... If these historical existences, events and institutions are of such a quality that they contradict the claims, hopes and visions which are stated to be both the basis for and the aims of Christian believing then Christianity is in fact contradicted.... But I also feel and believe that there is a vital sense in which God in and through Jesus speaks and is active precisely through and in this contradiction.[53]

David Jenkins's emphasis here is on not collapsing the tension between institutional failure and the conviction that God through Jesus can meet us in the midst of that contradiction. This stance is critical to acknowledging without reservation our failure, while maintaining hope that something new might emerge, if we do not flinch from facing the truth of that failure.

---

53. Jenkins, *The Contradiction of Christianity*, 9.

2

Stories Read "Otherwise"

The First Testament (Old Testament) has been read by Jewish and Christian scholars and political leaders over millennia as a source of wisdom and normative guidance on political engagement. As well as celebrating the Davidic monarchy, the First Testament records the traumas of imperial invasion, political subjugation, and the extended, disorienting experience of diaspora. All of these experiences were a matter of continuing theological interpretation and debate both then and now. The complexity of this heritage, the difficulty of untangling its various strands, and the paradoxes of its reception by the church during Christendom, are beyond the scope of this chapter. Mark Brett offers a warning about the risks of careless reception of this heritage.

> While most of Jewish history has embodied diaspora models of social life, Christendom made use of the very imperialism that biblical theology repeatedly resisted. In part because the idiom of resistance to empires was often borrowed from imperial language and ideas, when the Bible took its place in Christendom in later centuries, it could also be easily turned into a source of sanctions for medieval and colonial political power.[1]

This warning might best be translated as, "be careful how you read the political theology of the First Testament (Old Testament). If you read it through Christendom lenses you might end up reading it in opposition to its deepest intentions." With this warning in mind, I venture in this chapter to read "again" some of its narratives. My readings are undertaken from the perspective that the key actors in the stories had substantial power, but

1. Brett, *Political Trauma and Healing*, 7.

were not "in control." From this perspective, I probe the ambiguities and the silences in the stories, questioning inherited interpretations that are at ease with the trappings and language of empire.[2] Some of the insights I arrive at are "otherwise" than those that are frequently drawn out in preaching and exposition of the stories of Joseph, Esther, and Daniel. In these accounts of Jews grappling with the exercise of power in exile, implicated in imperial governance without being in a position of control, I explore the tensions of their involvement, what is suggested in the text about their faithfulness to God, and the maintenance of their Jewish identity. In discussing each of these stories, I provide a brief account of the narrative and the significance of the way it was told and taken up into the history of Israel, resulting in readings that are "otherwise" than those commonly associated with the stories in much Christian preaching.

I conclude this chapter by discussing the tensions in the book of Samuel around the emergence of the monarchy in Israel and the existence of a dissenting tradition that was critical of the monarchy. Unpacking this critique of the monarchy provides an interesting background for my discussion of kingship and the kingdom of God in the teaching and ministry of Jesus in the following chapter.

Joseph reconsidered

Genesis was compiled during the exile of the Israelites in Babylon, though the oral traditions on which it was based go back a long way. Chapters 37 to 50 are devoted to the story of Joseph and his family in an epic tale which has successfully jumped across millennia and cultural genres. It has been retold in a variety of forms, from Sunday school flannelgraphs, through Thomas Mann's epic four-part novel *Joseph and His Brothers*, to the musical *Joseph and the Amazing Technicolor Dreamcoat*.

Simply to sketch out the plot of Joseph and his family is to understand its continuing attraction. It has all the elements to drive a good Netflix series: a complex and dysfunctional family, a patriarch with several wives, lots of plotting by the siblings fueled by jealousy against the favorite son, with a plot to kill him thwarted at the last moment. When Joseph gets sold into Egypt there is an attempted workplace seduction involving a powerful woman. After a period in prison, Joseph makes it to the role of chief executive officer for Pharaoh, with a feel-good family reunion that ties up all the ends. Or at least that's how the story of Joseph in Genesis is normally read.

---

2. Brueggemann, *Inscribing the Text*, 16–17.

Stories Read "Otherwise"

Joseph joins the empire

In my reading "again" of the story of Joseph I focus on his activity as a policy adviser and administrator for Pharaoh. Given his opportunity, on being summoned from prison, Joseph not only interprets Pharaoh's dream, informing him of seven years of prosperity in Egypt, followed by seven years of famine, but offers a policy to deal with the threat of famine to the rule of Pharaoh. Joseph, given the responsibility by Pharaoh, implements the program successfully. That sounds straightforward enough. A successful public servant solves a major problem to the benefit of the community. Sounds good? Certainly, much of the preaching on this episode presents Joseph's involvement as Pharaoh's economic guru as an unproblematic success, and a good model for Christians in justifying their exercise of power in government. In the background God gets the credit for providential intervention to deal with a potential humanitarian crisis.

It is true that *Yhwh* is affirmed to be with Joseph in his elevation to a position second only to Pharaoh in power and authority. If we pay close attention to the way the story is told certain tensions, and perhaps even criticisms, are observable underneath the boilerplate stamp of approval that we tend to focus on.[3] What I will explore are the questions that are deliberately though unobtrusively registered by the compilers of the chronicles about the nature of God's approval of Joseph, along with questions about Joseph's faithfulness to *Yhwh*. We are warranted in reading the story of Joseph "otherwise" than as an account of the exercise of power, providentially engineered by God, without regard to its longer-term political and economic impact.

I start my reading "again" with Walter Brueggemann's discussion of Joseph, whom he describes pungently as "a fourth generation sellout."[4] The first theological issue raised by Brueggemann goes to the question of Joseph's identity. After Joseph's interpretation for Pharaoh of the dream of abundance and famine, and his recommendations for dealing with it, he is made second in charge under Pharaoh and the people are called to bow down to him. "He [Pharaoh] had him ride in the chariot of his second-in-command; and they cried out in front of him, 'Bow the knee!' Thus he set him over all the land of Egypt" (Gen 41:43). Think about this in the light of the history of Israel. Chariots were the technology of war used in the pursuit of Israel during the exodus, as well as by the conquering powers during the invasion that led to Israel's exile. The chariots are the symbol of military prowess and imperial

---

3. Pietersen, *Reading the Bible after Christendom*, 96–97.
4. Brueggemann, *Inscribing the Text*, 59–62.

might. This characterization of Joseph points toward his assimilation into the structure of Egyptian power. Joseph symbolically joins the empire, and the text draws this development explicitly to our attention.

The extent of Joseph's assimilation into the culture of Egypt goes a good deal further. Joseph is given an Egyptian name and takes an Egyptian wife, becoming assimilated as an Egyptian, without any sign of dissent or unease. Context is important here in interpreting what is at stake in this reference. Intermarriage with the surrounding nations is disapproved of throughout the history of Israel. Abraham sends back to his kinfolk to find a suitable wife for his son Isaac. Taking on an Egyptian name is also significant. It stands in stark contrast to the pattern of giving new names in much of the narrative in Genesis. Abram is renamed as Abraham, and Jacob is renamed as Israel by *Yhwh*, but Joseph's new name is given to him by Pharaoh. The text suggests implicitly that Joseph does not fit the pattern of relationship to God that is characteristic of the patriarchs, because of his assimilation culturally and religiously into Egyptian government and society.

Joseph's assimilation to Egypt results in Joseph being left out the affirmation of the ancestors. Here I return to the observation of Brueggemann about how Joseph is, and isn't, acknowledged in the narratives of Israel. Brueggemann discerns a subtle theological judgment by the wise people of Israel on the exercise of governing power by Joseph. Why, asks Brueggemann, isn't Joseph included in the formula, "The God of Abraham, Isaac and Jacob"? Why is there no recognition in this confession of a figure who receives such a large amount of attention in a narration that extends from Genesis chapter 37 to chapter 50?[5] The absence of Joseph from the confession, Brueggemann argues, points toward a critical assessment of him. He is not endorsed by the compilers of the tradition within Israel.

From a Christendom perspective, that assumes an automatic theological approval of the linkage of political success and access to power, there should be no reason why Joseph shouldn't have made it into the heart of Israel's story. He seems to be a critical element in God's providential care for his family who are carrying forward the promise to Abraham. Joseph has wisdom, and as an interpreter of dreams has achieved a position of authority at the center of Egyptian government. Yet nowhere is there any reference in the text to "the God of Joseph." He lacks the ultimate theological stamp of approval from the tradition, despite having his historical role in care for his family amply acknowledged. Brueggemann argues that at the heart of the decision of Israel not to include Joseph in its confession, a decision that he sees as both conscious and deliberate, is Joseph's linkage with Pharaoh, who

---

5. Brueggemann, "A Fourth-Generation Sellout."

stands in the First Testament (Old Testament) for all that threatens Israel's faith and existence.

It is with these observations in view that I now turn to an examination of Joseph's role in serving Pharaoh and its consequences undertaken by two distinguished Jewish scholars, Leon Kass and Aaron Wildavsky. In their respective accounts they draw on the Jewish tradition of scriptural interpretation of this narrative, with a perspective shaped by a history of being in a minority and vulnerable to the Pharaohs of every age. Their judgment aligns with that of Brueggemann while taking the critique of Joseph further.

Joseph and the shadows cast by his success

At the heart of the questioning the place of Joseph in the tradition of Israel is the policy that Joseph designs and implements to deal with the famine. In closing out his reading of the book of Genesis as a book of wisdom, Kass draws our attention to the close and continuing connection that quickly develops between Joseph and Pharaoh in the story. Not only does Joseph interpret Pharaoh's dream, but he acts as a consultant to provide a policy response to the nightmare of scarcity that stands as a risk to the survival of Pharaoh and his regime. Joseph has discerned that "Pharaoh is less interested in the meaning of the dream than in its implications for his reign and power. And the plan Joseph proposes is music to Pharaoh's ears: a prime minister loyal only to him, backed by an army of bureaucrats, will centralize control over the entire land and its food supply. A silent implication . . . is surely not lost on Pharaoh: during the years of famine the central administration will use the dispersal of food to further augment and consolidate Pharaoh's power."[6]

In appointing Joseph to be his executive officer, Pharaoh will rule but Joseph's word will govern the conduct of the nation. Joseph travels throughout Egypt during the seven years of plenty, gathering up the food and storing it up in the cities. It is not just a matter of taking up the surplus grain—Joseph takes it all (Gen 41:48). By his storing the grain in the cities, the rural areas lose their self-sufficiency and become entirely dependent upon the cities. This is a critical change that prepares the way for the transformation of administration in Egypt that will shortly follow. Kass observes that "this excessive gathering and storage of grain—at the expense of saving enough even for replanting—might itself have contributed to (not to say caused) the famine the years that followed."[7]

6. Kass, *The Beginning of Wisdom*, 566.
7. Kass, *The Beginning of Wisdom*, 570.

The policy that Joseph implements ruthlessly centralizes Pharaoh's control over the population of Egypt. Under pressure of famine when it arrives, the surplus from the community, whether money or livestock, accumulates in the hands of Pharaoh's administrators who dole out the food. People sell their land, and then sell themselves into bondage, to survive, and the land then accumulates in the regime's hands. In Genesis 47:23–26 the people, having sold their land to Pharaoh and receiving seed for sowing from him, are now required to provide 20 percent of the crop to Pharaoh. The peasants from one end of Egypt to another have now become sharecroppers, reduced to a status only a little short of slavery. Joseph, in exempting the priests from having their land claimed in return for providing food, shored up his support from a significant source of power. There is no indication that the very nature of this policy and its impact on the people of Egypt causes Joseph any concern. There is no moral dilemma for him in his work for empire. He has provided policy advice and managed the implementation efficiently, and effectively. What more could you ask of a public servant?

Kass suggests that the teachers and chroniclers of Israel in making their judgment about Joseph in the course of compiling the text seem to have asked the further and more difficult question that a public servant, at least one shaped by the history and commitments of Israel, must consider: namely, is the policy appropriate? This question requires paying attention to the consequences of the policy, bringing into view issues of ethics, questions about equity, questions about what sort of society people want to have and what the impact of the policy will be. What we have here as we contemplate the consequences of the policy is a stark contrast between the policy of accumulation that Joseph has designed, and implemented, and the policy of redistribution and forgiveness of debt that we find elsewhere in the teachings of the Torah. In his lack of concern with these questions, in his commitment to the service of empire and its fear of scarcity, in his silence on these issues, we find the ground on which Joseph has distanced himself from the covenant with Yahweh. Joseph certainly never utters a word about his own identity in relationship to the covenant and the God of the covenant in the course of his time as second-in-command in Egypt. Nowhere do the theological commitments of Israel enter into the narrative as being problematic for Joseph in undertaking his service of empire. There is no crisis of conscience, no conflict between the claims of the covenant and the claims of Pharaoh. The contrast with Daniel, as we shall see later, is striking.

None of this criticism brings into question Joseph's commitment to his family. Joseph in expressing his loyalty to his family shows no awareness of the claims of the covenant of his ancestors. Joseph's family has to go into exile because of the famine and he places them under the protection of empire, ensuring their safety and well-being. Joseph, though he remains apart from his family after their move into Egypt, treats them with generosity, gives them access to the best of the land and ensures they are well fed in the midst of the famine (Gen 47:11–12, 27). They are privileged, and would have been seen as such by the remainder of the population. Joseph's policy results in wholesale slavery in Egypt, a state to which Israel is reduced when the protection of Pharaoh is withdrawn by his descendants. All its prosperity will make it very difficult for Israel to return as intended to the promised land when the famine is over. Why go back when we are well off here? At some stage however this protection fails, and Joseph's descendants fall under the oppression of the centralized power shaped by Joseph's policy. His family becomes victims of the absolute economic and social structure of Egypt, and eventually they begin to cry for freedom.

Joseph's story of sustaining his family is told in detail, and faithfully remembered in Israel. His integrity in this dimension of his life is acknowledged without any reserve. Despite this there is an ambiguity, a tension arising from Joseph's association with oppression. Kass's judgement is aligned with that of Brueggemann, though expressed in slightly different terms—that the theological affirmation of Joseph's role in the covenant people is withheld from him by the scribes and wisdom writers of Israel. Perhaps Kass suggests Joseph is omitted in the end from Israel's theological confession because the wise people of Israel, when assessing his role, were unclear about who the God of Joseph actually was. Was the God of Joseph the Egyptian author of slavery, whose policy in the light of history victimized his own people? Perhaps the question that lingered in the mind of the compilers of Genesis was not whether God was with Joseph, but was Joseph with God? The narrative records no direct judgment, but there seems to have been an implicit judgment nonetheless.[8] In another hint, that there was such a judgment comes in the genealogy of Jesus in Matthew's Gospel. Joseph gets no explicit mention. The reference is to "Jacob, the father of Judah and his brothers" (Matthew 1:2).

Joseph and Moses

I now turn to a reading of story of Joseph by the distinguished public policy analyst Aaron Wildavsky, who reinforces the assessment of Brueggemann and Kass but does so by comparing Joseph with Moses. With a sensibility shaped by his career in researching public policy,[9] Wildavsky argues that in

8. Brueggemann, *Inscribing the Text*, 59–62.
9. Wildavsky, *Assimilation versus Separation*, 6–9, 203–6.

the Joseph saga the conflict between wisdom, behavior which is wise in the ways of humanity, and holiness with its fidelity to God's law, is played out and centers on the question: "Are serfdom and forced deportations morally acceptable because they involve foreigners?"[10] Responding to the story of Joseph, says Wildavsky, involves a judgment that is critical of wisdom insofar as it comes into conflict with holiness.

The genius of the stories about Joseph, Wildavsky concludes, lies in "their simultaneous rejection and wary appreciation of worldly wisdom.... The narrator makes us aware that with power comes the temptation to confuse evil with benevolence by persuading oneself that heinous acts like forced deportation are part of God's plan for man."[11] Joseph's path, Wildavsky argues, is not one that should be taken by a God-centered people. The account of Moses as leader in Exodus, coming as it does straight after the conclusion of the story of Joseph, demonstrates that at a very fundamental level, both religiously and politically, Joseph was fundamentally rejected by Israel when assessed in the light of the covenant.

> Now we know why the patriarchs stop with Jacob, why the line of succession goes from Abraham, to Isaac to Jacob and then stops before Joseph. The Torah peers over the precipice, sees the consequences of combining power with assimilation—Joseph's abandonment of God's moral law—and begins again with Moses.... Joseph is tried and found interesting, even admirable in some respects, but is ultimately found wanting... How can they follow Pharaoh's helper? Instead, they will follow his opposite Moses who proclaims God's law.[12]

In coming to his assessment of Joseph, Wildavsky continues with a comparison of the trajectory of Joseph with that of Moses, who becomes absolutely central to the story of Israel in the book of Exodus, where Moses is in fact the "anti-Joseph."[13] Quite strikingly there is no revelation, appearance of God, or word that comes from God to Joseph. The narrator observes that Yahweh is with Joseph, but that is as far as it goes. There is no promise of blessing associated with Joseph in the way that blessings were affirmed with respect to Isaac and Jacob. Yes, Yahweh is present with Joseph, but is very much behind the scenes in the way Joseph's story is told. Moses on the other hand frequently receives a direct word from God, and guidance as to

---

10. Wildavsky, *Assimilation versus Separation*, 7.
11. Wildavsky, *Assimilation versus Separation*, 202.
12. Wildavsky, *Assimilation versus Separation*, 196.
13. Wildavsky, *Assimilation versus Separation*, 192–96.

how he is to act in his role as the leader of his people.[14] The trajectory of the two leaders is very different, and the narrator repeatedly calls this to our attention. Joseph climbs to a position of high status in Egypt, while Moses starts off in a position of status in Egypt and renounces it. Joseph acts on Pharaoh's behalf to implement policy within Egypt, a policy that he himself proposed. Moses fights against Pharaoh to achieve the exodus of his people from slavery. Joseph helped to bring Israel from Canaan to Egypt, while Moses takes Israel from Egypt to the verge of Canaan.

When measured against Moses, Joseph is treated with reserve, and the comparisons uniformly count in Moses' favor so far as the compliers of the tradition are concerned. These oppositions are staged, Wildavsky argues, so that hearers and readers of the stories can envisage clearly the choices facing Israel. "Joseph's Egyptian wisdom in action reveals the true meaning of Egypt: prosperity, idolatry and in the end despotism. Joseph takes the Egyptian principles of human mastery and rational administration in the service of life, and longevity, to their perverse conclusion: land, patrimony and freedom are sacrificed to the goal of survival."[15]

Given these readings of the story of Joseph, we have good reason to interpret the story of Joseph "otherwise" than as the frequently unqualified endorsement by Christians of Joseph and his path in the exercise of power and its centralizing policy. The risk of becoming a chaplain and consultant for empire, and its nightmare outcomes, cannot be justified by Israel. The story of Joseph read "otherwise" is not one of approval of his assimilation and accommodation to empire, with no effort made to draw lines around the extent of his compliance. Certainly, we have in Joseph a model of personal integrity who is dedicated to his family's welfare, but who displays conformity exercised through technical competence in policy advising and policy implementation in the service of empire. We have here an approach to faithfulness in which the personal dimensions of responsibility by Joseph to his family, are divorced from faithfulness to "the God of Abraham, Isaac, and Jacob." This is demonstrated in public policy Joseph implements, with its lack of concern about questions of justice and equity.

While the short-term impact of Joseph's policy on the Egyptian people was oppressive, the long-term impact was to be disastrous for the people of Israel. "Israel is doubly cursed by Joseph's policies. The prosperity for his family produced by Joseph's favoritism will arouse the envy of the Egyptians, and even more importantly Joseph's consolidation of Pharaoh's power will result in the practice of wholesale slavery. Thanks to Joseph's agrarian

---

14. Wilson, *Joseph, Wise and Otherwise*, 100.
15. Kass, *The Beginning of Wisdom*, 634.

policies Egypt is transformed into a nation of slaves."[16] Joseph is seen here to have "out-Pharaohed" Pharaoh. The Israelites themselves in the longer term become oppressed under Pharaoh's yoke, and the move to freedom from that oppression, the exodus, was to become a central in accounts of the identity of the people of Israel. Mark Brett nicely summarizes some elements of this criticism in the light of the longer narrative of Abraham.

> In many respects the characterization of Joseph inverts the narrative of Abraham. Instead of removing himself from the center of an empire, Joseph rises through a series of bitter ironies to command all the coercive power of Egypt. . . . Genesis 47 presents a chilling picture of imperial politics which has often been obscured by readerly affections for the family of Joseph. The narrative is quite explicit in describing the painful economic realities. Having accumulated all the available land and wealth Joseph establishes a totalitarian rule based on debt slavery.[17]

In the light of this reading, Joseph is clearly not an example for us to follow in our transition beyond Christendom. Precisely the opposite. The tale of Joseph is of a person committed to personal integrity and family values, who implements a strategy shaped by accommodation to empire. The stories of Esther and Daniel that I now turn to show an awareness of the story of Joseph and deliver in their narration an implied judgment on him and the path he took.[18] The narrators of the stories of Esther and Daniel strike differing balances in their respective accounts of the engagement of the protagonists with imperial power. Neither of the comparisons, though, count in favor of Joseph's choice. It is his attachment to family that emerges most strongly in the final word from Joseph when he acknowledges that eventually the Israelites will return to the land that God swore to Abraham, Isaac, and Jacob. "When God comes to you carry up my bones from here" (Gen 50:24–26). The emphasis at this last moment in his life is on the family connection, not the return to the land of promise. Egypt still has a word in this, though. Joseph is embalmed and placed in a coffin in Egypt to wait for his family to begin their return, a return that will be driven by the figure of Moses, who finally stands over, and against, Joseph in the tradition of Israel.

---

16. Kass, *The Beginning of Wisdom*, 630.
17. Brett, *Locations of God*, 69–70.
18. Wildavsky, *Assimilation versus Separation*, 126–34.

Stories Read "Otherwise"

Esther and the tensions of exile

The story of Esther deals with exile, power, and empire. I will make clear in the following discussion when I am referring to the book of Esther, in which the story is narrated, as opposed to the character Esther, who actually shares the stage in the book with other significant figures, including the king, Haman, Mordecai, and just possibly God. In the book of Esther, the story leaves open a number of questions. How we decide to answer these questions will shape our reading of the story.

The book of Esther is set in the midst of the Persian Empire, probably around the third or fourth century BCE in a specified historical location, and that location provides us with some guidance on the way we are to read the book. It is a story about survival of the Jewish community in exile and the use of power by exiles when their assimilation is not yet an accomplished fact. The story is told as a response to the perceived threat to Jewish identity felt by many Jews in the shift from exile to diaspora. It seems to be intended, among other purposes, to provide guidance for the exiles on negotiating the difficult path between assimilation and maintaining their identity through sectarian withdrawal. There is little by way of explicit reference in the story to the God of Israel. The significance of this silence, though, is disputed, and I will say a little more about that shortly. Despite the serious issues at stake in the narrative, matters of life and death, there is a good deal of humor in the way the incidents are developed, and the characters are sketched out. The story is also notable for accounts of a large number of parties involving lots of drinking, during which various denouements occur, announcements are made, and the plot is advanced in important ways.

The specific audience to which the book of Esther was directed is those Jews who remained in exile, who in this story are portrayed as being relatively well off. The exiles in view here clearly had taken the advice of Jeremiah to settle down and seek the welfare of the city, and by doing so succeeded in doing well for themselves. These were Jews who had remained in the Persian Empire and not returned to Jerusalem. They now felt threatened by the communities in which they had settled, who in turn felt threatened by an emerging prosperous community that could be portrayed as the dangerous "other."[19] Exile as a reality had to be continually renegotiated by those who did not return to Jerusalem. The book of Esther thus records the hidden private transcripts of resistance and negotiation by the exiles, that is, it is a response from the perspective of those who are not "in control," but who were not without a degree of power and influence.

---

19. Grossman, *Esther*, 20–21.

We are at the point in this story where the exile has given way to diaspora. This is a tale dealing with the crisis of the Jewish life in the diaspora, a crisis that it shares in common with Daniel. The story of Esther demonstrates the possibility of maintaining Jewishness for the diaspora, that is for those who were now not going to return to Israel.[20] When the exiles are embraced in some sense by the prevailing culture, how are they to retain their Jewishness? The feast of Purim, with which this story concludes, is seen as a celebration of the outcome of this process of identity maintenance.

The story of Esther

The story of Esther begins with Ahasuerus, king of Persia, who having deposed his queen makes arrangements to choose a new one from a selection of beautiful young women from throughout the empire. A Jewish orphan named Esther, brought up by her uncle Mordecai, is entered into the quest, and having received the royal stamp of approval, is crowned as his new queen. All this takes place without Esther revealing her Jewish heritage. Shortly afterwards, Mordecai discovers a plot by two courtiers to assassinate the king. The conspirators are apprehended and hanged, and Mordecai's service to the king is recorded by the bureaucrats in the royal archives, though the event is then forgotten by the king. The next turn in the plot is that King Ahasuerus appoints Haman as his viceroy. Mordecai, who sits at the palace gates, falls into Haman's disfavor. Haman discovers that Mordecai refused to bow to him because he, Mordecai, was a Jew. Haman in revenge plots to kill not just Mordecai, but all the Jews in the empire. He obtains Ahasuerus's permission to execute this plan. A royal decree is issued throughout the kingdom to slay all Jews on a specific date.

When Mordecai discovers the plan, he goes into mourning and implores Esther to intercede with the king. She is afraid to present herself unsummoned, an offense punishable by death. She directs Mordecai to have all Jews fast for three days for her, and vows to fast as well prior to going to Ahasuerus, who on her entry stretches out his scepter to her to indicate that she is not to be punished. She invites him to a feast in the company of Haman and then at that feast she asks them to attend a further feast the next evening. Meanwhile, Haman is again offended by Mordecai and has gallows built to hang him. That night, Ahasuerus cannot sleep and orders the court records be read to him. He is reminded that Mordecai interceded in the previous plot against his life, and that Mordecai never received any recognition for this action. Haman appears to request the king's permission to hang

20. Treloar, *Esther and the End*, xxi.

Mordecai, but before he can make this request, Ahasuerus asks Haman what should be done for the man that the king wishes to honor. Assuming that the king is referring to Haman himself, Haman suggests that the man be dressed in the king's royal robes and crown and led around on the king's royal horse. To his surprise and horror, the king instructs Haman to do so to Mordecai.

At Esther's second banquet the king promises to grant her any request. She now reveals that she is Jewish, and that Haman is planning to exterminate her people, including her. Overcome by rage, Ahasuerus leaves the room; meanwhile Haman stays behind and begs Esther for his life, falling upon her in desperation. The king returns at this very moment and thinks Haman is assaulting the queen; this makes him even angrier and he orders Haman hanged on the very gallows that Haman had prepared for Mordecai. Unable to annul a formal royal decree, the king instead adds to it, permitting the Jews to join together and destroy any and all of those seeking to oppress them.

Who is at the center of the story?

Who is the protagonist of the tale? The answer is not as obvious as it may seem. Mordecai dominates the early chapters, while Esther takes up the key role from the middle of the book, where she largely replaces Mordecai as the key human agent in the salvation of her people. Jonathan Grossman, a Jewish commentator, places a stronger emphasis on the presence and providence of God at the critical turning point in the conversation between Mordecai and Esther than do many Christian commentators (Esth 4:14–16).[21] Certainly, while there is no obvious ritual observance by the leading Jewish characters in the story, Esther and Mordecai, there is both a providential appeal and a subtle acknowledgment that God is hidden but not totally absent in a story that highlights the trajectory of human action in response to emerging challenges to the safety and well-being of the exiles.[22]

There are interesting parallels between the stories of Esther and Ruth, to cast our net wider for a moment. Both women employ the tactics of the "trickster," the person without power who seeks to leverage their limited power indirectly, and perhaps involving sharp practice as they each develop in narrative status from lowly origins to positions of significance. They do this through managing the tension between private and public transcripts of their action and status. The wisdom "trickster" engages in sharp and shrewd

21. Grossman, *Esther*, 31–32.
22. Treloar, *Esther and the End*, 150–56.

tactics, while functioning as underdog.²³ Esther reveals the politics of a community that is not "in control," even if it has become well established in a life and a future away from Jerusalem. Esther is certainly not the chosen representative of her community, though at critical moments she speaks for her people. She is chosen by the ruling powers, in this case the king, and is dependent on his favor for her power. The accountability to her people for the exercise of power that Esther exercises is self-chosen. Here we have a form of Jewish exilic politics where key actors are struggling to maintain their identity without a separate king, officials, and priests. Brueggemann reads the message of Esther as the affirmation of Jewish ethnic identity as a strategy within empire. "The urgent teaching of the book of Esther is the urgency that Jewish identity must not be hidden. The book assures its readers that courageous self-assertion within the counsels of empire will help bring support and well-being in the empire."²⁴

The turning point in the tale comes in this case not through a dream, but in the darkness when the king cannot sleep and there is the reading of his acts, and the question of justice to Mordecai arises. This sudden and unexpected change of fortune exposes the inner contradictions of the political system in its various components. The king, the court, decision-making, the maintenance of records, the plotting and counter-plotting all reveal an instability in the environment in which the diaspora Jews must live.²⁵ It is the exercise by Esther of power and influence, though braving a high degree of vulnerability in their exercise, that makes the difference for the community.

The presence and absence of God

On one reading the book of Esther leaves open the theological question as to the role of God in achieving the salvation of the people. The apparent absence of God in the book of Esther reflects a theological ambiguity. Is God involved in driving the plot, or is it chance that is ruling here? It is an open question for the reader as to whether this is read as a truly secular or as a religious story, noting that the secular may be a location in which God may be active. The hiddenness of God for some scholars of this story is "a clear and undeniable reference to the presence of God in this story world. . . . That is, the absence of any explicit reference to God is taken by those with eyes to see and ears to hear to be a clear affirmation of God working

---

23. Walzer, *In God's Shadow*, 116–17.
24. Brueggemann, *Out of Babylon*, 149.
25. Treloar, *Esther and the End*, 140–41.

providentially on behalf of the Jews throughout the story."[26] The book reflects the life of most people who do not experience God's speech directly, as did the biblical patriarchs and prophets. Actions and decisions taken as an exercise in responsibility to the Jewish community remain wrapped in theological ambiguity. If we choose to read this as a secular tale in which God is not visibly present, or directly acknowledged, we are still able to read it as a story about how God works through the normal processes of human life in dealing with the problems we face in everyday existence. The threat of Jewish extermination is met with "fasting, meeting, and lamenting" but without any specific cry to the God of Israel. Esther has "a genuine choice to make in this particular situation . . . but there is no immediate guidance from the Torah on how to deal with the terrible particularities of her situation."[27]

Despite this relative absence of God, and dispute over the story's theological weight, the story of Esther is very biblical in its structure.[28] The story is patterned after that of Joseph, with which it has a good deal in common. There is the setting in a foreign court, the rise from humble origins to a high political position that enables Esther, like Joseph before her, to help her people in a crisis. The story connects these Jews in Persia with the larger story of Israel, from the point of view of Israel in exile.[29] The lesson of Esther when read in the context of the stories of Joseph is that it is not necessary to worship foreign gods or adopt foreign customs to achieve high office. The story of Esther is an implicit critique of the choice Joseph made in aligning himself with the empire.

Readers after Christendom, in a situation where loss of privilege is now a commonplace, may find this book, if not directly instructive, at least providing us with a cautionary tale. We are in a situation where access to substantial power is still a possibility, and where community tensions and identity can become a focus for forms of ethnic jealousy and cleansing. It is imperative to remember too that we read the book of Esther after the Shoah, so that our interpretation of this story must take account of the reality of genocide and an underlying anti-Semitism in much Christian practice and scriptural interpretation. It would be perilous therefore to read the violence by the dispersed Jewish diaspora communities in this story as "a statement about Jewish nationalism, treating the story's violence as normative and essential to Judaism rather than as a defensive response to mortal danger."[30]

26. Beal, *Esther*, xxi.
27. Brett, *Locations of God*, 123.
28. Day, *Esther*, 18–19.
29. Wildavsky, *Assimilation versus Separation*, 131.
30. Day, *Esther*, 21.

The book of Esther then is a story of a response to a clear and present danger to an ethnic identity. I say "ethnic" because the religious character of the Jews does not receive much emphasis. Here is where it gets difficult. The result of the exercise of power under the influence of Esther and Mordecai is that their place in the empire becomes firm, they end up as the ones with power, and are no longer vulnerable. Exile becomes here a location in which a minority identity can lead to a self-reinforcing fear of the "other" on both sides of the community boundary.

The key achievement in Esther is the official recognition of a public feast that celebrates the Jewish community's continuing existence. Perhaps the "otherwise" reading here is of the need for caution in seeking to claim God's presence and support for the specific exercise of power. We have here a woman who acts in a key role, exercising a practical form of wisdom. The apparent lack of presence of God, and the emphasis on human responsibility, is a frame of action that speaks to a post-Christendom context for serving the community. Here the ambiguity relates to the question, which community is being served? Esther is focused on her ethnic religious group of exiles. The question of the "other" as the surrounding community remains a question. How wide do we envisage the scope of the community that we are called to serve? Is the "other" within the scope of our attention and responsibility?

Daniel: wisdom and the prophetic stance

As was the case with Esther, I will distinguish between the character Daniel, and the book of Daniel as I proceed. The writing and the compilation of the book of Daniel seems to have been occasioned by the crisis of 167–164 BCE, the attempt by Antiochus IV to eradicate Judaism through a program of radical Hellenization.[31] Commentators from the rabbis onward have continued to debate the tension between the themes of identity and resistance in the book. The story of the struggle for survival includes a focus on dietary issues as a subtle form of resistance to the pressures of assimilation. Though the actual context of the Jews at that stage was that they were back in Jerusalem, the story with its challenge to identity is set in a context in which the Jews are envisaged to be still in exile. Though they were actually "at home," they felt as though they were in exile under the heel of an oppressive empire.

---

31. Pietersen, *Reading the Bible after Christendom*, 128–30; Smith-Christopher, *A Biblical Theology of Exile*, 191.

Stories Read "Otherwise"

The location in the First Testament (Old Testament) of the book of Daniel is ambiguous and disputed.[32] The Jewish canon places the book of Daniel in the Writings as a form of Wisdom literature, along with the books of Job, Esther, and the Song of Songs. Christians have placed the book of Daniel as one of the four major prophets, in the company of Isaiah, Jeremiah, and Ezekiel. This difference in the way the book has been understood and received by the respective communities points to different, though admittedly overlapping, ways in which it can be read.

Exercising power in exile

For the purposes of my reading the story of Daniel "again," it is important to acknowledge that the book has a strong wisdom character in the first half that suggests comparisons and connections with the stories of Joseph and Esther in the experience of serving imperial authority while in exile. In chapter 2, for example, we have a parallel with the Joseph story in the presentation of Daniel as the prototypical wise man.

While falling into two distinct parts with respect to both style and theological focus, the book of Daniel offers a rich and complex resource for reflection on the exercise of power while in exile. This divided character leaves us with an unsettled question as to whether the character Daniel should be interpreted as a wise courtier or an interpreter of visions speaking truth to power. Or is he both? Given these different possibilities, I will first pay attention to the stories in the first half of the book, which concern themselves with Daniel's role as an adviser to the court, followed by readings which acknowledge the prophetic strain that is present.

The first few chapters are devoted to stories about Daniel as the model Jewish practitioner of wisdom, in exile and serving the imperial court. Daniel and his friends rise to prominence in the court of the Babylonian king, yet despite this demonstrated loyalty in service to the court, Daniel and his friends notably refuse to bow down to royal power on the grounds that it would manifest a form of idolatry. These narratives suggest it is possible to function, and indeed to prosper, in serving within empire provided you maintain at the same time an unswerving loyalty to Yahweh. When the empire demands worship, that is, it asserts its priority and claim on the Jewish people in defining how life is to be lived, this claim must be resisted unflinchingly.

In functioning as a court tale, chapters 1 to 6 of Daniel point to a context of ethnic and religious tension. Within a theological frame, the book

---

32. For a survey of the complexities of the text of Daniel see Newsom, *Daniel*, 1–12.

offers a strong response to what are identified as idolatrous imperial claims. Rhetorically, the narrator brings to our attention the respective relationships of divine and human sovereignty. The power claims made through the imperial rhetoric is met with a counterclaim of a power which the exiles name variously as the God of heaven and the God most holy. The claim of this God remains in tension with that of the empire and is a claim that can never be finally settled ahead of the risk of commitment of those who desire to remain faithful to him.

In the conflict reported in the tale in Daniel chapter 3, between the respective claims of the king and the God of the Jews on Shadrach, Meshach, and Abednego, the three acknowledge that there is no certainty that God will deliver them. Yet the three affirm that they must obey their God rather than the king, whether or not they survive the fiery furnace. It is interesting to ask where we the contemporary readers locate ourselves in this story. Are we among those on the sideline, not under the pressure of confession, but associated with those who exercise power over against the vulnerable? Our intuitive response is to locate ourselves with the three Jewish witnesses in their faithfulness. The historical record of the churches when faced by moments of extreme conflict would suggest that we are likely to be located on the sidelines rather than with those who pay the price of being faithful. We need to constantly ask who we are and where we are located in moments of crisis such as those sketched in Daniel. It is this questioning of the hearer that the tales in Daniel are designed to provoke.

In critique of Joseph

The stories of Daniel in the first half of the book point to the importance of wisdom used in pursuit of the faithful survival of a minority community that acknowledges that it is not in control of its destiny. Daniel here represents an alternative to an ethic of violence for self-preservation, drawing on the tradition of a wisdom-oriented peace ethic. Daniel is a wise man who is used to convey a message from the past to the here and now. He shows how a wise Jew of the diaspora can function at the highest levels in the life of the ruling gentile community. According to Wildavsky, "the serious purpose of the first part of the Book of Daniel is to contrast the behaviour [of one] taken in captivity from Jerusalem to Babylon and trained in the sciences of the local wise men with that of Joseph."[33] The first part of the book is in his view "a polemic against Joseph's surrender to foreign ways by indicating in

---

33. Wildavsky, *Assimilation versus Separation*, 126.

the person of Daniel what Joseph ought to have done."[34] Daniel for example not only interprets the dream, but actually tells the king in detail what the dream was, thus outdoing Joseph in the competition of wisdom. The story of Daniel presents him as greater than Joseph.

In the light of that context let me offer a brief summary of the first half of the book of Daniel, as a story of the public servant as resident alien, whose heart was attuned to the God of Israel, while his life was lived out in Babylon. Daniel in this narrative is identified for his potential and taken from his homeland to be trained as a principal adviser at the center of the empire. He lived out his life as a government official in a religiously alien environment. He continued to exercise his vocation while practicing his faith, even under threat of death. The distinctiveness of his faith was not an intellectual spiritual orientation, but a matter of what he ate and how he prayed. He remained, according to the story, the public servant par excellence, providing as an exile frank and fearless advice to the imperial power that had destroyed his nation. Daniel exercised his gifts in seeking the welfare of the city in which God had placed him, while remaining loyal to the God of Israel.

In the story of Israel and its faith, the exercise of Daniel's gifts and the integrity of his life was recognized and honored by his community. As the story is told, Daniel did not withdraw from the world, he lived faithfully in the middle of it, unwavering in his trust that the God whom he worshipped was ultimately the key to history, rather than the earthly ruler whom he served. The story offers Daniel as one who was sustained by the disciplines of his faith, by the faithfulness of the God whom he worshipped, and by the company of those who shared his faith and his vocation. In other words, he was shaped in his response by a community that did not recognize a distinction between the "sacred" and the "secular," or the "material" and the "spiritual." "The Hebrews maintained their own religious and cultural identity, as a witness to the God of Israel, even as they worked for the good of Babylon."[35] They were a visible witness in public affairs in the midst of a society where they had no control over the reigning political authority. The story of Esther carries a similar meaning and was similarly retold to encourage such witness.

---

34. Wildavsky, *Assimilation versus Separation*, 127.
35. Wildavsky, *Assimilation versus Separation*, 187.

A prophet against the empire

The Jesuit priest, poet, and anti-war activist Daniel Berrigan reads the book of Daniel in the context of the prophetic tradition of Israel, rather than as an account of a model wise person. In his reading from a position of radical opposition to much of contemporary US policy, he offers an extended midrash on the book of Daniel, drawing attention to its contemporary relevance as an account of resistance to authoritarian power. The ancient story according to Berrigan tells of conflict of conscience in opposition to the powers. The story concerns worldly power striking against the discipline of the believing community. In this struggle, the costly faith of Daniel and his friends reveals itself as a new form of anti-imperial power. In the Christian tradition Daniel "is honored as one of the sublime quarternity of the major prophets. In a window of the Cathedral of Chartres an astonishing image [shows]: Daniel and his other 'major' compatriots—Isaiah, Jeremiah, and Ezekiel—bear upon their shoulders the four evangelists."[36]

Daniel, in Berrigan's poetic reading, lives out a response of conscience that is clear and uncompromising in its opposition to the claims of empire. There is a danger in this reading. While Daniel's is undoubtedly a heroic response, it is not always the only option that is available, or indeed required. Being bedazzled by the "heroic" choice can sometimes encourage us to dismiss its relevance to our time, and help us rationalize away, or indeed completely avoid noticing, the claim on us to be faithful in the face of less extreme and less stark conflicts. The distinction between a prophet and a wise person speaking truth to power may rest on discernment and attention to a range of possibilities rather than a simple choice between resistance and conformity.

Overall Berrigan assesses that Daniel was "an improviser of ways and means. An icon for the people of his time and for those to come an heroic image of fidelity. All of these and a high mystic as well."[37] Berrigan makes it clear that the account of Daniel as offered to us over the centuries has a symbolic character. In Daniel's dreams there is a suggestion of a power that challenges the imagination and the certainties of empires, and in so doing calls them all into question. His reading of the appearance of the rock in the dream in chapter 2 points to the way it cuts a swathe through the imperial powers in an account that carries with it the passion of an anti-war activist and a poet.

---

36. Berrigan, *Daniel*, 5.
37. Berrigan, *Daniel*, 5.

> The rock is an image of preeminence. It nullifies all other images of power, all kingdoms no matter how lowly (those feet of clay) or grandiose (the head crowned of gold).... It takes to itself the anger of Christ confronting as it must... hardness of heart, claims and counterclaims of omnipotence, worldly systems whether of church and state, their pretensions, ruthlessness, legalism, violent contempt for the victims they themselves create ... The image of the rock implies an invitation and urging. In our times we are invited to consider (and to undertake) startling forms of nonviolent activity. To set the rock rolling striking against self-deifying images of authority. To the crowned heads let us offer the truth. The truth includes this: their feet are of clay...[38]

The second half of the book of Daniel moves away from questions of faithfulness while serving the empire, to a theological account and critique of empire. That is, it is an account in which the earthly realities of political and religious power, for there is no meaningful distinction between the two, are projected onto a cosmic screen. Nations can exercise opposition to the will of God, delay it but not actually thwart it. Exile now becomes understood not just as divine punishment, but as the result of being caught up in a divine conflict in which angels or spiritual powers are manifest. Daniel in his interpretation of dreams here introduces a third element beyond Israel and God, the powers, a concept which is taken up in the Second Testament (New Testament) in Paul's account of the principalities and powers.[39] Here we have an interplay between divine and human figures, all set on a cosmic stage in which the current struggles of a subject people are relativized, or perhaps even secularized, through their insertion into this broader theological frame.

In this brief reading of Daniel "otherwise," I have acknowledged the differing locations of the book of Daniel in the Jewish and Christian traditions, and the range of possible responses that emerge on how we might work within, and perhaps even on behalf of, empire. The stories and dreams of Daniel remind us that grand gestures of resistance may be appropriate but are not always our only option.

---

38. Berrigan, *Daniel*, 41.
39. William Stringfellow addresses these issues in *An Ethic for Christians*.

Provisional soundings

The stories of Joseph, Esther, and Daniel as we have seen can be read in ways that offer interpretations and understandings that are "otherwise" than those in much preaching and devotional literature. This is particularly true of the story of Joseph. To read it "otherwise" is a response for which we find support in the stories of Esther and Daniel. The Jewish people in exile experienced a complex relationship with empire and told stories of a range of possible responses on how to live in exile, within the shifting character of empire. They do not offer direct parallels to the situation we are in after Christendom. They do however offer resources to inform our imagination, and to encourage us to ask fresh question about how we might approach community engagement in our context. The stories of both Esther and Daniel stand as a critique of the choices Joseph made. It is not necessary to conform to the culture of the empire to rise to positions of power and be able to act on behalf of its people.

Joseph enacted a strategy of accommodation and assimilation to Egypt in which his identity and the possibilities of faithfulness to the God of Israel is submerged in the management of imperial power. The story of Joseph as it is told in Scripture does not offer a direct criticism of his activity. Rather it withholds approval, and its criticism is implicit in the silences in the text. His story is one in which, while his family benefits from the protection of empire in the short term, in the long term they do not escape the political and economic impact of centralized power and economic servitude. The story suggests that there are severe risks in putting aside our ethical frame in providing pragmatic policy advice and undertaking program implementation.

Esther takes the risk of publicly exhibiting her Jewish identity and wins over the empire to provide care and support for her people as an ethnic group. The story of her venture offers little by way of theological justification. The pressures and the vulnerability of that identity are very visible to us in reading this story in the light of the Shoah. In the story of Esther, the question is raised as to whether God is in the decisions and their outcomes. The answer to this may be very difficult to determine, even retrospectively. The question lurking here is whether God is present in the secular as a silence in which substantial responsibility is left with those taking the decisions.

The book of Daniel offers us multiple readings on the exercise of power by those working with, and for the empire, while in exile. In the first half of the book, Daniel and his companions engage in the service of empire, while retaining a clear boundary setting disciplined life within an overarching framework in which the claims of the God of Israel override the claims of empire when they conflict. Daniel's visions and their interpretation point to a theological deconstruction of the claims of imperial powers by placing them in a broader eschatological framework. Being able to imagine possibilities beyond the claims of the powerful is an exercise in worship of God, and an act of desecularizing the claims of the political deities.

The monarchy viewed "otherwise"

Despite the limited period during which the kings of Israel and Judah actually exercised effective sovereignty over independent nations, this period in Israel's history has received disproportionate weight in influencing the political reading of the First Testament (Old Testament) during Christendom. This perspective has underpinned the presumption of the normative character of monarchy as being at the heart of the story of Israel, but does not reflect the predominant experience of exile in shaping Israel's identity and worship, living as it did in the geographical shatter zone of empires. There is another perspective from which we can challenge the predominant, indeed taken for granted, focus on the monarchy in the history of Israel. The tradition of Israel records a minority strand that articulated a questioning of the rationale and theological justification for the monarchy. The prophet Samuel in the records passed down to us is the key figure in this other reading of the role and theological status of monarchy.

> The prophet Samuel's denunciation of the establishment of a monarchy and his continued subversive behaviour with regard to the king who marked the transition to dynastic succession, Saul, indicate the depth of feeling against it. According to the memories of Israel settled in the Promised Land, there was a tradition of charismatic leaders, the Judges. God raised up leaders to meet particular needs, whether administrative or military. In the midst of the stories told about this period, suspicion attached itself to the ambitions of those who would make themselves kings.[40]

In 1 Samuel, chapter 8, the people of Israel, represented by the elders, come to the prophet Samuel seeking a king. This is a central passage in beginning to read kingship "again" and to read it "otherwise."

> Then all the elders of Israel gathered together and came to Samuel at Ramah, and said to him, "You are old, and your sons

40. Rowland, "A Kingdom, but Not as We Know It."

> do not follow in your ways; appoint for us, then, a king to govern us, like other nations." But the thing displeased Samuel when they said, "Give us a king to govern us." Samuel prayed to the Lord, and the Lord said to Samuel, "Listen to the voice of the people in all that they say to you; for they have not rejected you, but they have rejected me from being king over them. Just as they have done to me from the day I brought them up out of Egypt, to this day, forsaking me and serving other gods, so also they are doing to you. Now then, listen to their voice; only—you shall solemnly warn them, and show them the ways of the king who shall reign over them."
>
> So, Samuel reported all the words of the Lord to the people who were asking him for a king. He said, "These will be the ways of the king who will reign over you: he will take your sons and appoint them to his chariots and to be his horsemen, and to run before his chariots; and he will appoint for himself commanders of thousands and commanders of fifties, and some to plow his ground and to reap his harvest, and to make his implements of war and the equipment of his chariots. He will take your daughters to be perfumers and cooks and bakers. He will take the best of your fields and vineyards and olive orchards and give them to his courtiers. He will take one-tenth of your grain and of your vineyards and give it to his officers and his courtiers. He will take your male and female slaves, and the best of your cattle and donkeys, and put them to his work. He will take one-tenth of your flocks, and you shall be his slaves. And in that day you will cry out because of your king, whom you have chosen for yourselves; but the Lord will not answer you in that day."

This passage presents the people as coming to Samuel asking for an improved system of government that would bring Israel into line with the governments of the surrounding nations. We need, they argued, to get with the program, to get over the inefficiency and uncertainty of relying on the judges, and the unpredictable and uncontrollable movement of the Spirit of God. The sociologist and theologian Jacques Ellul comments that viewed from a human standpoint "Israel feels that monarchy would be an organizational advance, that it is both more efficient and more secure, that it allows of political planning in a way that the system of the judges did not."[41] In response the prophet Samuel points out to them the consequences of shifting to a monarchy, and they were not going to be pretty. Efficiency and effectiveness in government might have its downside. Monarchy would end up causing them a good deal of unhappiness and social disruption.

---

41. Ellul, *The Politics of God*, 17.

> [T]he text is ambivalent, if not downright comical. When the Israelites ask Gideon, the judge, to be their king, he refuses because God is king (Judges 8.22ff). Yet Gideon's son is named Abimelech, which means "my father is king"! Samuel is equally ambivalent: he is the one whom Yahweh instructs to anoint both Saul and David, yet he tries to dissuade the people when they ask for a king (1 Samuel 8.4ff).[42]

More importantly, monarchy was a form of governance that would be at odds with the social structure and economic character of Israel as it had been up till then. If you want a king, Samuel told them, you are asking for conscription of your youth, the creation of a standing army, exorbitant taxation, social oppression, and economic impoverishment.[43] We find out later in the Naboth story that the creation of monarchy would lead to their land being taken as well (1 Kgs 21). "Never mind all that," the people said, "We want a king." Beyond the social and economic consequences, the theological implication of shifting to a monarchy was that the people were implicitly rejecting God as their ruler. Those who put the chronicles together faithfully recorded the prophetic dissent against this decision despite the fact that the shift was made to the monarchy. Despite the high status given to David in Israel's memory, the texts not only preserved this tradition of dissent, but also left a record that did not exactly burnish David's reputation. While David is granted a dynastic covenant, and is presented as being responsive to Yahweh on many occasions, his falls from grace are also recorded and left as a witness to the follies of the contemporary monarchy.

The other passage on kingship that we need to consider in tracking this tradition of dissent is Deuteronomy 17:14–20, where Moses allows for the possibility of a king. The qualifications attached to kingship though are so severe that by the standards of the surrounding culture a person so limited would hardly be a king at all. Moses like Samuel is not presented as being enthusiastic about kingship. The qualifications he places on kingship, if placed as a template over the account of the kings in the line of David, would see a black mark entered against nearly all of them.

> When you have come into the land that the Lord your God is giving you, and have taken possession of it, and settled in it, and you say, "I will set a king over me, like all the nations that are around me," you may indeed set over you a king whom the Lord your God will choose. One of your own community you may set as king over you; you are not permitted to put a foreigner

---

42. Hurcombe, "Disestablishing the Kingdom."
43. Brett, *Political Trauma and Healing*, 172.

over you, who is not of your own community. Even so, he must not acquire many horses for himself, or return the people to Egypt in order to acquire more horses, since the Lord has said to you, "You must never return that way again." And he must not acquire many wives for himself, or else his heart will turn away; also silver and gold he must not acquire in great quantity for himself. When he has taken the throne of his kingdom, he shall have a copy of this law written for him in the presence of the levitical priests. It shall remain with him and he shall read in it all the days of his life, so that he may learn to fear the Lord his God, diligently observing all the words of this law and these statutes, neither exalting himself above other members of the community nor turning aside from the commandment, either to the right or to the left, so that he and his descendants may reign long over his kingdom in Israel.

After King David, whose status and charisma left an enduring impression on Israel and its traditions, though as I have noted David's failings were also documented, the kings who followed him were never able to claim the unquestioned divine status and authority that was usually ascribed to the monarchy in the surrounding political/religious culture. The prophets claimed a divine calling or authority for their proclamations over against the claims of the monarchy that they were challenging.[44] Given that David despite his charismatic standing did not escape challenge from the prophets, it is hardly surprising that most of the kings who followed him were subject to even more substantial and unrelenting critique. The balance in the overall appraisal of monarchy is nicely summarized by Christopher Rowland.

> The Torah hardly contemplates monarchy with equanimity. Its vision of society is of a community of the elect which, if not exactly egalitarian, works according to a vision of social intercourse in which injustice is corrected, whether through the release of debts (Deuteronomy 15) or the Jubilee (Leviticus 25, though even here the exigencies of the "real world" demand some kind of dilution of the ideal). Even in Deuteronomy, where the likelihood of kingship does seem to be contemplated (Deuteronomy 17.14ff), it is a grudging acceptance in which the effects of monarchy are duly rehearsed.[45]

Despite its apparent centrality, the existence of the monarchy was remembered as being problematic, and theological contestation over it

---

44. Walzer, *In God's Shadow*, 75.
45. Rowland, "A Kingdom, but Not as We Know It."

remained in the record. The economic historian Michael Hudson in the course of his account of biblical law notes that there is an anti-royalist spirit in the law in the First Testament (Old Testament).[46] Evidence of that contestation was left prominently in the text, even though there was every opportunity for it to have been downplayed or omitted. The historians of Israel came to the conclusion that kingship in Israel was a matter of human choice. It was an optional rather than an indispensable feature of government, and could not claim an unqualified divine mandate, as was the case with the prevailing nations whose governing model Israel had sought to emulate.

Christian readings of the First Testament (Old Testament) on this issue have tended to overlook the significance of this counter-tradition, and to read kingship in Israel from beginning to end through an entirely approving and uncritical frame of reference. Christopher Rowland highlights the difference between popular remembering of the Davidic dynasty and what the critical character of the record on which that remembering is based.

> The curious thing about the story of the Davidic dynasty, with its central position in the story of God's people, is that in large part it actually serves to point out the inadequacies of that particular structure. Throughout the books of Kings, in particular, we are offered a catalogue of travesties of the divine righteousness. Even beacons of hope such as Hezekiah are shown in less than flattering light. The same is true for those founding figures, David and Solomon, whose heroic deeds and empire-building are viewed with a mixture of admiration and suspicion.[47]

The unease about kingship, its political/religious failures, and devastating social and economic impact, accompanied by a theological undercutting of its status, offers an important challenge to any attempt to leverage the First Testament (Old Testament) into a source of uncritically sourced divine support for Christendom. The critique of kingship in this counter-tradition acknowledges that the structure of monarchy was a human choice, subject to criticism on its social and economic failings, not an arrangement that carried an automatic divine sanction. Kingship in Israel's memory is desacralized and subject to prophetic judgement. Claims for divine support for kingship in Israel were just that, claims that were always vulnerable to theological questioning and critique.

Daniel Berrigan pushes this questioning of kingship further, suggesting that in the books of Judges, Samuel, and Kings we have a diagnosis of

---

46. Hudson, . . . *and forgive them their debts*, 182–83.
47. Rowland, "A Kingdom, but Not as We Know It."

the pathology of power, not an affirmation of kingship.[48] The historical sociologist Philip Gorski in a more nuanced judgment concludes the political theology of the First Testament (Old Testament) involves a rejection of all political idolatry, and therefore a distrust of monarchs, that was accompanied by a demand for social justice, along with a distrust of the well-to-do who often horde riches for themselves.[49] This critique of kingship has implications that run through to a theological orientation on the way we engage with government. Indeed, there will be echoes of this stance when I return to reimagining kingship in the Gospel writers' account of the teaching and ministry of Jesus in the next chapter.

48. Berrigan, *The Kings and Their Gods*, 6
49. Gorski, *American Babylon*.

3

Teaching and Performing a Different Kingdom

This chapter marks a shift in style. Apart from the introduction dealing with the theology of the kingdom of God,[1] the material in this chapter originated in several sermons that I have preached over the years on Jesus' teaching and practice of kingship. These sermons when I revisited them while writing this book went to the heart of what I wanted to say in this chapter. I decided on retaining something of the original informal rhetorical style that goes with preaching.

The Second Testament (New Testament) is a rich source for reading Scripture "again" in the cause of reimagining community engagement after Christendom. My choice of material in this chapter came down to my conviction that a good deal hangs on our ability to gain a fresh take on the theology of kingship and kingdom. Christendom after all was marinated in images, theology, and worship that laid out a theological warrant for kingship. Still now in post-Christendom, this language and the associated images powerfully haunt our theological imagination, even if we don't always explicitly acknowledge their presence and power. We still carry these images with us as "the unthought" through which we read, and reflect on, the teaching and practice of Jesus in the Gospels. Certainly, I still find myself reaching automatically for images of "kingship" and the patterns and assumptions about power that are carried by that terminology.

It's easy to simply drop back into habits of mind and imagination shaped by our current cultural assumption when we come to read the Scripture, chief among them that religion is a matter of individual choice with no wider frame of reference or claim on our life. But the Gospel writers didn't

---

1. I have relied on the survey of scholarship on the kingdom of God in Marshall, *Kingdom Come*.

view "religion" and "politics" as distinct and separate dimensions of human life. These realms were deeply entangled in the time of Jesus. We need to read the Second Testament (New Testament) in a way that takes account of that reality and doesn't import twenty-first-century assumptions about two distinct and different realms into the exercise. The reality of empire is pervasive throughout the Second Testament (New Testament). Caesar was lord and claimed a response of worship from those he ruled that was both political and religious in its claims. Jesus asks: "To what can we compare the kingdom of God, or what parable will we use for it?" (Mark 4:30). Through the medium of the parables Jesus rolls out a rich variety of images to help us envisage what God is up to, and how we might envisage that rule. He did not avoid using language that carried political claims.

In beginning my discussion of the kingdom of God, I acknowledge that I am rereading the accounts of the kingdom of God in the Gospels from a comfortable location as a member of a church that is a beneficiary of the British invasion and colonization, though Christian churches are no longer so closely linked to political power as they were at the time of the invasion.[2] My view is that we will be better placed to tackle these issues front on if we scrape away the barnacles of the Christendom mindset, and I proceed on that basis.

The kingdom of God

Jesus' teaching of the kingdom, and his inauguration of it, took place in an occupied nation under the rule of Rome. The *Pax Romana* was proclaimed by the Romans as an arrangement of unique benefit to all the nations and tribes that it ruled. The proclamation of the benefits of Roman rule had an unquestioning self-assurance that has remained a commonplace of imperial propaganda by authoritarian rulers down to the present day. The preferred Roman policy for managing their empire was one of indirect rule. While ultimate power was held by Rome, local rulers were allowed to maintain jurisdiction over their own territories, provided that they acted in the interests of the empire. During the time of Jesus, Galilee was ruled by Herod Antipas, while a Roman governor was in charge of Judea, with internal affairs under the control of the Jewish Sanhedrin. Implicating the subjects of imperial rule in the exercise of that rule had substantial benefits in dividing their loyalties and separating their interests from those of their fellow subjects proved effective. Reading the Gospels with that perspective in mind reveals

2. This reality has only just started to receive serious theological attention in Australia. See Budden, *Following Jesus in Invaded Space*.

a world of tension and conflict throughout moments of engagement with Jesus.

Jesus confronted these different levels of authority, and engaged in criticism of them all, with a criticism that was both "religious" and "political." Christopher Marshall observes that the "basic presupposition of his political critique was that sovereignty or kingship (*basilea*) belongs to God. God alone possesses ultimate authority in human affairs and God's character, God's demands, God's standards are the measuring rod against which the exercise of human power is to be evaluated."[3] Just as significantly as Jesus' critique of the abuse of power by political leadership is his discussion of how power is to be exercised by, and within, the kingdom of God. Prevailing patterns of power and greatness are turned upside down by Jesus in his teaching, and the hierarchy of status is brought under severe question.

There is to be no domination of the weak by the powerful within the community, in contrast to the practice of the Gentile rulers. Marshall summarizes this strand of teaching as demonstrating that true greatness is to be shown by striving to be of least account. Leadership is to be practiced as servanthood. This normative account of the exercise of power is radical enough for a range of Christian theologians and political activists to discern it as being compatible with at least some accounts of anarchism.[4] There is no easy step then from Jesus' account of kingship to an endorsement of monarchy. The Gospels are full of challenges to conventional wisdom in Christendom of an endorsement of monarchy, as in the character of the Messiah that is rendered for us in Matthew's Gospel.

> Jesus is presented as a humble king (21.5), contrasted with Herod who is no true king of the Jews (2.2). Herod slaughters the innocents (2.16ff) whereas the true king reacts positively to children (18.2, 19.14, 20.31). Those who are pronounced blessed share the characteristics of this humble king (5.3ff) who engaged in acts of compassion and healing which affected crowds rather than leaders (9.36, 14.14, 15.32). Final judgement (25.31ff) is based on response to the Son of Man hidden in the destitute lot of his brethren (cf. 7.21ff, 10.42f) who will be revealed as in some sense identified with "the least" at the moment of "apocalypse" on the Last Day. Concern for one's final destiny is a present response to those who, like the earthly Son of Man, have nowhere to lay their heads (8.20).[5]

3. Marshall, *Kingdom Come*, 84–85.

4. On the connections between Christianity and anarchism, see Christoyannopoulos, *Christian Anarchism*.

5. Rowland, "A Kingdom, but Not as We Know It."

Jesus radically reinterpreted the messianic nationalist and militarist hopes that were present in the traditions recorded in the First Testament (New Testament). The form of messianic hope that he teaches and practices does not lead us in the direction of a purely spiritual kingdom detached from the concrete reality of social and political life. Jesus' understanding of the kingdom included a strategy for transforming social life based on both a prophetic critique of violence and injustice, and the creation of a human society attempting to live now in a way that anticipated the age to come. So, what happens if we go back to reread the Second Testament (New Testament) taking into account the political context in which the Christian movement emerged?

Tom Hurcombe reminds us that to speak of "Jesus as Lord" is to use a metaphor that was both political and religious. We tend to remain oblivious to the political dimension. "But what a metaphor! It is filled with irony, because Jesus is an un-lordly lord. He does not lord it over his friends (Mark 10.42ff), nor do his followers. Even stranger is the Lamb who conquers—a conquering dead sheep! In this apocalyptic metaphor is an ironic back talk, a secret language in which words seem to mean the very opposite of what they usually do."[6]

We can't get away from the political character of the metaphor of the kingdom of God. The metaphor points to both a form of government, as well as a location and space where that government is exercised. Despite this, Christians when they have used the language of kingship, to justify a Christendom connection between church and government, have frequently interpreted Jesus' teaching of the kingdom in purely abstract terms, detached from any lived political reality. Christopher Rowland in criticizing this stance reminds us that "kingdom language is no less real than scientific language; it is another way we struggle to fully describe the world in which we live. . . . In the telling of the story, the parable, the metaphor, something happens. This peculiar upside-downness, this back-talk, that is the language of the kingdom of God evokes the very presence of the divine that it describes."[7]

The parables relating to the kingdom of God have multiple frames of reference. The kingdom, as Jesus taught and practiced it, is about both individual and communal healing. The parables of the kingdom are also about judgment. Jesus frequently tells a parable in a way that directly involves the hearer or concludes with a question to them. The parables call forth a response from the hearer, and that response places the hearer then, and the

---

6. Hurcombe, "Disestablishing the Kingdom."
7. Rowland, "A Kingdom, but Not as We Know It."

hearer now, under the judgment of the kingdom. The judgment, if we dare accept it, opens up possibilities of release and forgiveness, of belonging, acceptance, and transformation.

The extent to which our imagination about the kingdom has been dulled by the association of kingship with the absolute monarchical power during Christendom can be difficult for us to fully realize. It is helpful to be confronted with blunt statements such as that of Symon Hill, who reminds us that "a carpenter's son executed as a political troublemaker by an oppressive regime does not conform to our understandings of monarchy; even less so when he teaches that the first will be last and the last first."[8] The Marxist literary critic Terry Eagleton in a moment of theological engagement, to which he is prone from time to time, asserts that the "only authentic image of this violently loving God is a tortured and executed political criminal who dies in an act of solidarity with the *anawim*, meaning the destitute and dispossessed."[9] Now that is a challenge to our imagination, and to our ingrained assumptions of Christian respectability. After all good, respectable, middle-class people don't get arrested, let alone crucified.

Street theater in Jerusalem as a clue to Jesus' kingship

In following Jesus, we are not taking up a private religion, or a solely interior spirituality. Rather, if we follow Jesus how are we to respond in public to injustice and violence?[10] Scripture does not address a world detached from the reality of conflict, a world that would differ absolutely from the world in which we live. With this perspective in mind, I turn to consider the account of Jesus' entry to Jerusalem on Palm Sunday, on the way to his crucifixion, as recorded in Mark 11:1–11. It is a carefully narrated dramatic account that richly repays close attention as we begin thinking about kingship.

> When they were approaching Jerusalem, at Bethphage and Bethany, near the Mount of Olives, he sent two of his disciples and said to them, "Go into the village ahead of you, and immediately as you enter it, you will find tied there a colt that has never been ridden; untie it and bring it. If anyone says to you, 'Why are you doing this?' just say this, 'The Lord needs it and will send it back here immediately.'" They went away and found a colt tied near a door, outside in the street. As they were untying

---

8. Hill, "The Subversive Feast."
9. Eagleton, *Reason, Faith and Revolution*, 23.
10. William Stringfellow riffs appropriately on this theme in *The Politics of Spirituality*.

it, some of the bystanders said to them, "What are you doing, untying the colt?" They told them what Jesus had said and they allowed them to take it. Then they brought the colt to Jesus and threw their cloaks on it; and he sat on it. Many people spread their cloaks on the road, and others spread leafy branches that they had cut in the fields. Then those who went ahead and those who followed were shouting,

"Hosanna! Blessed is the one who comes in the name of the Lord! Blessed is the coming kingdom of our ancestor David! Hosanna in the highest heaven!"

Then he entered Jerusalem and went into the temple; and when he had looked around at everything, as it was already late, he went out to Bethany with the twelve.

In reading this Gospel passage we need to pay attention to the context in which it was written. It seems likely that Mark was written just before, or perhaps even during, the uprising of Jewish nationalists against the imperial power of Rome in a war that lasted from 66 to 70.[11] Jewish forces sought to regain political and religious control of their nation through a bitter guerilla war that raged across Galilee and Judea, ending in defeat following the Roman siege of Jerusalem. It was a time of struggle for survival by peasant farmers, with guerillas raiding the countryside making up for their lack of numbers and limited military resources with tactics that involved a willingness to give their lives in killing Roman soldiers in what they saw as God's cause. If that was the case, Mark recorded the story of Jesus' entry into Jerusalem for a church that was asking questions about what faithfulness to Jesus as the crucified and risen Messiah meant during a time of war. Should they support their fellow countrymen in the uprising? Were they being disloyal if they did not join the military struggle against Rome?

Mark tells the story of Jesus' approach to Jerusalem in a way that challenges his listeners to align themselves with Jesus' practice of kingship. Jesus approaches Jerusalem not on a war horse, as a conquering military figure would, but on a colt, not a form of transport normally associated with royalty. No Jewish king or Roman emperor would choose to ride such an animal when entering in triumph into a conquered city. Certainly, Jesus attracts attention from the mob, and there are crowds yelling approving slogans during Jesus' approach to Jerusalem. But after all the buildup of a dramatic entry into Jerusalem, and being received with popular acclaim, Jesus does not claim sovereignty as the incoming ruler who is taking over from the powers that be. He simply looks around and then wanders off to

11. Myers, *Binding the Strong Man*, 40–41. See also Shepherd, "Facing, Naming and Engaging Violence," 3.

supper with friends. It is a total anticlimax. The scene as developed by Mark presents Jesus as one who, if not getting ready for a coup, is preparing for a confrontation with the authorities, but nothing happens. What's going on here? What's Mark suggesting about the nature of Jesus' kingship in the way he tells the story?

Mark drops clues all the way through that would have led his first reader/listeners toward anticipating that here we have a warrior, or at least a political Messiah. Mark, though, doesn't follow through to provide a stunning political conclusion in the way that his readers were no doubt anticipating. Certainly, we have the reference to David, the warrior-king par excellence in Jewish history. Mark does not deny the political dimensions of Jesus as Messiah, but instead challenges the accepted conventions as to what the politics of the Messiah will be. Mark points to a Jesus who does not take up the role of warrior.[12]

The account of Jesus' procession into Jerusalem can be understood as a form of street theater in which Jesus signals his claims as Messiah, but as a very different kind of Messiah from that which was expected at the time. Mark's account implicitly challenges the assumptions of three groups. There were those who were committed to getting rid of the Romans by military means, such as the Zealots, a political movement in first-century Second Temple Judaism, which sought to incite the people of the Judea province to rebel against the Roman Empire and expel it from the Holy Land by force of arms. Then there were those who wanted to withdraw into a spiritual or religious response that avoided issues of economic injustice and Roman imperialism. Finally, there were those who simply wanted to get along with business as usual with whoever was in charge, running interference for the Romans as the ruling powers.

According to Mark, none of these ways is open to the followers of Jesus. The kingship of Jesus is of a completely different character. Jesus simultaneously lives out a rejection of the politics of violence, the politics of withdrawal, and the politics of accommodation. Here we find a pointer towards a culture and practice of community engagement and service. Mark's Jesus challenges the customary culture and practice of rule. In Mark 10:42 the disciples make the claim to join Jesus in his exercise of kingship but are only offered by Jesus the possibility of joining him in his baptism and supping from his cup of suffering. The disciples are challenged here to move beyond these dominant and dominating ways of engaging with the world. Taking

---

12. The contrast between this reading of Jesus and the militarized warrior reproduced by white US evangelicals over the past decades is striking. For a detailed account linking this militaristic reading of Jesus to an overt Christian political agenda in the US from the 1950s onward, see Du Mez, *Jesus and John Wayne*.

these themes forward to the point of Jesus' crucifixion, at the moment of Jesus' death Mark tells us the economic, institutional, and spiritual power of the temple is destroyed and replaced by a kingship based on service.

At this point I want to draw attention to the Scripture readings that accompanied Mark's Gospel in the lectionary readings for the day, from the prophet Isaiah 50:4–9, the suffering servant, and Philippians: 2:5–11, the self-emptying character of Jesus. These fill out our understanding of the sort of Messiah that Jesus is. The account of the chosen one in Isaiah 50:6 includes the sentence, "I offered my back to those who struck me and my cheek to those who pulled at my beard." This line is confronting in its gut-wrenching directness that speaks of the physical and psychological experience of abuse. In reading this passage my imagination jumped immediately to both the treatment of Jesus during his trial and crucifixion, and to the patient and nonviolent response of participants to the violence experienced by participants in the civil rights movement in the USA during the 1950s and 1960s.

"Were you there when they crucified my Lord?" intones a Black spiritual that has a fitting place in the worship of Good Friday. The congregation in a Black church responds wholeheartedly with a "Yes, we were there." But there is more to this "yes" than the congregation joining in a call and response that places themselves "again" imaginatively at Calvary than one may at first recognize. They affirm that what happened back then in the crucifixion of Jesus is being lived out now in their experience of suffering, first as slaves, and then in daily discrimination of white racism and police violence. In this passage in Isaiah, where the servant confesses his trust in God and a willingness to absorb the violence inflicted by his enemies, we can sense the connection with Jesus as the suffering Messiah. The story of Jesus in its turn opens up and shapes the witness in the now, to the redemptive power of suffering by a Martin Luther King, a John Lewis, or a Fannie Lou Hamer, during the civil rights era in the US, figures who sought the transformation not only of their own people but the moral healing of their oppressors and enemies. Isaiah did not know when he penned this oracle how it would be taken up by later generations. But once we hear the story of Jesus in his passion, we can see and affirm the connection between what was done and said then by the prophet, and what was lived out by Jesus, and we recognize this pattern when we see parallels of its enactment in our own time.

The Gospel reading does not stand alone, but has deep connections with the arguments advanced in Paul's letters. I turn our attention to Philippians 2:5–11. This is the famous hymn to Jesus as servant that fills out with remarkable poetry and profound theology what Mark was hinting at in his story.

> Let the same mind be in you that was in Christ Jesus, who, though he was in the form of God, did not regard equality with God as something to be exploited, but emptied himself, taking the form of a slave, being born in human likeness. And being found in human form, he humbled himself and became obedient to the point of death—even death on a cross. Therefore, God also highly exalted him and gave him the name that is above every name, so that at the name of Jesus every knee should bend, in heaven and on earth and under the earth, and every tongue should confess that Jesus Christ is Lord, to the glory of God the Father.

We have here a distilled account of the meaning of Jesus' life, ministry, death, and resurrection. Paul is very clear that in the resurrection of Jesus we have the vindication by God of the suffering servant anticipated in the servant song of Isaiah. What was anticipated then in deep trust by the prophet in the faithfulness of God is claimed now in Paul's account of what God has done in Jesus. We have in this poem the same spirit of subversion of assumptions about power that appears in the street theater by Jesus in Mark's Gospel. In this hymn the call by Paul to the church at Philippi is a call to suffering service that resists the violence of the world. We are called to a response that trusts in God for results.

Trust in God was expressed by Jesus throughout his life and death. This trust was demonstrated in his rejection of the offer of the tempter in the desert, in his resistance to the temptation offered by the zealots with their willingness to use violence to bring in God's kingdom, in the call of the crowds for another greater David who would lead to military victories and achieve economic prosperity and well-being through an extended imperial reach. In Paul's call to the church at Philippi (Phil 2:5), "Let the same mind be in you that was in Christ Jesus," he is not talking about a response to an ideal that is external to us. What we are called to is to open ourselves to Jesus taking shape within us. So, what kind of Messiah is this anyway?

Jesus was, Mark tells us, a Messiah who called into question the hope for a warrior with its assumption that violence is king and military power is the key to history. Isaiah testifies to the patience and endurance of personal and indeed social abuse that does not respond to violence with violence but absorbs it and trusts in God for vindication and judgment. In our day it is hard to think what else except trust in God could sustain the witness of people in Christian Peacemaker Teams in areas of conflict, who have stood between warring parties at risk of their own lives on the West Bank, in Colombia, Afghanistan, and Iraq.

Paul affirms with all the passion that he can command that we are in good company in taking the way of patient service rather than that of overbearing, self-focused power. We are called here to the company of Jesus, who forms in us the character of the suffering servant that we worship. As we reject the path of violence and overbearing power, we are on Paul's account working with the grain of the universe, placing ourselves in tune with God's intention for human life and all creation. Paul is clear about what sort of Messiah we have been given to follow. All things in creation shall bend their knee at the name of Jesus, not a military conqueror but a suffering servant vindicated by God in the resurrection. Here we have a complete reformulation of the meaning of kingship that suggests the possibility of another sort of kingdom than that imaged in our media and popular culture.

Subverting images of kingship

While Mark is my favorite Gospel, it is not the only one that if read with attention can help us re-envisage the kingdom of God. Take the Gospel of John. We misunderstand this Gospel if we allow the tag sometime applied to it of "the spiritual gospel" to stand unchallenged. At key moments in the story the author draws our attention to its profound political implications. The story that I turn to is the feeding of the five thousand (John 6:1–15). This story as presented to us has strong connections with the story of the exodus.

> After this Jesus went to the other side of the Sea of Galilee, also called the Sea of Tiberias. A large crowd kept following him, because they saw the signs that he was doing for the sick. Jesus went up the mountain and sat down there with his disciples. Now the Passover, the festival of the Jews, was near. When he looked up and saw a large crowd coming toward him, Jesus said to Philip, "Where are we to buy bread for these people to eat?" He said this to test him, for he himself knew what he was going to do. Philip answered him, "Six months' wages would not buy enough bread for each of them to get a little." One of his disciples, Andrew, Simon Peter's brother, said to him, "There is a boy here who has five barley loaves and two fish. But what are they among so many people?" Jesus said, "Make the people sit down." Now there was a great deal of grass in the place; so they sat down, about five thousand in all. Then Jesus took the loaves, and when he had given thanks, he distributed them to

Teaching and Performing a Different Kingdom

those who were seated; so also the fish, as much as they wanted. When they were satisfied, he told his disciples, "Gather up the fragments left over, so that nothing may be lost." So they gathered them up, and from the fragments of the five barley loaves, left by those who had eaten, they filled twelve baskets. When the people saw the sign that he had done, they began to say, "This is indeed the prophet who is to come into the world."

When Jesus realized that they were about to come and take him by force to make him king, he withdrew again to the mountain by himself.

John here is here referencing Moses, the Passover, and the exodus, while looking forward to the passion. At the Passover Moses led the people out of Egypt, in an act of political and religious liberation. John offers parallels between the people being fed by the manna in the wilderness, and the people being fed by Jesus. John keeps the images of exodus and liberation in view in telling this story. John, while emphasizing that something extraordinary happened in Jesus' feeding of the crowd, does not tell us the story in a way that answers the sort of questions that our modern scientific curiosity tends to raise. To chase that rabbit down a long and winding burrow is to miss John's point. The significance of this event is the issue that John is trying to get his readers and hearers to attend to. What does the story tell us about Jesus? Poverty and oppression were the common condition of most of those who came to listen to Jesus. Many were peasants suffering under the exploitation of local tax farmers supporting the political puppets of Rome who were ruling the province. A ruler who could provide them with enough to eat, as seemed likely with Jesus, rather than a ruler slugging them for more taxes, would have been extremely attractive option for those who shared this meal.

According to John, though, the crowd was not simply responding to the attraction of having enough to eat. The people interpreted what they had just experienced in the light of the exodus story. They drew the conclusion that Jesus is the one who is to come, the prophet like Moses, who will again lead them from slavery to freedom. They want to make him a king by force. But Jesus resists this move. The crowd here has got something right: a new liberator has arrived, the one who is going to bring in a new kingdom. However, in their enthusiasm they haven't properly understood the character of that kingdom and its king. John has given clues to enable those present then and those of us who are hearing the story now to see Jesus as a liberator in the line of Moses. Jesus has the credentials—why then does he walk away? For the answer to this question, we need to move forward and consider the exchange between Jesus and Pilate in John's passion narrative in John 18:33–37.

> Then Pilate entered the headquarters again, summoned Jesus, and asked him, "Are you the King of the Jews?" Jesus answered, "Do you ask this on your own, or did others tell you about me?" Pilate replied, "I am not a Jew, am I? Your own nation and the chief priests have handed you over to me. What have you done?" Jesus answered, "My kingdom is not from this world. If my kingdom were from this world, my followers would be fighting to keep me from being handed over to the Jews. But as it is, my kingdom is not from here." Pilate asked him, "So you are a king?" Jesus answered, "You say that I am a king. For this I was born, and for this I came into the world, to testify to the truth. Everyone who belongs to the truth listens to my voice."

What John tells us here about Jesus' kingship explains why Jesus rejected the crowd's attempt to make him a king after the feeding of the multitude. Jesus does not deny here that he is a king. It is the exact character of Jesus' kingship and the nature of his kingdom that Pilate does not seem to understand, and perhaps could not understand, given his imperial frame of mind and his realpolitik assumptions about power. Jesus' reply to Pilate, "My kingdom is not of this world," is not a statement about the location of God's kingdom as somewhere in some disembodied ethereal world detached from the material world you and I live in. Jesus' kingdom is not of this world in the sense that it is an alternative style of kingdom to that of those who exercise kingly authority from the top down with the help of military force.

In sketching Jesus' confrontation with Pilate, John gestures towards an alternative form of kingship in the ministry of Jesus to that assumed by Pilate. This king, Jesus, is one who washes his disciples' feet and calls them his friends. Pilate's questioning will serve to stand in for all of us who still find it hard to imagine kingship except in terms of violence and force exercised by centralized political power. Jesus accepts the title of king, but his kingdom is not of the kind that is established by violence. It is certainly not an ethereal, vague, mystical, and feel-good sort of kingdom. But it is a kingdom for all that, a polity that is rich in politics, economics, social relationships, and its affirmation of the goodness of the earth and our material existence. It is a kingdom that is manifest in the practice of truth and faithfulness in relationship, not in force or emotional violence. It is tough and uncompromising in it for the long haul, as Dorothy Day, Martin Luther King, and Oscar Romero, to name just a few recent examples, have demonstrated. Miroslav Volf helpfully unpacks the dynamics of what is at stake in the exchange between Pilate and Jesus on the character of kingship.

> In the exchange with Pilate Jesus argues against "the truth of power" and for "the power of truth." . . . Jesus does not refuse the title "king" but alters its contents. His kingship is "not from here," not "from this world" (18:36). After all he came "into the world" (18:37) and his disciples are "in the world" (17:11), inserted into the play of social forces. As a "king" he does not stand in the same arena with other contenders to power, fighting the same battle for dominance. His kingship does not rest on "fighting" and therefore does not issue in "handing over" people to other power. The violence of eliminating other contenders for power or holding them in check by treating them as things is not part of his rule.[13]

John's so-called "spiritual" Gospel turns out to be instead a witness to an alternative practice, and an alternative consciousness, of power and rule in this world. The fourth Gospel engages in a radical redefinition of kingship. Jesus' kingship is not "of this world" in that its origin and practice are different from the way power is exercised by Caesar and his underlings. "By calling for adherence to a king, the authority and pattern for whose kingship is 'not of this world,' the followers of Jesus do not fight but remain in the world bearing witness to the truth before the rulers of synagogue and empire."[14]

This account of kingship and power offered by Jesus is not just a matter of politics, but of the exercise of power in the church and in the way we engage with our community. How can we live as followers of Jesus, this most unusual king, whose "upside-down kingdom" is characterized not by the usual forms of hierarchy, status, and power, but by a new order of service, humility, and love? How are we to live as witnesses to this strange kingdom as people who do not accept business as usual and are not content to hang around simply waiting for a kingdom detached from the pain and suffering of the creation, while enjoying the privileges of wealth and power as if they are ours by right?

This is a challenge to our imagination about the character of the church and our discipleship. "In place of his tortured body, which exposes the lie behind all torture and death dealing, Jesus' followers are therefore invited to become a new Body, a new social reality . . . , [and] this new political reality is not based on hierarchy, exclusion and domination. Instead,

---

13. Volf, *Exclusion and Embrace*, 266–67.
14. Rowland, "A Kingdom, but Not as We Know It."

it is an invitation to discover concrete practices which move in precisely the opposite direction to 'politics as usual.'"[15] The Gospels never suggest that discipleship expressed in such community engagement is an easy option. We are called to pray: "Your kingdom come, your will be done on earth as it is in heaven," that is for a kingdom that is lived out now in this actually existing world, in an anticipation of the age to come, that points in its peaceable commitment to justice and human flourishing, the kingdom in all its fullness.

The Feast of Christ the King

For one more take on kingship in the Gospels, I turn to the readings for the Feast of Christ the King, a feast in the liturgical calendar immediately prior to the first Sunday of Advent. This celebration is best known to Christians in the Anglican and Catholic traditions. Having spent some time churching with Anglicans, I was struck by its potentially subversive character. I acknowledge that in the Catholic Church this feast day has been taken up in support of a reactionary theo-politics. Despite this, there is I think something important here that can help us reimagine our understanding of kingship. The reading from the lectionary that I preached on was the Revelation of John 1:4–8.

> John to the seven churches that are in Asia: Grace to you and peace from him who is and who was and who is to come, and from the seven spirits who are before his throne, and from Jesus Christ, the faithful witness, the firstborn of the dead, and the ruler of the kings of the earth. To him who loves us and freed us from our sins by his blood, and made us to be a kingdom, priests serving his God and Father, to him be glory and dominion forever and ever. Amen. Look! He is coming with the clouds; every eye will see him, even those who pierced him; and on his account all the tribes of the earth will wail. So it is to be. Amen. "I am the Alpha and the Omega," says the Lord God, who is and who was and who is to come, the Almighty.

What does kingship mean to John the Revelator? Many of the Caesars had divinity ascribed to them and the political power of many rulers was inextricably bound up in religious claims.

> The claim that Christ is king not only subverts common expectations about the nature of power. It is also a reminder that

15. Barrow, "How Easter Brings Regime Change."

> no-one can serve two kings. If Christ is king, then no other person or institution can demand our total loyalty. . . . Many early Christians attracted extra persecution by refusing to declare that "Caesar is Lord." If Christ is Lord, they reasoned, then Caesar cannot be. After the coming of Christendom—when the Church became allied with the forces of power and wealth—this claim was softened. In order to get round the problem, earthly monarchs were presented as representatives of Christ.[16]

The early church ran headlong into conflict with the Roman Empire for precisely this reason. The Christians were tagged as atheists, as dangerous subversives, because they didn't worship Caesar, but claimed to worship another king, Jesus. They lived out their claim to the point of dying, because they were citizens of another kingdom whose claims preceded those of Caesar. To confess Jesus as king was therefore a stance loaded with political meaning. It was not just an individual choice in the religious supermarket of the time, an age with some similarities to our own in the diversity of options available. To be a follower of Jesus was to acknowledge a claim that extended to all areas of life, rather than a choice about how one filled in one's leisure time one day a week.

Other readers in the radical tradition have thought that the language of kingship was too difficult to recover for a reading of Scripture and practice of discipleship that would free us from cultural and political co-optation by the state and market. Is there a word or phrase that expresses in our age some of the breadth and depth of the terms *king* and *kingdom* and that expresses the breadth of a call to discipleship beyond the narrow frame of "religion"? God's commonwealth? The republic of God? The "God movement"?[17] These terms are not worn out by overfamiliarity, and they focus attention on the political and social dimension of God's activity in a way that sidesteps the unhelpful dimensions of the term *kingdom*. While not completely satisfactory, they offer translations that might help us begin the task of revisioning the politics and communal dimension of our discipleship.

To learn a little more about the different nature of Jesus' kingship and how authority and rule are exercised in God's commonwealth, I will return to the passage from Revelation. The key phrase around which the rule of Jesus revolves is that which describes him as the faithful witness, and from that faithfulness his power and rule flows. He is the first born from the dead, the ruler of the kings of the earth. He is faithful in suffering a highly political death that was a scandal to all the religiously respectable. This is the paradox

---

16. Hill, "The Subversive Feast."
17. McClendon, *Biography as Theology*, 96; Marsh, *The Beloved Community*, 81.

at the heart of our faith, which we keep wanting to collapse into something merely "religious." It is out of this faithfulness—in dying a death that left Jesus identified with those who rebelled against Rome and identified with all those who were outcasts and marginal—that Jesus is affirmed by God to be ruler of the kings of the earth.

The stunning force of John the Revelator's claim needs to be fully registered if we are to seriously consider our own commitment to following Jesus. There is so much that seems at first to count against the claim. To glance at the newspaper headlines, or the lead stories on television any day of the week, is to be bombarded with evidence that suggests that whoever, or whatever, is in control it surely doesn't seem to be God. Perhaps John is suggesting that is not what God is about: God's claims are overarching but perhaps God's preferred mode of working is not by the exercise of top-down control. Indeed, the claim of death to be the power that rules our age seems to confront us once we stop and ask the question. The newspaper headlines may be part of our problem because they already assume who the rulers of this world are and how rule should be exercised. The media are shaped by the visions they claim to merely report on, that what is done by the powerful, and the state, is all that is important for shaping our future and guaranteeing us peace and safety. This implies that it is in the spectacular, the momentary, and the exercise of state power that success is to be measured and our hopes located.

Perhaps we don't see the signs of God's activity and rule in the power of service because we are looking for the wrong thing, and we are looking in the wrong places, with the wrong assumptions about how God's power and rule are to be discerned. To change our sight, our vision, our expectations about the kind of kingdom or commonwealth Jesus was talking about is going to be necessary before the evidence of God's activity will become apparent for us to see with the eyes of faith.

What was the result of Jesus' faithfulness? According to John the Revelator it was that we might become kings and priests to serve God in the exercise of his rule. In other words, Jesus' faithfulness is exercised so that we might become rulers who serve by building community, empowering those we serve. The rule of Jesus is power that disturbs the status quo, offends the respectable, challenges the certainties of those who think they have God worked out and boxed up within their system. The rule of Jesus is manifest in preaching good news to the poor, healing the sick, eating with the unclean, touching the lepers (the AIDS victims of his day), and announcing the Year of Jubilee, a time of economic redistribution. These are the signs we should be looking for, and I suggest, looking forward somewhat, the shape of our community engagement.

Teaching and Performing a Different Kingdom

The commonwealth of God is not to be found in the worship of gods who depend on violence as a means for maintaining our physical and emotional security as a community. This commonwealth cannot be found for Christians in the anger of nationalism or a rhetoric that classifies the person who is different as the enemy. We are as the church joined in that commonwealth that includes all peoples and nations, that great cloud of witnesses of those who have sought to be faithful disciples. In John's vision, and in the prophet Isaiah's vision, God's commonwealth is not bound by race or nationality. Our community extends beyond such boundaries. Nor is it found in a culture of self-fulfillment or frantic anything-goes economic growth.

This is the feast of victory for our God, that the Lamb who was slain has begun to reign, not as the despot wielding the power of the tyrant, but through the empowering of faithful witnessing to the truth even in the face of death. All this is out of tune with the stories that drive our age and dominate our media and political discourse. Yet our calling as disciples is to follow and be shaped by that faithful witness. To be empowered by that compassionate prophetic spirit, to be nurtured by that sustaining comforter as we face the powers of violence and death as they manifest themselves in the organizations and communities in which we are engaged, trusting in the faithfulness of a God who takes upon himself the suffering and pain of the world.

The association of the church with status, wealth, and force is inappropriate for followers of Jesus. We should be committed to ways of being good news to the poor, the powerless and persecuted, while being cautious about our engagement with the state. The kingship of Jesus is in great tension with the kings and authority patterns of Christendom and its residue in the thinking of many church leaders.

Reading kingship "again"

The account of kingship and the kingdom of God that emerges from reading Jesus' teaching and life "again" is challenging on whatever level we consider it. But if we bring it into conversation with the way many churches and not a few church-related agencies have been run in recent decades it is explosive. I find it hard to read these passages from the Gospels in the light of the behavior of church leadership and the cover-up of sexual abuse driven by concern for institutional self-preservation without becoming deeply judgmental, and for that I need forgiveness.

If we claim, as evangelicals do, that we have a "high" view of the authority of Scripture, then applying that "high" view to the teaching and practice of Jesus as presented to us in the Gospels would be, I have thought, non-negotiable. But here we are. Christendom has left us with a legacy in which we have continued an attachment to the language of kingship sourced in the teaching of Jesus, but not unpacked the radically challenging character of that kingship. Following Jesus and beginning to live into the character of his kingdom is a matter of practice rather than affirming correct theological beliefs. Working out what following this strange, disconcerting king means for our community engagement is a matter for ongoing reflection and discernment that engages enthusiastically with a context in which we are not "in control." Some indications of what this means will emerge in some of the case studies in Part III and in the reflection on the Beatitudes in the Epilogue.

4

Exile: Community Engagement in a Shifting Location

The grief arising from physical and psychological dislocation may hit us in a rush, or be experienced gradually over time, as we come to explicitly acknowledge that much that we have taken for granted in our life is now gone beyond hope of recovery, except in memory. I have been reminded of the intensity of grief that follows from dislocation while watching media interviews with survivors of bushfires as they reported on the loss of their homes and the destruction of their communities. For refugees, living in the long-term exile of UNHCR camps, or waiting in a foreign land hoping for recognition of their claim for protection and a safe future, the response of grief can take a long time to find articulation, parked as it is behind the need to focus on the day-to-day struggle for survival for themselves and their families.

Today the dislocation of exile is a reality for large numbers of people, to an extent rarely paralleled in human history. Exile as an experience of dislocation remains the experience today for millions of people living with lives on hold in massive refugee camps in Jordan, Kenya, and Bangladesh, and scattered across the Indonesian archipelago. Reading the theme of exile in Scripture "again" is important, not only in helping us to imagine an identity and mission lived out in a position of not being "in control," but also for helping us shape our engagement with those for whom exile is a defining and ongoing experience.

Taking up a scriptural account of exile as a theme is not straightforward, though. Many Christians and church congregations in the English-speaking world are now claiming an exilic identity frequently attached to a claim of victimhood arising from the shift beyond Christendom. Living with the unsettling of much that they regard as essential to their identity, many feel they are living on the edge of the abyss, as they enter what they feel to be an exile with the loss of political, cultural, and social hegemony.[1] Many white evangelical Christians in the US, and some Christians in Australia, have taken up this theme, by which they seem to mean, among other things, that they are no longer culturally and politically "in control." I am conscious that exile is being used by this group of Christians in a way that appeals to a nostalgia for Christendom, and that disrespects the gap between their claim of victimhood and the traumatic and long-lived experience of the exile of many people. Having flagged the contestation over the use and misuse of the terminology, I will trace the theme of exile through this chapter, reading Scripture around this theme "again," because I think it is both relevant and helpful to our imagining of community engagement after Christendom. The risk of misuse of exile as a theme that I have identified speaks to its relevance.

Exile in the history of Israel

A narrow focus on the Davidic monarchy skews our perception of the context in which most of the First Testament (Old Testament) was written and results in a lack of attention to the importance of the exile in the history and tradition of Israel. Exile was the crucible for Israel's faith and a central theme in its interpretation of its history. Brueggemann makes the case that exile "did not lead Jews in the Old Testament to abandon faith or settle for abdicating despair, nor to retreat to privatistic religion. On the contrary, exile provoked the most brilliant literature and the most daring theological articulation in the Old Testament."[2] I have already explored some of this theological response in the questioning of kingship, and the narratives of faithful living in exile in the stories of Joseph, Esther, and Daniel.

In this chapter I look at a series of shifting theological responses to exile, with the experience of dislocation and not being in control, starting with the letter of Jeremiah to the exiles in Babylon. I move through the discussion of Christian discipleship as diaspora in 1 Peter, and subsequently in the Epistle to Diognetus. I conclude by pointing to connections of this theme with the Anabaptist response on issues of community engagement and location that I take up in Part II.

---

1. Brueggemann, *Theology of Jeremiah*, 192–96; Brueggemann, *The Word Militant*, 132–35.

2. Brueggemann, *Cadences of Home*, 3.

Exile: Community Engagement in a Shifting Location

Jeremiah's letter to the exiles

Following the Babylonian invasion in 567 BCE, the prophet Jeremiah wrote to the Jews who were in exile in Babylon. His letter to the exiles is short and lapidary in its guidance. The recipients of Jeremiah's letter had not chosen their destiny. The Babylonians had invaded their nation and then deported them. In such a situation it would not be surprising if Jeremiah had given advice that emphasized maintaining social and cultural barriers and keeping a clear line of demarcation from their enemies, while looking forward to returning home. A strategy of maintaining purity and distance from surrounding communities was to emerge later under Nehemiah and Ezra, when the exiles returned to Jerusalem and had to manage relationships with the people with whom they were sharing what had previously been their land. Jeremiah commends a very different approach that emphasizes engagement by the exiles in the basic activities that sustain human life, and community.

> These are the words of the letter that the prophet Jeremiah sent from Jerusalem to the remaining elders among the exiles, and to the priests, the prophets, and all the people, whom Nebuchadnezzar had taken into exile from Jerusalem to Babylon.... The letter was sent by the hand of Elasah son of Shaphan and Gemariah son of Hilkiah, whom King Zedekiah of Judah sent to Babylon to King Nebuchadnezzar of Babylon. It said: Thus says the Lord of hosts, the God of Israel, to all the exiles whom I have sent into exile from Jerusalem to Babylon: Build houses and live in them; plant gardens and eat what they produce. Take wives and have sons and daughters; take wives for your sons, and give your daughters in marriage, that they may bear sons and daughters; multiply there, and do not decrease. But seek the welfare of the city where I have sent you into exile, and pray to the Lord on its behalf, for in its welfare you will find your welfare. (Jeremiah 29:1–7)

Rather than simply waiting to be able to return to Jerusalem, Jeremiah advises the exiles that they should take for themselves the small pieces of Babylon that they occupied to construct their homes and plant their vegetables. Building a house is the sort of activity that entangled the exiles with the government of Babylon and the surrounding community. Owning land, or renting it in a way that permits construction, has always required some sort of civic recognition of your rights to the property. Jeremiah goes further with his call to seek the welfare of the city, that was the capital of their enemies. "[T]he exiles must learn that their world is no longer separate from that of their captors. There is no arrangement in which destruction and evil can fall on Babylon without also falling on the exiled Israelites as well; even more importantly, the exiles must bring themselves to actively seek the good of the community in which they find themselves."[3]

Settling on a translation for the Hebrew term *shalom* as the goal of this exilic activity is not straightforward. The term has multiple resonances, envisaging a movement towards wholeness and completeness, that is both grounded in looking forward to each Israelite being at peace under their own vine and fig tree, and transcendent, longing for the peace associated with the coming of the Messiah. The resonance of shalom rules out any clear divide between the "material" and the "spiritual," or the "political" and the "religious." The common translations, "peace" and "welfare," don't quite convey all the possible meanings of the term. I suggest that while all of these translations I have just noted are useful, the term "flourishing," which has a forward-looking, always-underway, and yet-to-be-completed resonance, allows within its lexical scope reference to the commonly used terms "well-being," "welfare," and "peace." How then can we best describe the task of faithfully responding to Yahweh while in exile? I suggest that the response that Jeremiah is advising here can be specified as one of living out human diversity after Babel, as a community without access to coercive power.

The sociological and ecclesiological implications of living "as if exiles," yet "seeking the flourishing of the city," as advocated by Jeremiah, runs contrary to the assumption that living an exilic identity requires a separatist, socially withdrawn, and disengaged ethic. The matter is more subtle and complex. Brueggemann is helpful in articulating this, observing that "Israel is not a sect. It does not withdraw into its own life. It is always a community of exiles intensely aware of the hegemonic community with which it lives in tension. Thus in Jeremiah 29.7, Israel is enjoined to pray for Babylon because upon the peace of Babylon depends its own peace. Israel is not offered any 'separate peace' by Yahweh."[4]

The Jewish exiles, facing the reality of living under an imperial government, developed forms of social life that claimed independence and significance in their rootedness in a competing narrative in which Yahweh was Lord. In doing this they direct our attention to the role of institutions, and cultural innovation, that are beyond the initiative of the state, though engaging with it, contributing to furthering human flourishing and developing a specific form of politics. Based on studies of subordinate communities, the political anthropologist James Scott observes that as "long

---

3. Dow, "The Politics of Exile."

4. Brueggemann, *Cadences of Home*, 52. See also Brueggemann, *A Commentary on Jeremiah*, 256–58.

Exile: Community Engagement in a Shifting Location

as we confine our conception of the political to activity that is openly declared we are driven to conclude that subordinate groups essentially lack a political life . . ."[5] If we drop this assumption, we will be able to discern the reality of political activity below the level and sometime beyond the comprehension of those who are in control. What we find when we do that are patterns of resistance to domination that may be limited, but nevertheless have real significance for subordinate groups' day-to-day life.

Daniel Smith-Christopher in his theological account of Israel in exile makes a similar point. Exiles, he reminds us, "are not merely sufferers, nor are they inevitably incomplete, nor are they always handicapped without the trappings of statehood. This is not to deny the often debilitating conditions under which many exiled peoples must function; it is rather to recognize the creativity and resourcefulness through which these people remain firmly engaged in the world . . ."[6] Patterns of activity by exilic communities that simultaneously enact both accommodation and resistance are a form of faithful agility by which they seek to accommodate to the reality of the power of the empire while maintaining an identity and ethic grounded in their own tradition.[7] While Jeremiah certainly held out the hope of a delayed homecoming, his exhortation laid the basis for a life within the Persian Empire for those exiles who remained. This imaginative positioning has a "flexible capacity to float with interpretive power from one context to another."[8] In so doing it provides authorization for similarly imaginative responses in the future. We have to acknowledge that those who complied many of the texts in the First Testament (Old Testament) shaped a powerful cultural and societal response to a disruptive and traumatic policy of deportation and relocation.

Jeremiah's instructions encouraged a practice of living patiently while waiting with the hope of homecoming. While some of the exiles returned to Jerusalem, many did not, and exile became a permanent location. The question become one of living between accommodation and resistance.[9] In discharging their vocation to seek the flourishing of the city, Jews increasingly served the imperial community through engagement as translators, scribes, sages, and merchants, while maintaining a distinct Jewish identity. Exile, living in the tension of seeking the flourishing of the city while maintaining a particularistic identity, is not necessarily a sectarian stance. Exile

---

5. Scott, *Domination and the Arts of Resistance*, 199.
6. Smith-Christopher, *A Biblical Theology of Exile*, 197.
7. Brueggemann, *Out of Babylon*, 131–34.
8. Brueggemann, *Out of Babylon*, 111.
9. Brueggemann, *Out of Babylon*, 130–35.

is the vocation of living as not being in charge, while contributing to the flourishing of the community.

> Jeremiah's political vision is juxtaposed to that of the false prophets (Chapters 28–29) who argue that the exile is only a brief interruption of the house of David's rule as a nation like other nations; that is, they insist that a spatial politics will quickly be restored. Instead, Jeremiah prophesies that Israel's political vocation of possessing the land for the Lord is being transformed into a more temporal politics, whereby the Jews go forth to other lands for the sake of seeking the salvation of the peoples to which God sends them.[10]

The path Jeremiah charted for the exiles, however, was not without its risks. The narratives of Esther and Daniel in their different ways open up questions about the difficulties and possibilities of exercising power and influence, as exiles closely engaged in seeking both the welfare of the empire and their own community. Positioning the community in this way rejects both separatism and an uncritical accommodation to the prevailing social order. It involves an effort to learn the languages that will enable conversation about a common life. In discharging their vocation, the exiles served the imperial community in Babylon over the succeeding centuries. Such a "diaspora" ethic points beyond the choice offered by Reinhold Niebuhr, between an ethic of "withdrawal" and an ethic of "responsibility," and H. Richard Niebuhr's rejection of Anabaptist thought as being "against culture." A "diaspora" ethic involves making discriminating judgments on issues as they emerge in diverse areas of human culture, allowing for the possibility of transformative responses in the dynamic tension of engagement.

Church, society, and difference in 1 Peter

During the first century of the Christian movement there were a variety of approaches to engagement with the prevailing political order. The continued appearance of the exilic theme and assumption of familiarity with the experience of diaspora in Christian reflections on location and identity is not surprising. The missionary journeys of Paul hitchhiked as it were on the existing network of synagogues of the Jewish diaspora who lived out their faithfulness in permanent dispersal as a given reality. It's the taken-for-granted background to the Pauline letters.

---

10. Bell Jr., "Jesus, the Jews," 103.

Exile: Community Engagement in a Shifting Location

The exilic theme helpfully for my purposes here receives explicit attention in 1 Peter. This discussion serves as a helpful starting point for tracing the reworking of Jeremiah's injunction to the exiles in the early church. Here the primary location of citizenship for Christians is the church, a citizenship that was lived out in parallel with their identity as strangers, or exiles, within the earthly polis.[11] This duality and tension of Christian identity and engagement is reflected in Christians being spoken of as "exiles in the Dispersion" (1 Pet 1:1), "a chosen race, a royal priesthood, a holy nation, God's own people" (1 Pet 2:9) and "aliens and exiles" (1 Pet 2:11).[12] The terms used in the epistle suggest an identity generated at least partly by a distinction between insiders and outsiders, generated by a fundamental loyalty that was not comprehended within the polity of the Roman Empire.

The images used in this epistle in discussing the identity of the Christian movement add a layer of complexity to the distinction between the exiles and the imperial rulers in Babylon in the direction from Jeremiah to the exiles. Christians here are not called to be outsiders to the social world seeking accommodation to their new home, as is often the case with second-generation migrants in a new homeland. Nor are they called to shape their new home in the image of the world they have left behind, as would be the case with colonizers, or those who establish a ghetto in a new world. These analogies do not provide an accurate mapping of location and behavior of Christians.

Miroslav Volf in his discussion of the issue offers the following helpful suggestion on how to envisage this relationship. The form of church-society relationship that is envisaged in 1 Peter is of Christians as insiders, whose relationship of difference to their culture is set by their status of being "born again." "Christian difference is therefore not an insertion of something new into the old from outside, but a bursting out of the new precisely within the proper space of the old.... Christians ask, 'Which beliefs and practices of the culture that is ours must we reject now that our self has been reconstituted by new birth? Which can we retain? What must we reshape to reflect better the values of God's new creation?'"[13]

On the basis of the directions in 1 Peter, there is no reason for categorizing the community to which it was addressed as a sect, a minority practicing a self-focused withdrawal. The task of the community was to live in faithfulness to God's kingdom and to invite others to do the same. The approach suggested here was that of a patient living out of an alternative way

---

11. Harink, *1 & 2 Peter*, 31–35.
12. Winter, *Seek the Welfare of the City*, 12.
13. Volf, "Soft Difference," 18–19.

of life, transforming the host society in so far as it was possible to do so from within that society, and giving public witness to a new form of social life.[14]

According to Bruce Winter, who has thought a good deal about the implications of 1 Peter for Christian community engagement, the key to understanding the injunction of the author is to be found in exploring the role of benefactor in the culture of the time. The social positioning of Christians in this letter highlights both the complexity and the revolutionary character of Christian participation in the community as both benefactors and citizens. This epistle has both a heavenly and an earthly focus in its instructions in which, as the diaspora, the exiled people of God, the Christians were to direct their hope towards the grace coming through the revelation of Jesus Christ, a mandate that directed them to seek the welfare of others in the public as well as the nonpublic dimensions of life. The community was thus to participate in public life in response to the will of God.[15]

This Petrine injunction required an engagement in the social order that went beyond the accepted limits of the benefactor-client relationship that governed public engagement in the empire. In 1 Peter all in the community who could were called as Christians were to participate in seeking the welfare of the broader society, a calling that was not limited to those who were of a particular social rank. This involved an effective, even if it was understated, subversion of the prevailing social structure with its status rules and distinctions. The call to seek the flourishing of the city in all its dimensions was the task of the all the members of the Christian community, not just a minority with a certain social standing. This Christian difference could be justified through either the negative process of rejecting the beliefs of others or positively through pointing toward a new and alternative allegiance. First Peter points to the positive process for establishing difference where the marker is not an issue of ethnicity. The connection to Jeremiah's injunction is clear and the shift is one of development of the theme in a new context, generated by the coming of the Messiah.

First Peter offers the possibility of participation in politics by presupposing that politics would be able to renounce its totalizing character "and that its conception of citizenship would move away from the claim that this status has to dominate all others. But from this perspective it becomes evident that through its very resistance Christianity contributed decisively to the demolition of any such claim."[16] Here we have a subversion of the

---

14. Volf, "Soft Difference," 20.
15. Winter, *Seek the Welfare of the City*, 220.
16. Wannenwetsch, *Political Worship*, 143.

totalitarian claims of the empire on its citizens, suggesting such involvement secularizes the claims of the empire to a sacred unchallengeable status. It thus offers a challenge to the prevailing culture rather than by undertaking a movement towards developing a "counterculture."

Living "as in exile": Christian identity in the Epistle to Diognetus

The next reworking of the exilic tradition that I want to draw attention to is laid out in the Epistle of Mathetes to Diognetus, a late second-century apology addressed to a certain Diognetus who is otherwise unknown. The Epistle develops an account of the dual citizenship of Christians in language in which there is both a shift in vocabulary, and a continuity of reference to that which was used in 1 Peter.[17] In the Epistle to Diognetus we have an account of the duality of Christian citizenship and the participation by Christians in everything as citizens that takes us beyond the Christian difference articulated in 1 Peter, but does so in a way that retains the fundamental tension.

> Christians are distinguished from other men, neither by country, nor language, nor the customs which they observe.... But, inhabiting Greek as well as barbarian cities . . . and following the customs of the natives in respect to clothing, food, and the rest of their ordinary conduct, they display to us their wonderful and confessedly striking method of life. They dwell in their own countries, but simply as sojourners. As citizens, they share in all things with others, and yet endure all things as if foreigners. Every foreign land is to them as their native country, and every land of their birth as a land of strangers. They marry . . . [and] they beget children; but they do not destroy their offspring. They have a common table, but not a common bed. They are in the flesh, but they do not live after the flesh. They pass their days on earth, but they are citizens of heaven. They obey the prescribed laws, and at the same time surpass the laws by their lives.[18]

This account retains the "as citizens" character of the Christian community, while retaining the tension of being at the same time "as foreigners," "as in exile." The grounding of the Christian community in the common material practices of human life is accompanied by the emphasis on maintaining a Christian identity that is different in its practices from

17. Winter, *Seek the Welfare of the City*, 12.
18. *Epistle of Mathetes to Diognetus*, chapter V.

the surrounding culture. What empowers the addressees is the Christlike embrace of their paradoxical condition, of living in a given context without exclusively belonging to it. Alan Kreider draws our attention to a range of writings by early church fathers who articulated this living of the tension between indigenizing and being pilgrim, between affirmation and critique or, alternatively, as between being at home and being strangers in which both dimensions of identity and sociological location were maintained.[19] Abiding with this tension represents a form of patient Christian involvement in the community.

In his discussion of the Diognetian account of what he describes as the dual citizenship of the Christian, the philosopher Nicholas Wolterstorff argues that the Christian "occupies a unique location in the space of politics and nationality: citizen of the church but also citizen of some natural nation."[20] This tension in the Christian calling to a dual citizenship belongs to the given structure of our common humanity. The shift here is that the tension is registered in the conflict of two forms of citizenship. According to Wolterstorff this dual citizenship is opposed to the Augustinian stance on the two cities. The Augustinian account obscures from our view "the paradox, namely that the Christian is a citizen of Christ's kingdom and also a citizen voluntarily and by conviction of some natural and political order . . . and that the jurisdiction of the sovereigns of these two citizenries overlaps."[21] Wolterstorff's argument points to an account of Christian living that acknowledges the reality of dual citizenship and the tension between them, a tension that is maintained through articulation of the theme of living "as in exile."

The maintenance of the tension, between the affirmation of engagement and the antithesis of identity, is in this view healthy and requires ongoing cultivation rather than a shift of emphasis that will lead to a collapse of the tension. The tension needs to remain in our living and in our discernment of appropriate responses to specific situations. When we get to this point, we are moving beyond an ethnically shaped exilic identity in Jeremiah's account, or an active engagement by non-ethnically driven community of difference in 1 Peter.

In the Epistle to Diognetus we have a reimagining of the character of Christian social involvement in a new social context through an identity "as citizens," yet at the same time "as sojourners." The tension of living as citizens in two societies, the nation-state and the church, brings into focus

---

19. Kreider, *The Patient Ferment*, 91–130.
20. Wolterstorff, "Christian Political Reflection," 167.
21. Wolterstorff, "Christian Political Reflection," 163–64.

the role of critical discernment in maintaining the tension as the church learns how to embody "an alternative cultural vision that provides the basis for its mission and involvement in the cultural setting . . . as a creative pioneering community."[22] A minority community can bring about social change through the practice of an ethos of compassion, hospitality, and nonviolence, modeling possibilities for the wider community. There is the possibility of developing alternative institutional responses to social need and the provision of community service, working for new possibilities of participatory democracy and partnership, and protest and resistance against prevailing social and governmental policies.[23] The exilic orientation has a parallel in contemporary Anabaptist theology that does not require a single fixed stance or a rigid pattern of response, but rather looks to *ad hoc* initiatives in response to the diversity of social settings and power structures, without relinquishing attachment to particular territories, or rejecting concern for human security. In this it stands as a counter to nationalism, offering an alternative to forms of political liberalism that would erase or homogenize ethnic and cultural difference.

The implications of this paradigm for the mission of the church and church-related agencies are substantial. The Jeremian approach, which identifies the scattering of the people and their exile to Babylon as "mission," can be understood as an anticipation of Christ's approach to the Gentile world. A recent ethnographic account of the appeal by contemporary socially active evangelicals to Jeremiah's injunction points to an interesting contemporary rereading of the passage, as a mandate for social involvement. Importantly, the exilic element in the theme was usually elided in these discussions, avoiding the tensive relationship with the wider society that would be implied by the exilic designation.[24]

Augustine and the Anabaptists on "seeking the flourishing of the city"

My final stop in the course of tracing the development of the exilic theme from Jeremiah's call to seeking the flourishing of the city, through to the Anabaptist stance that I will explore in the following chapters, brings me to a note struck by Augustine.

---

22. Friesen, *Artists, Citizens, Philosophers*, 40.
23. Friesen, *Artists, Citizens, Philosophers*, 214–20.
24. Elisha, *Moral Ambition*, 193–94.

> The Heavenly City, while on its earthly pilgrimage, calls forth its citizens from every nation and every tongue. It assembles a band of pilgrims, not caring about any diversity in customs, laws and institutions whereby they severally make provision for the achievement and maintenance of earthly peace. All these provisions are intended in their various ways among the different nations, to secure the aim of earthly peace. The Heavenly City does not repeal or abolish any of them, provided that they do not impede the religion in which the one supreme, and true, God is taught to be worshipped.[25]

Augustine's metaphor here for the church's relation to the world is not that of citizenship, but one of pilgrimage, an image not identical but not too distant from that of being an exile.[26] We are faced here again with the tension of engagement while maintaining identity. "The City of God may cooperate with the City of Man in the pursuit of temporal goods, but only with a distinct sense of her own identity and a certain wariness of the fragility and accidental character of such alliances. For citizens of the Heavenly City can never make their final home in earthly institutions; they are on pilgrimage in this temporal existence."[27]

As we move forward

The trajectory of exile and engagement that I have traced in this chapter highlights not only how it has developed over time, but also the continuing tensions of engagement. The questions raised in carrying out the injunction by Jeremiah have never gone away, as the theological accounts in this chapter demonstrate. These accounts provide a theological resource for reflecting on the tensions of identity and mission after Christendom. In none of the accounts I have reported on is there a mandate for withdrawal from the task of seeking the flourishing of the community. The entanglement of the heavenly and the earthly cities, to use Augustine's terminology, without fixed geographical locations and including the ready transgression of boundaries, is a given, not a problem. "What Augustine portrays in terms of the city of God's pilgrimage on earth, Jeremiah heralds as Israel's diaspora, which is no less a political vocation and even a conduit of divine grace."[28]

---

25. Markus, *Christianity and the Secular*, 40.

26. For a helpful discussion on the use of the term "pilgrim" in marking Christian identity in an age of mobility, see Cavanaugh, *Migrations of the Holy*, 69–87.

27. Lee, "Republics and Their Loves," 574.

28. Bell Jr., "Jesus, the Jews," 103.

Exile: Community Engagement in a Shifting Location

Possibilities for practicing such a boundary-transgressing approach to engagement may include inculcating a culture committed to the transforming initiatives of the Sermon on the Mount that attends to the significance of institutions beyond the control and ideological shaping of both state and market. It may involve forming and/or sustaining nongovernment social movements and "ministries" dedicated to implementing restorative justice practices and giving priority to "raising up the lowly," providing a voice for the voiceless, while looking for opportunities to contribute to the transformation of public institutions through analysis, critique, imagination, example, and advocacy.

"Living in Babylon," while originally directed to those Israelites who had been taken off to the capital of the empire, has been taken up in recent theological debate as a metaphor for a stance and practice of engagement for the people of God who are not in control of their destiny and are distant from their homeland. It is a stance that takes account of place even though the location may be, as the title suggests, a babel, a place of confusion. The injunction then is one that points us to making a commitment to the elements of human life that are the foundation of human flourishing even though the broader context may be one of hostility and confusion.[29]

In sketching the contemporary significance and imaginative appropriation of the metaphor of exile, Brueggemann reminds us that we do not need a tight analogy between Scripture and our contemporary context.

> [W]hen the preacher proclaims in the baptised community in our present social context, the preacher speaks to a company of exiles. This does not mean that the exiles will all be weak, powerless, inept people, for many are formidable.... It means simply that such people are at work seeking to maintain an alternative identity, an alternative vision of the world and an alternative vocation in a societal context where the main forces of culture seek to deny, discredit, or disregard that odd identity. The great problem for exiles is cultural assimilation.[30]

The vocation of community engagement involves a refusal to choose between a false binary of participation versus nonparticipation, but rather requires a grappling with complex choices about the shape of public

---

29. On thinking imaginatively with and around this metaphor, see Brueggemann, *Out of Babylon*, 92–108.

30. Brueggemann, *Cadences of Home*, 41. On the background to the letter, see Smith, *The Religion of the Landless*, and Smith, "Jeremiah as a Prophet of Nonviolent Resistance."

cultural, political, and economic engagement, while maintaining an identity grounded in faithfulness to the call as an exile.

> [T]he people of God are to be about the welfare, the peace, the justice of all persons. There can be no question of withdrawal, no renunciation of responsibility, no self-absorption.... Christians concerned with faithful political witness—that is about appropriately heeding the call to work for the wellbeing of the cities of our exile—learn from the story of Daniel that service to the state, engagement in what the world calls politics, can have a legitimate place. But we also learn that such service is contingent and conditional...[31]

The theme of exile envisages political and cultural possibilities beyond those grounded in an imagination shaped solely by borders and boundaries. Jeremiah offers us a starting point for developing a vision in which politics, culture, and mission are all interwoven, and the development of this theme through the early church points to a continuing rethinking of what patient presence means for those who find their calling in exile.

---

31. Weaver, *States of Exile*, 81.

Part II

"Anticipating" Community Engagement
after Christendom

5

Pilgram Marpeck: A Biographical Approach to Community Engagement

In a book written in the conviction that moving beyond Christendom is something to be welcomed, it probably won't be a surprise that I have turned to Anabaptist history[1] as a resource for reimagining community engagement after Christendom. What may be a surprise is that I have chosen to provide a biographical sketch of Pilgram Marpeck, a significant Anabaptist leader but one not very well known outside Anabaptist circles.

As a form of storytelling, biography can be a powerful means to shake up our settled convictions, provoke questions, and open up conversation. I hope I can achieve some of that with my sketch of the life of Pilgram Marpeck, a sixteenth-century Anabaptist for whom community engagement was central to his understanding and practice of Christian discipleship. Ever since I discovered his story two decades ago, he has been a constant, if challenging, presence.

Pilgram Marpeck, it must be said, was a rather unlikely and quite atypical Anabaptist. At varying stages of his life, he worked as a mining magistrate, a municipal engineer, served on a town council, and provided pastoral leadership for scattered Anabaptist communities across Moravia, southern Germany, and Switzerland, all the while engaging in extensive theological debate with mainstream Protestant Reformers and diverse radical critics. Though Marpeck lived in a time in which Christendom was very much alive, his life and theology provide us with what I have termed

---

1. For an introduction to Anabaptism's history, I would recommend Snyder, *Anabaptist History and Theology*, while Weaver, *Becoming Anabaptist*, provides a good discussion of its contemporary significance.

as an "anticipation" of post-Christendom as a context for community engagement.

Who was Pilgram Marpeck?

Until the late nineteenth century, Marpeck remained a shadowy figure in the history of the Anabaptist movement. Since then, scholars burrowing through the municipal archives of Europe have uncovered a substantial corpus of theological writings and correspondence that has brought Marpeck and the Anabaptist movement in southern Germany into much clearer focus.[2]

The available documentation doesn't tell us much about Marpeck's childhood and education. He was born in 1495, in Rattenberg, a town on the Inn River in the Tyrol region of Austria. His father, Heinrich, served the town as a councilman, mayor, and district magistrate. The Marpeck family was well-to-do, with a town gate near the Marpeck house named after them. Based on an analysis of his theological writings it seems likely that Pilgram was educated at the Rattenberg Latin School. The municipal records provide us with some intriguing details of his life after leaving school. He worked in the city hospital, organized the city's crossbow competition, and acted as a purchasing agent for the mining guild's infirmary. He followed his father into the local administration, serving on the Rattenberg city council for several years, including a one-year term as mayor in 1522. He also represented Rattenberg at a session of the Tyrolean Diet in 1524. In 1525 Marpeck was given responsibility for organizing the supply of firewood for the town.

The extent of the Marpeck family wealth can be gauged from the fact that Pilgram was assessed at the highest level for a special imperial tax, as well as making a substantial loan to Ferdinand I, then Archduke of Austria. The source of the Marpeck family wealth almost certainly lay in their participation in the mining industry, where Pilgram worked as a contractor, managing the transport of silver and copper ore from mines in the Tyrol. His reputation and standing in the community were such that he was appointed as a mining magistrate by the Archduke of Austria in 1525, a position that he served in until his resignation in January 1528. This was one of

---

2. I have drawn heavily on Walter Klaassen and William Klassen's account of the life and times of Pilgram Marpeck, *Marpeck*, in writing this chapter. For those who come away from this chapter curious about Marpeck, I highly recommend their account of Marpeck's life and its social and political setting in southern Germany. Marpeck's theology, including its connection with that of Luther, is discussed in Blough, *Christ in Our Midst*, while the influence of south German mysticism on Marpeck is explored in Boyd, *Pilgram Marpeck*.

only five such positions in the empire, and carried significant political and economic responsibility. The mining magistrate adjudicated the competing interests of the princes, foreign investors, local investors, miners, and the neighboring cities in granting exploration and mining rights. Marpeck was also responsible for mediating disputes within the mining industry, giving him almost complete civil jurisdiction within the community. He had to ensure that the monarch received royalties from the industry, and that all fines were forwarded to the imperial financial office. With the local mining community structured in the form of a guild, the magistrate also had oversight of the care of widows, orphans, and retired miners, thus being responsible for performing a significant social welfare function, in what was a dangerous industry. In carrying out his responsibilities in this role Marpeck would have been one of the most significant figures in Rattenberg, with responsibility for making decisions on issues that were central to the economic and social functioning of the community.

The 1520s were a period of considerable religious and social upheaval across the Tyrol. Lutheran influence on the reform movement in the church in southern Germany and Austria didn't last long, and the Swiss reformers had little impact in the region. When we turn to Marpeck's stance on church reform prior to 1527 we don't have much information. He seems to have been favorably disposed toward the reform of the church. He was active in seeking to ensure proper provision of zealous and active clergy at the local level to ensure proper teaching and the regular conduct of worship. He negotiated the release of a local reform-minded preacher, Stephan Castenbaur, a spokesman for church reform, who was arrested by the authorities in 1522. Marpeck, acting at least partly on behalf of the mining guild, was also involved in pushing forward the hiring of a priest to fill the pastoral office in the city's parish church.

Marpeck has left us with little evidence on what led him to turn from his involvement in reforming the existing church, to joining the Anabaptists. In the record of his discussion with Bucer in Strasbourg in December 1531 the council minutes of that meeting leave us with only a tantalizing (and not especially clear) brief summary of his experience. "Since now in the whole world the fight and quarrel is only about the faith, he had been brought to this faith by his God-fearing parents in the papacy. Then he found a notable contradiction in the writings. For since at those places where one preached the gospel the Lutheran way, in which fleshly liberty was felt, this made him hesitant, since he could find no peace in it."[3] This account suggests his connection with Lutheran reformers was only brief.

---

3. Klassen and Klaassen, eds., *The Writings of Pilgram Marpeck*, 22.

Anabaptism emerged as the major carrier of the Reformation in the region, receiving strong support from the mining community. Given Marpeck's involvement with miners, it seems highly implausible that he would have been unaware of Anabaptist missionaries and their teaching activities in the region. The impact of the Anabaptists in the region was such that on August 20, 1527, Ferdinand I issued a mandate against all "sectarians and heretics." This proclamation was followed by a further mandate in October 1527. This second mandate required "the population to denounce Anabaptists and hand them over to the authorities for punishment . . . [since] heretics not only threatened Christian unity but also fostered enmity, rebellion, disobedience to the government and the seduction of the common man."[4] In a word, the Anabaptists were challenging Christendom, and the authorities did not want to risk the economic and social disruption that they assumed would accompany this movement directed at the reform of the church.

Becoming an Anabaptist

In late 1527 events came together that resulted in Marpeck throwing in his lot with the Anabaptist movement. Correspondence held by the imperial bureaucrats in Innsbruck provide us with a good record of the sequence of events and indirectly some insight into Marpeck's thinking. On November 25, 1527, Leonhard Schiemer, an Anabaptist missionary, was arrested in Rattenberg. On the basis of Schiemer's confession under torture he was sent to trial, and the Innsbruck administration ordered Marpeck to be ready for the apprehension and punishment of Anabaptists arising from Schiemer's confession. It must have been an anguished Christmas for Marpeck because on January 1, 1528 the civil magistrate at Rattenberg reported to his superiors in Innsbruck that Marpeck had asked to be relieved of the responsibility of handing over Anabaptists. The reported grounds for this request were that this was not part of the mandate of the mining magistrate. This was clearly a bureaucratic technicality advanced to try to distance himself from carrying out orders that he was opposed to. It seems unlikely that Marpeck really believed that this interpretation of his responsibilities would be accepted by his superiors. Perhaps it was nothing more than an attempt to buy time in the hope that something would turn up to get him off the hook, or to give himself time to make a decision with huge consequences for his future.

What turned up was another imperial mandate on January 4, 1528. "[T]he death penalty was the appropriate punishment for rebaptism under

---

4. Goertz, *The Anabaptists*, 122.

ecclesiastical and secular law, and . . . [it was thought that] the Anabaptists were plotting the overthrow and abolition of all government. The emperor reminded the authorities of their duty to act vigorously against the movement."[5] In the light of this mandate the authorities in Innsbruck were not impressed with Marpeck's plea to avoid participation in persecuting Anabaptists. They informed the civil magistrate in Rattenberg that, "they wish to deal seriously with him [the mining magistrate] in these matters pertaining to the Anabaptists, together with you, in obedience to the royal mandates and orders . . . If he persists in not following the royal prescription you must report it to us."[6] Correspondence from Innsbruck dated January 10, 1528 suggests that Marpeck changed his mind and agreed to comply with the mandate against the Anabaptists, a change of stance that did not last long.

On Sunday, January 12, 1528, the Anabaptist missionary Leonhard Schiemer was tried in Rattenberg. The record shows that someone who was not identified in the court records argued that the mandate only required imprisonment and confiscation. The tantalizing possibility, based on circumstantial evidence of both the timing of events, and Marpeck's subsequent decision to join the Anabaptists, is that this person may have been Marpeck. But Schiemer was sentenced to fire and the sword, beheaded on Tuesday, January 14 in the castle tower of Rattenberg and buried in the embankment behind the tower only 200 yards from Marpeck's home. Marpeck must have written his resignation as mining magistrate shortly after the execution, because by the following Saturday, January 18, his request to be discharged from his responsibilities had been acknowledged by the authorities in Innsbruck. While Marpeck may have had substantial sympathy with the Anabaptists previous to these events, the execution of Schiemer seems to have pushed him to throw in his lot with them. The request for discharge of Marpeck from his role in the imperial administration was granted on January 22, accompanied by instructions to hand over the books to his successor.

The events I have sketched suggest the difficulty and the anguish of Marpeck's decision. There were substantial consequences flowing from his commitment to join a group of radical reformers, whom the Duke of Bavaria was pursuing with all the power and authority available to him. The mandate against the Anabaptists had the death penalty attached to it. Beyond that, Marpeck had much to lose in giving up his position as mining magistrate in terms of financial security, professional status, and the

---

5. Goertz, *The Anabaptists*, 122–23.
6. Klassen and Klaassen, eds., *The Writings of Pilgram Marpeck*, 19.

certainty that in going into exile he would never be able to return home to Rattenberg. Little wonder at the uncertainty, second thoughts, and some good old bureaucratic bush lawyering prior to his resignation.

Of Marpeck's family up to this point in the story we know little, beyond the fact that his first wife died of the plague in 1527, and that after resigning as mining magistrate before leaving Rattenberg he handed over guardianship for his daughter and made arrangements for her financial support. We can only guess that his decision to leave his daughter was informed by the risks of his future as an Anabaptist, and his assessment of the difficulties of carrying her with him into exile. Following his departure Marpeck's property in Rattenberg, valued at 3,500 guilders, was confiscated by the authorities.

Marpeck's choice of Moravia as a location of exile following his departure was not surprising, given its reputation for tolerance and the willingness of its rulers to allow Anabaptist communities to establish themselves there. A number of significant changes came in Marpeck's life in the months following his move to Moravia. He remarried, was (re)baptized, and became actively involved with the Anabaptist communities that we now know under the title of the Austerlitz Brethren. Marpeck was quickly commissioned by them as an elder with authority to baptize.

Of his second wife, Anna, we have only fragmentary glimpses in the written records. Marpeck's mentions of her in his surviving correspondence across the years are warm and carry a note of real affection. Her presence is also acknowledged in correspondence directed to him from groups of Anabaptists, suggesting that she was seen as having a significant role in their joint pastoral activity. The leading Reformer in Strasbourg, Martin Bucer, despite his substantial theological disagreements with Marpeck, spoke of Pilgram and Anna as having an unblemished character. This in Bucer's view meant that they were particularly dangerous, as it made their theological stance more attractive and plausible to the unwary. A backhanded compliment indeed.

The move to Strasbourg

The political landscape of early sixteenth century Europe looks strange to us in the twenty-first century, with our experience of closely monitored and clearly defined borders. The relative openness to movement by dissenters and exiles across borders was a result of the fact that the Holy Roman Empire from Lyon in France in the west, to Cracow in Poland in the east, was a patchwork quilt of independent political units, duchies, kingdoms, and city-states. These territorial units had separate governments, each with its own jealously guarded interests and rights, and by our standards, minimal police forces and limited border controls. Dissenters, provided they were careful about their choice of route, had a reasonable chance of finding a safe haven. Pilgram and Anna were able to travel from Moravia to Strasbourg without great difficulty, though no doubt with some anxiety. They purchased citizenship in Strasbourg on September 19, 1528. Their move to Strasbourg seems to have been with the intention of working with emerging Anabaptist congregations in the city.

Strasbourg due to its reputation for relative tolerance to dissent was at this stage a magnet for Anabaptist refugees of all stripes. Marpeck came quickly to the notice of the Strasbourg authorities through being arrested as a member of a group of Anabaptists involved in undertaking a communal collection for the poor and refugees. It wasn't the charitable activity itself that attracted the unfavorable attention of the authorities. The activity was seen as problematic because it was an implicit criticism of the failure of the town council to take care of the poor, which failure reflected badly in the public view on its implementation of the Reformation in the city. This arrest did not prevent Marpeck's subsequent employment shortly after by the Strasbourg City Council. Perhaps his professional reputation, presumably based on his previous experience in Rattenberg, overrode any concerns about his theological commitments.

From late 1528 until December 1531, Marpeck worked as a municipal engineer for the city, with responsibility for managing the purchase of harvesting rights and the supply of firewood. He consequently spent a substantial period outside the city in the adjacent Kinzig and Leper river valleys, organizing the purchase and management of timber to be floated down the rivers to supply Strasbourg with firewood. Marpeck helped establish Anabaptist communities in these areas and maintained a pastoral correspondence with them over many years, while also exercising leadership of Anabaptists within the city that were associated with the Moravian strand of Anabaptism.

While working as a public servant, Marpeck contributed to a three-sided theological debate between the Anabaptists, other strands of radical dissent, and mainstream Reformers. In 1531 Marpeck published two works directed at spiritualist dissenters from the Reformation, as well as a work critical of the evangelical Reformers for their willingness to take up the sword on behalf of the Reformation. Given the anonymity of authorship of these publications, it has only been recently that scholars have been able to confidently attribute the authorship of all three publications to Marpeck. The first, *A Clear Refutation*, was written in response to radicals of spiritualist inclinations, who were questioning the necessity of the sacraments, a stance that was accompanied by an emphasis on the inner nature of the spiritual life. Against this Marpeck contended for both the legitimacy of the sacraments and for the validity of their continued use. Humans, he argued, are led to God by that which is visible. Indeed, all creatures according to Marpeck are a source of revelation of the gospel. Theologically his critique of spiritualism rested on the communal nature of the church, and the significance of the created order. There can be no purely private faith. The gifts of the Holy Spirit are given for mutual upbuilding, and for service manifested in love and faithfulness. The second publication, *A Clear and Useful Instruction*, dealt with a similar range of issues, this time with a strong christological emphasis in the argument. Marpeck argues that we find our way to the inner spiritual Christ through Christ's humanity. Christ's humanity was manifested in his teaching, his deeds, and his baptism, and was passed on to us by the disciples for our guidance. On the evidence of these theological manifestoes, Marpeck did not have any marked differences with the Reformers on issues such as Christology, the Trinity, and eschatology.

The third work was a critique of the mainstream Reformers, despite a title, *The Uncovering of the Babylonian Whore*, that may have led us to anticipate an attack on the Roman Church. In it Marpeck criticized the decision of the Lutherans to defend the Reformation by militarily opposing the emperor if he decided to take military action to force them to withdraw from their confessional statements. The political background to the Reformers' stance is that in February 1531 Strasbourg became a member of the Schmalkaldic League, which involved a commitment to a theological justification for military resistance to the emperor's threat of violence against the "Lutherans." Marpeck seems to have written this theological polemic in response to these developments, offering an Anabaptist critique of the use of military force in defense of the church. Marpeck did not believe that Christians had any mandate from Christ to use the sword to defend the gospel, or to suppress dissent within the church.[7] I will pick up some elements from his polemic on these issues in an account of some key themes in his political theology and approach to community engagement in the next chapter.

Marpeck's polemic prefigured a range of theological differences with the mainstream Reformers in Strasbourg that emerged more decisively in late 1531. Marpeck had a vision of church life that called for a loving and disciplined, but not legalistic, community. He could not agree with the

---

7. Blough, "The Uncovering of the Babylonian Whore."

polity of the Reformers because it involved support for what, in his view, was an undisciplined church that deferred to the civil authorities on the enforcement of moral standards within the church. Marpeck focused on developing smaller disciplined groups of believers that were not controlled by the governing authorities. Anabaptist ecclesiology here had substantial political implications.

The theological differences between the Anabaptists and the Strasbourg Reformers were brought to public notice when Marpeck was imprisoned in Strasbourg on October 22, 1531 on charges of misleading the citizens about theological issues to do with the relationship of church to government. Martin Bucer, the leading Reformer in the city, complained that Marpeck refused to endorse the annual oath of loyalty to the city, and further refused to urge members of his group to bear the sword. This, along with the refusal of Anabaptists in Strasbourg to have infants baptized, was in Bucer's view leading to a weakening of the city's social fabric. The Christendom assumptions of the mainstream Reformers were clearly behind this controversy.

The early release of Marpeck from prison reflected the reality that the Strasbourg Council was walking a tightrope in its handling of Anabaptist dissent. While the Anabaptist refusal to take the oath, and the perceived threat to public order from their ongoing public criticism of the evangelical preachers was of concern to the Strasbourg Council, the Council was equally concerned about taking any action against the Anabaptists and other dissenters that might concede too much power to Bucer and the evangelical preachers. The Council sought to retain its overall authority and did not want to be seen as operating at the beck and call of the leaders of the mainstream Reformation. This led to an interesting three-way dynamic in the events leading up to Marpeck's expulsion. The Council refused requests from both Bucer and Marpeck for a public debate, but agreed that a discussion between them would be held in front of the Council, in closed session. The debate, perhaps not surprisingly, changed no one's mind. On December 18, 1531, the Council resolved that Marpeck would be expelled from Strasbourg, unless he was willing to retract his assertion that infant baptism was unchristian, and to also commit to abstaining from rebaptizing of adults. Debates about baptism and rebaptism were not narrowly theological issues but were matters of significance for the shape of the public order, and political in the broadest sense of that term.

Marpeck agreed to obey the Council's order of expulsion. However, he could not promise the Council that he would not return to Strasbourg in the future if he were led to do so by the Spirit. He subsequently sought, and was granted, an extension of time from the Council, to sell his household goods and finalize business arrangements. Marpeck during this period made another attempt at dialogue with the Reformers. He sought from Bucer a written defense of infant baptism. Upon receipt of this defense, he sought a further two-week extension and prepared a *Confession of Faith* in response. The confession dealt particularly with the relationship of the First Testament (Old Testament) and Second Testament (New Testament), which he discussed as having a relationship of promise and fulfillment that represented a development in divine history. He also discussed the ordering of the relationship between the spiritual and the secular powers. In Marpeck's view Jesus as the initiator of the new age had refused to be a secular king and did not use earthly power to coerce and dominate. His resurrection was the beginning of a kingdom in which violence, vengeance, and coercion are forbidden.

On January 12, 1532 the Council agreed to a further hearing, in the light of this theological exchange, though again it was not held in public. The hearing took place the following week and resulted in confirmation of Marpeck's expulsion by the Council. The drawn-out character of this episode suggests a degree of respect for Marpeck's character and theology, a willingness to take time to participate in dialogue, and a refusal to be seen to be acting at the behest of Bucer and his colleagues. It is interesting to speculate just how confidential these dialogues before the Strasbourg Council actually were. It seems unlikely, given the public interest in theological controversies during this period, that the substance of the exchanges did not leak out to the general public.

Once again in exile

In leaving Strasbourg, Pilgram and Anna once again became exiles. Marpeck's awareness of the price being paid by those who were forced into exile as a matter of conscience is captured in his farewell to the Strasbourg Council. "I hope that you completely avoid any persecution of the miserable people who have no place in the world and who flee to you, especially if they are innocent of crimes, to find a haven from their misery without any coercion of their conscience."[8] This plea on behalf of refugees has a very powerful resonance in our own time.

Evidence of Pilgram and Anna's activities, and their location for the next decade, is limited. There are glimpses of their movements in the correspondence that has survived, but little firm evidence of prolonged residence in any one location. The most that can be said with confidence is

8. Marpeck, "Letter to the Strasbourg Council (1532)," 308.

that Pilgram probably worked as an engineer supervising the construction of water flumes for the St. Gallen weaving industry during 1535, an important contribution to the economic well-being of the local community. His movements were clearly limited by his need to remain hidden from the authorities, both Catholic and Protestant, given the increasingly draconian measures to suppress Anabaptists in the aftermath of the violent revolution in Munster in 1534. Despite the crackdown during this period, he apparently undertook some pastoral visitation, and wrote letters of advice and encouragement to groups of Anabaptists across Moravia and southern Germany. In cooperation with co-worker Leupold Scharnschlager, Marpeck also embarked on a theological work on the sacraments termed *The Admonition*. It offered instruction on the use of the term "sacrament," the nature of baptism and the Lord's Supper and the church. His sacramental theology included an account of the church as a prolongation of the incarnation as the "unglorified body of Christ."

Marpeck and Anna emerge from over a decade of obscurity in February 1544, with his employment by the Augsburg City Council as the public works director for the city, to manage the city's wood supply, and to oversee improvements to the water supply system. This employment by the city council of a known Anabaptist in a public, highly visible position took place during a period in which neither the Reformers nor the Catholics in Augsburg had effective political control in the city. Marpeck's work must have been regarded as satisfactory during the early years because from 1549 onward he was provided with a horse and an expense account for work for the Augsburg Council undertaken outside the city. As a registered resident and city employee, Marpeck was exempt from city taxes and military service. Employment of someone of Marpeck's theological background is hard to explain aside from his technical competence and professional reputation.

During his time in Augsburg, in addition to having a full-time job supervising the construction of an improved water supply to the city, Marpeck provided pastoral and theological leadership for an Anabaptist group that had gradually reemerged following the wave of arrests and persecution during 1527 and 1528. He also conducted a vigorous theological controversy with the spiritualist theologian Caspar Schwenkfeld, in which issues of the incarnation and the character of the church were central themes. In 1547, with the help of Anabaptist colleagues, he compiled and published a topical concordance *The Explanation of the Testaments*, which dealt with the relationship of the First Testament (Old Testament) and the Second Testament (New Testament) on topics of specific interest to Anabaptist communities.

There is strong evidence that during his time in Augsburg Marpeck sponsored a printing press for Anabaptist literature. The Augsburg Council was clearly aware of these activities and issued warnings to him on a number of occasions. In July 1545 Marpeck was directed to desist from working amongst the Anabaptists. In May 1550 inquiries were made about a major biblical concordance that he had published. In September 1553, an investigation was ordered by the Council into whether Marpeck was holding Anabaptist meetings with the direction that if he was, he was to be punished. A record of the council in September 1554 suggests that his activities with the Anabaptist community were again causing concern and noted in an interesting wording that "if it is ascertained that Pilgram is spreading his error, he shall be told to go and spend his penny elsewhere."[9] Beyond recording the various reprimands against him over the years, no follow-up action seems to have been taken by the Council. Minutes taken for the record followed by discreet inaction is a bureaucratic and political tactic with a long history. It suggests that Marpeck's work was valued by the Council and that it didn't want to go looking for a replacement.

Unlike many of the other Anabaptists in the sixteenth century, Marpeck died peacefully at home, sometime in the week prior to November 7, 1556. A sign of the changes during Marpeck's lifetime was that when he was growing up in Rattenberg there was only one Christian church. By the time of his death in Augsburg there were two major churches along with a number of illegal smaller groups of dissenters in the city.

Reflections on a life in exile

Put into contemporary terminology, Marpeck provides us with a case study of an urban professional who had a lot at stake in the political and religious status quo. Despite this, he walked away from a life of relative privilege to live out a new, and peaceable, vision of Christian discipleship engaged in the community to the extent to which his conscience allowed him and the political situation made it feasible. As a public servant, theologian, and pastor, Marpeck constructively sought the peace of the city, attempting peaceful dialogue over matters of substantial theological difference, making the theological case for rejecting the taken-for-granted practice of coercion in matters of faith. For much of his life, Marpeck was on the road as a refugee because of his commitment to a non-Christendom form of church life and discipleship. Writing out of a context of dislocation, he developed a theology that celebrated the incarnation and was positioned against a detached "spiritual" form of Christianity. In taking this stance he affirmed the church as a sacrament and a continuation of the incarnation, the

9. Klassen and Klaassen, eds., *The Writings of Pilgram Marpeck*, 41.

"unglorified body of Christ." The implications of this theological approach pose substantial questions to us in a time in which the institutional church has become preoccupied with itself and its own survival.

Marpeck's life of community service, pastoral care, and theological reflection was one in which he brought his skills and experience to the service of both the political and church communities. The record demonstrates that Marpeck engaged with those in power, whether theologians or politicians, with the confidence of one who was their equal in terms of status and education. In addition to his administrative and technical skills, he was theologically assertive despite being theologically self-educated. Critically for our purposes, Marpeck practiced a form of Christian life that rejected the Christendom entanglement of state and church. He undertook with the theological tools available to him a scriptural deconstruction of Christendom with its entanglement of church and state, drawing as he did so on his own experience as a public servant. His theological account of the relationship of church and state pointing to a separation is one that we shall explore in the next chapter. It substantially predates the Enlightenment critique and leans toward a politics of tolerance.

Aside from the uncertainties during the period of making his fundamental decision to align himself with the Anabaptist movement to surrender a position of power and relative affluence, his engagement with those in authority in both Strasbourg and Augsburg displays a measured and considered character. In Strasbourg where theological dialogue was, he judged, both possible and possibly productive, he pushed his case in discussion with both the church and civic leadership as far as he could. During a period of severe persecution of Anabaptists, he sought to serve the community in support of its economic development, while quietly maintaining pastoral support for scattered groups of Anabaptists. In Augsburg, the complex balance of forces on the city council between Catholic and Protestant was such while he was working for the Council there that he seems to have judged that a quiet Anabaptist presence and the maintenance of a printing press publishing Anabaptist literature was feasible without generating repercussions for himself and his wife, or the local Anabaptist community.

Having explored in this biographical sketch Marpeck's practice of community engagement in its lived tension with Christendom, I turn in the next chapter to his theological critique of Christendom, an important step toward imagining and grounding a form of community engagement after Christendom.

6

Theologically "Anticipating" Post-Christendom

In this chapter I unpack Marpeck's theological account of community engagement, which in many ways anticipates a helpful theological approach to our post-Christendom context. Marpeck wrote as an exile, and with a consciousness of being a minority voice in the arguments that he was advancing. Marpeck's theology, while it emerged from reflection on Scripture, was undertaken in the course of a life lived in service of the civil community, while at the same time he was involved in nurturing a church that was independent of the state.[1] For much of his life, after completing his daytime work as a municipal engineer, he must have spent his evening poring over Scripture, developing his theological arguments, and consulting with printers.

Before I embark on a discussion of some of Marpeck's key theological themes that underpin his critique of Christendom, I want briefly to draw attention to the importance of his emphasis on the incarnation. While Marpeck affirmed the divinity of Christ, he also stressed the importance of Christ's historical, physical humanity. The "un-constraining Spirit" gathered those who willingly received it into the "unglorified body" of Christ on earth, that is the church, which awaited union with the "glorified body" of Christ in heaven. In Marpeck's understanding, the reception of the Spirit, which is sealed by baptism, the "covenant of good conscience," in effecting sanctification, leads to a commitment to justice, not only internally before God, but also externally before humanity. Because of his understanding of the "un-constraining" nature of Christ's Spirit, Marpeck criticized the pursuit of justice by means of either the civil sword, or a theologically

---

1. A key source on this topic is Boyd, *Pilgram Marpeck*.

coercive legalism. This theological theme sits in the background of my discussion of his political theology in this chapter.

Marpeck's critique of Christendom

Marpeck's biographers make two points that are relevant to the discussion of Marpeck's political theology. The first concerns the relationship between creedal orthodoxy and discipleship. For Marpeck "the mark of the truly Christian life was not an isolated creedal orthodoxy but a life of conformity to Christ . . . [entailing] a conscious choice to be a disciple of Jesus and to be part of the church of Christ in which neither government nor the state had a determining function."[2] The second is that despite living a life of dissent "Marpeck was politically quite traditional. He upheld the legitimate authority of emperors, kings and councils for the maintenance of social order. He had no vision for a new social or political order such as was held by the Anabaptists of Munster in Westphalia or by John Calvin. But he believed in the autonomy of God's kingdom in the midst of the kingdoms of this world, and he devoted himself to that vision."[3]

Elements of Marpeck's critique of the Constantinian settlement, and his normative account of the relationship of church and state, are found throughout his theological writings. Marpeck's treatment of these themes was occasional, rather than systematic. He wrote in response to pressing issues and to questions raised by groups of dissenting Christians across southern Germany. Nevertheless, his topical and polemical approach provides the basis for an interesting account of a relationship between church and state that we can legitimately describe as being post-Christendom in its character.

I begin my account of Marpeck's political theology with a sketch of three key themes concerning the relationship between church and state that point beyond Christendom. The first relates to the use of coercion in matters of faith, the second concerns the relationship of the church and secular authority, and the third deals with the question as to whether Christians can be magistrates and rulers. I have sought to let his voice be heard through substantial quotations from his writings. I like to think that something of his character, and his voice, comes through in these quotations.

---

2. Klaassen and Klassen, *Marpeck*, 25.
3. Klaassen and Klassen, *Marpeck*, 26.

Coercion in matters of faith

During Christendom the church disclaimed the direct use of force in underpinning theological orthodoxy. However, offenders were handed by ecclesiastical authorities to the civil authorities for punishment. Marpeck does not accept this casuistical distinction. He is unequivocal in rejecting the use of coercion in matters of faith. "Christ was subject to all Authority and never responded with violence. . . . Christ does not distribute earthly inheritance or imperium, His own whether they are treated justly or not requite and repay with justice and love. All external things including life and limb are subjected to external authority. But no one may coerce or compel true faith in Christ."[4] In his *Strasbourg Confession* he asserts that "there is no coercion, but rather a voluntary spirit in Christ Jesus our Lord. Whoever does not desire [this spirit] let him remain outside . . ."[5]

Marpeck's opposition to the use of violence to enforce uniformity of faith also emerges in his *Letter to the Strasbourg Council*. "[T]he Lord has so far been gracious to you in matters of faith and has preserved you from the shedding of blood—not a small grace from God—so that this highly praised city of Strasbourg, by the grace of God, has been preserved from that more than all other places in the world."[6] Marpeck undertakes an extended exposition of the parable of the Weeds to underpin his argument against using violence in pursuit of Christ's kingdom. According to Marpeck, Christ "also instructs his own by the forgoing parable to wait. He commands no one to condemn and kill with the sword."[7] The only sword Christians are to exercise is that of the Word. Marpeck's argument against coercion has a strong christological grounding. "The criterion for judgement about how church and government should function in the new age . . . could only be Christ inasmuch as God had revealed his will to the world in him. . . . Christ must be the mirror by which these things are judged. . . . This Christ did not exercise coercion or arbitrary power over others."[8]

The broader political implications of Marpeck's stance on the state's role in enforcing matters of faith is given a clear articulation in the *Address to the Strasbourg Council* in 1534, by Marpeck's close theological collaborator Leupold Scharnschlager.

---

4. Marpeck, "Exposé of the Babylonian Whore," 10. I note here that the translation of the Marpeck document uses the term "Exposé," while Blough uses the alternative translation of "Uncovering."
5. Marpeck, "Pilgram Marpeck's Confession of 1532," 112–13.
6. Marpeck, "Letter to the Strasbourg Council (1532)," 306–7.
7. Marpeck, "Exposé of the Babylonian Whore," 41.
8. Klaassen, "The Anabaptist Critique of Constantinian Christendom," 225.

> Your suspicion that I and my associates should we become the majority would immediately drive you out the door ... as you now seek to do to us—since we do not consider such a work of the Spirit, nor as the ban, power and order of Christ, I see no possibility of doing. If I and my colleagues would number even one hundred thousand it would be more useful for us before God, that we all would move away from you or allow ourselves to be driven away rather than that we should drive you away with force and cause such a scandal against God's love ...[9]

The church and secular authority

Arising from Marpeck's rejection of the use of coercion to enforce matters of faith at a society-wide level is the rejection of the use of power by the state to interfere in matters that are internal to the life of the church.[10] Marpeck took a clear stand on the importance of withdrawing the exercise of temporal power from enforcing matters relating to the life of the church and rejected the use of external power from influencing the government of the church.[11]

> I admit worldly carnal and earthly rulers as servants of God in earthly matters, but not in the kingdom of Christ; according to the words of Paul, to them rightfully belongs all carnal honour, fear, obedience, tax, toll and tribute. However, when such persons who hold authority become Christians ... they may not use the aforementioned force, sovereignty, or ruling in the Kingdom of Christ. It cannot be upheld by any Scripture. To allow the external authority to rule in the kingdom of Christ is blasphemy against the Holy Spirit ...[12]

In 1532 in his *Letter to the Strasbourg Council*, Marpeck denied the right of the Council to rule on the theological issues that were at stake in his debate with the preachers in Strasbourg. "[T]he altercation between me and the preachers with respect to the Word of God is known to my gracious lords. You are not authorities over us but are listeners to it and have occasion to hear both sides of the question. However, no one can judge in these matters except God alone."[13] Marpeck develops his argument over the

---

9. Scharnschlager, "Leupold Scharnschlager's Farewell," 217–18.
10. Klassen, "The Limits of Political Authority."
11. Marpeck, "Pilgram Marpeck's Confession of 1532," 112–13.
12. Marpeck, "Pilgram Marpeck's Confession of 1532," 150.
13. Marpeck, "Letter to the Strasbourg Council (1532)," 306.

limited scope of temporal authority in the church on historical as well as biblical grounds. Here Constantine comes into view.

> The early Christians to the time of Constantine exercised no temporal rule or sword among themselves. The command of their master did not allow it. He granted them only the sword of the Word. Whoever after sufficient admonition would not listen was regarded as a Gentile and unbeliever [Matt 18:17] But when at that time the pope as the servant of the church was married to Leviathan, that is the temporal power but in the disguise of Christ, the Antichrist was conceived and born as has now been revealed.[14]

Marpeck returned to this theme on a number of occasions, arguing that given that the pope has no right to exercise coercion in the church, "much less ought worldly magistrates to be put into the holy place. . . . They should be allowed to remain in their proper service of God to fulfil it according to God's will through the fear of God and that wisdom which is necessary and requisite for all worldly pagan authority whom Paul calls servants of God regardless of faith."[15] Marpeck was in tune here with the overall stance of the early Anabaptists, who regarded the fusion of church and government under Constantine as the "fall" of the church. In challenging that development, the Anabaptists held that questions of faith and the internal life of the church should not be enforced by secular authority. Such issues were to be resolved within the community of faith and could not and indeed should not be settled by any outside authority.[16] The worldly authorities have no place within the internal life of the church. These authorities have their own job to do, which is to focus on the work of maintaining justice in the community, not on intervening in the church, where they have no right to use coercive power.

Christians as magistrates and rulers

Beyond the issue of the proper limits of the exercise of temporal power, Marpeck also discussed the question as to whether, and to what extent, individual Christians should exercise civil authority. Here he focused his argument on the question of whether a Christian could become a magistrate. While many Anabaptists absolutely rejected the possibility of exercising

---

14. Marpeck, "Exposé of the Babylonian Whore," 38–39.
15. Marpeck, "Explanation of the Testaments," 558.
16. Klaassen, "The Nature of the Anabaptist Protest," 299.

power in the realm of the secular, that is as part of the civil authority, Marpeck took a slightly more qualified stance. He does not rule out Christians being involved in the exercise of secular power, though he thinks that such involvement is likely to be severely limited and would need to be assessed on a case-by-case basis. It seems clear that Marpeck's experience in positions of responsibility in the Rattenberg Town Council, and his role as a mining magistrate, shaped his approach to this issue. A decision on whether a Christian could serve in such an office would need to be made on the basis of what was expected of a person exercising authority in a specific post.[17]

In a letter written in 1545, Marpeck set out some of the criteria for such an assessment, asserting that Christians "have been appointed by Him not to rule over, judge, condemn, destroy or inflict any evil or suffering on men . . ."[18] Marpeck advised that, while it might be possible for a Christian to be a magistrate, perhaps reflecting his experience as mining magistrate under the Hapsburgs, he was of the view that "it is hard for a Christian to be a worldly ruler. . . . If he does rule over the things of the kingdom of this world, according to God's just and human order, how long will he remain a ruler of this world? He would have the weight of its misuses and distortions on his conscience and need to bear with them. How long would his conscience let him be a ruler?"[19]

If the possibility of Christians exercising the authority of the magistrate or ruler is not absolutely closed off by Marpeck, the option of Christians undertaking that role to exercise vengeance is rejected. "When that Authority does not bear the sword as it should, but rather protects wickedness, destroys godliness, loves the lie and persecutes the truth, you must be content to admonish that Authority, which is God's servant, to be converted and leave the vengeance to God. No other sword or deterrence has Christ commanded his own to use."[20]

The view that Christians will automatically make better rulers than those who are outside the faith, a position that has been advanced by many evangelical Christians today, was dismissed by Marpeck. In a passage that represents him at his most eloquent, he points to the importance of the experience of suffering, and self-reflection on our own failures, before we undertake the role of rulers. Character, he suggests, matters. Claiming the label of Christian is not enough basis for exercising power appropriately.

---

17. Klassen, "The Limits of Political Authority," 349.
18. Marpeck, "An Epistle Concerning the Heritage and Service of Sin," 415.
19. Marpeck, "Response to Caspar Schwenckfeld's Judgement," 97.
20. Marpeck, "Exposé of the Babylonian Whore," 29.

> There are many rulers, many temporal and spiritual tyrants who while appearing to be Christian, violate, judge and condemn. They run ahead of Christ and seize his power like thieves and murderers, they rob him of his honour and glory and arrogate it to themselves. They rule before [they have known] patience, distress and suffering even though tribulation has to precede glory. They become powerful before they have humbled themselves, they rule and govern before they serve, they condemn and judge before they have judged themselves.[21]

Based no doubt on his observations of the push and shove to gain positions of authority among imperial authorities, Marpeck responds to the question about what will happen to government if Christians withdraw from the role of magistrate with a wry observation. "We don't need to be concerned about governmental authority. There will always be those who want to rule. Let us see that we remain Christians, live patiently and accept the victory of the Lamb."[22]

In summary, Marpeck took a cautious stance on the possibilities of participation in government by Christians. Commentators on his writing tend to disagree on exactly how and where he drew the line on such participation. I am inclined to agree with the assessment by Arnold Snyder.

> Marpeck refused to erect an ethical or legal barrier between the church as "the perfection of Christ" and "the world" as the realm of Satan. There was no polarity in Marpeck that forbade as an ethical principle, the participation of Christians in governing functions. On the other hand, neither was Marpeck very hopeful that Christian love and mercy would be compatible with the "political wisdom" needed to serve in public office.[23]

Marpeck in both Strasbourg and Augsburg worked as a municipal employee, accountable to a town council with whom he was in substantial theological disagreement. Stephen Boyd suggests that "Marpeck's quarrel was with those magistrates" who wanted to "use such bodily force to reign or rule in the realm of Christ." He did not say that magistrates could not be Christians, nor that civil power did not maintain a certain needed order. He only objected to those Christian magistrates exercising coercive power in matters of religious conscience and church reform.[24] Marpeck lived his

---

21. Marpeck, "An Epistle Concerning the Heritage and Service of Sin," 416.
22. Marpeck, "Expose of the Babylonian Whore," 42.
23. Snyder, "An Anabaptist Vision for Peace," 199.
24. Boyd, "Anabaptism and Social Radicalism in Strasbourg," 72.

life negotiating on a case-by-case basis how and where he could serve the political order.

"Anticipating" a post-Christendom pluralist/secular order

The issues that I have just discussed provide a sketch of Marpeck's critique of Christendom. In his theological arguments Marpeck "anticipates" the possibility of post-Christendom as a normative frame for Christian life and witness. Christians do not need to be "in control." In using the term "anticipation" in respect to post-Christendom, I am not suggesting that we find in Marpeck's writings a fully worked out theological account of the pluralist/secular political space that is characteristic of our current post-Christendom context. What I am suggesting is that in Marpeck's responses on a range of issues, along with his attempts to provide guidance for his fellow Anabaptists in his own day, we find in principle a commitment to a post-Christendom order.

Marpeck's stance points towards being able to imagine a thoroughgoing deconstruction of the Constantinian settlement. Historically Marpeck's theological influence on questions of community engagement by Anabaptists did not survive in any direct way in Anabaptist communities beyond the sixteenth century. His theological writing was lost to history, at least until recently. Thinking with and beyond Marpeck is nevertheless a helpful exercise in developing a theologically informed response to community engagement after Christendom. I suggest the following political commitments are consistent with Marpeck's situational theological discernment and scriptural argument:

- Rejection of the use of coercion by the state either to uphold a single religious option, or to enforce participation in a particular religious institution as an essential element of citizenship. This commitment makes possible pluralism of belief and practice, and clearly involves a limitation on the powers of government.
- Withdrawal of the state from the role of judging, deciding, and enforcing matters of policy, belief, and structure within the life of religious organizations. This implies the independence and integrity of the church and opens up the space more generally for a civil society with a variety of value-based organizations independent of the state.
- Rejection of the use of coercion by government against individuals in the exercise of religious conscience. This creates space for conviction

by argument within a society or political community and the exercise of witness to that community.

- The limitation of the responsibilities of the state to the maintenance of social order and justice. This withdraws religious sanctions from the armory of the state and implies the de-sacralization of government in both its character and authorization.

These commitments collectively point to the structural and functional independence of the church as a social organization, with the potential for it to be in a relationship of greater or lesser tension with the state. The assertion of the independence of the church as a social organization enables the possibility of independent action by Christians outside their formal roles in society and provides space for them to act directly on the biblical call to seek the good of the city. Marpeck therefore "did more than simply 'allow' Christians to participate in the world; he also urged loving action in the world by Christians. According to Christ's example, believers should resist evil and overcome it by means of good, by means of loving patience."[25]

Thinking about the state

In his discussion of the political and ecclesiological implications of Marpeck's stance, the following comments from the Marpeck scholar and biographer William Klassen provide a useful starting point for an account of Marpeck's thought. Marpeck "believed that the church must exist as a social structure in tension with the state. When it was suggested to him that a community which rejects the basis of power on which the state rests, in fact challenges the legitimacy of the state, he replied that obedience to God is more important than obedience to Caesar. . . . [E]ven if Anabaptists were to become a majority, they would not force their faith on others. Faith must come out of the willingness of the individual to accept it and coercion has no role in promoting faith."[26] As I shall discuss in some detail below, Marpeck's "critique of Constantinian forms of Christianity made it possible for him to separate the unity of the church from the unity of empire,"[27] in both practice and theology.

Marpeck affirmed both the positive and the negative aspects of the state. He understood the role of civil power as the protector of the just, punisher of the civilly unjust, and as a good ordinance of God. The civil

---

25. Snyder, "An Anabaptist Vision for Peace," 200.
26. Klassen, "The Limits of Political Authority," 350.
27. Blough, "The Uncovering of the Babylonian Whore," 55.

Theologically "Anticipating" Post-Christendom

power though should be limited in scope. At its best the civil power can sustain an environment in which justice might be extended, but it cannot guarantee the extension of justice and produce faith or bring about receptivity to the work of the Spirit. This appreciation of both the possibilities and limits of state activity was no doubt informed by Marpeck's experience in dealing with government at the highest levels. Due to his emphasis on the decisive character of the incarnation, Marpeck insisted that the Bible is properly understood only in the context of, and interpreted by, the whole community of believers. His surviving correspondence with the scattered communities of Anabaptists displayed a strong pastoral concern to find the path of Christian freedom exercised between the extremes of legalism and lawlessness.

Boyd concludes that "Marpeck apparently came to the conviction that true social justice and therefore the civil order was impossible without respect for the sovereignty of the individual conscience. Hence his critical participation in civil life was also governed by his commitment to social responsibility and respect for the sovereignty of the individual conscience."[28] The shape of Marpeck's account of state and church is centered around freedom. "[T]he new community is to be the new community and thereby extend the justice of Christ to others in the world, [so] it must be free. The state must be separated from the church for the sake of the church and for the sake of social justice."[29] Klassen further insists that the "most important theological contribution of Marpeck and his fellowship was their insistence that the humanity of Christ had relevance for the structuring of the church and its common life as well as for the shape of the ethical life. Freedom was important because Christ was free and died to make others free.... [F]or Marpeck the potential for human freedom opened up for humanity through the human Christ was a value that dare not be lost."[30]

Limited participation in positions of authority by Christians did not imply withdrawal from the public space or from attempting to influence public debate on specific issues. Marpeck urged those who called themselves Christians who were serving in government to live up to their own self-proclaimed standards. Government that helped the poor and oppressed and punished those who afflicted them in his view deserved the support of both Christians and unbelievers.

The practice of church as a voluntary community is also a rejection of the totalizing character of Christendom. Marpeck in undercutting the

---

28. Boyd, *Pilgram Marpeck*, 162.
29. Boyd, "Anabaptism and Social Radicalism," 72.
30. Klassen, "Pilgram Marpeck," 175.

assumed and politically enforced identity of membership of the state, or political community with the membership of the church, is suggesting the creation of a society that allowed for participation according to gift and opportunity, and the exercise of mutual responsibility and accountability. To establish an independent church as a community not under the control of the government was a political as much as a religious proposal and involved a more confident approach to political action arising from within society, rather than depending upon a top-down direction.[31] The rejection of religious unity as the taken-for-granted basis for political order, that follows from Marpeck's affirmations, is a movement towards a pluralist political order. The mainstream Protestant Reformers could not imagine a pluralist political order, or to the extent that it entered their horizon they viewed such a possibility with horror—as nothing less than a step toward anarchy and social collapse.[32]

As Marpeck's life demonstrated, independence of conscience and limited participation in positions of authority by Christians did not imply withdrawal from the public space or from attempting to influence public debate. Marpeck in his insistence on a church separated from secular control positions the church so that it is able to confront the secular order in placing an implicit limitation on the claims of the state. "Even though government was instituted by God and should be obeyed wherever its dictates did not violate Christian conscience, a Christian, they argue, could not directly participate in its coercive and lethal activities. Love for the neighbour could not include killing that neighbour . . ."[33]

The withdrawal of religious sanctions from the state as a means of enforcing social and political control implies a deconstruction of its sacral character with the recognition that a Christian's ultimate loyalty is to Christ. Marpeck's reading of Romans 13 sees him place limits on the status of the state. It is only by remaining within its limits that the state can be regarded as having divine authorization and a specific vocation. Government on this reading has, in Bonhoeffer's terms, a "penultimate" character as an institution.[34] Marpeck "knew that with his position of removing the religious sanctions from all that the state demanded which was against conscience he had in fact robbed the state of that which it cherished most: the ability

---

31. Klaassen, "The Nature of the Anabaptist Protest," 300.
32. Klassen, "Pilgram Marpeck," 175.
33. Heilke, "Locating a Moral/Political Economy," 221.
34. Klaassen "The Anabaptist Critique of Constantinian Christendom," 226.

Theologically "Anticipating" Post-Christendom

to demand unlimited loyalty, the supreme sacrifice. The kingdom to which Marpeck pledged his unlimited allegiance belonged to Christ alone."[35]

The Anabaptist critique of Christendom, which challenges in theological terms the linkage of church and state government, offers the apparently paradoxical conclusion that the state can only realize its highest potential in serving the community when it is not allowed to absolutize itself. The "Anabaptist believer is thus positioned in the most difficult of social locations: a space that acknowledges the political legitimacy of the civil authority without accepting its spiritual validity or foundation. . . . Put differently Anabaptists were called to be subject to an Authority whose ultimate validity they did not accept."[36] To shift the emphasis slightly, Anabaptists saw themselves as called to be subject to an authority whose ultimate validity as they understood it was grounded in God, and consequently gave that authority a purely provisional and limited character.

> One of the most baleful results of the state taking an active role in the functioning of the church in Christendom was that the church had become necessarily dependent upon, and inextricably tied to, the exercise of military power by the state. For Marpeck the union of Christ and the secular is a hopeless confusion of the distinct and independent functions of spiritual and secular authority. There is no biblical warrant for it. First of all, Marpeck argued the appeal that rulers in the Old Testament used the sword at the command of God is misplaced because the whole of the Jewish law had been abrogated by Christ. "Christ is the end of the law" (Romans 10:4), he reminded readers. More importantly, he said, there is no record whatsoever that Christ ever committed the sword of steel to his followers. The only sword he gave them was the sword of the Spirit. And Christ's own example totally negated their argument. He subjected himself to the authority of Pilate and Caiaphas and did not resist. Never did he dominate or coerce anyone. His is the example that Christians are called to follow.[37]

Marpeck here raises the issue as to whether churches could be true churches when they used the sword against each other, an action Marpeck described as being "in the semblance of Christ" but in fact denying to Christ his role in the church.[38] The test of the unity of the church is to be found in

---

35. Klassen, "The Limits of Political Authority," 359.
36. Biesecker-Mast, *Separation and the Sword in Anabaptist Persuasion*, 130–31.
37. Klaassen and Klassen, *Marpeck*, 160.
38. Klaassen, "The Anabaptist Critique of Constantinian Christendom," 227.

its commitment to the practice of peacemaking, not a creedal orthodoxy upheld by military coercion.

Conclusion

As a theologian and public servant, Marpeck developed a theological argument for rejecting association of the church with state coercion. He also argued for and demonstrated in his life a practice of limited and critical community engagement, rather than either a Christendom assimilation or an absolute withdrawal from society. Marpeck stands as a witness to a stance that "anticipated," in important ways, the possibility of community engagement after Christendom. We are the richer for that resource in both his practice and theological reflection. The other issue that I want to briefly note is that Marpeck's deconstruction of Christendom in his life and theology was underpinned by a commitment to a practice of the church as the "unglorified" body of Christ. This is an image that gives a strong theological affirmation of the church's identity, while reminding us that the church does not have a glorified character in its earthly existence and cannot claim a status that places it beyond criticism.

7

Community Engagement after Marpeck

Pilgram Marpeck's theological "anticipation" of community engagement after Christendom that I sketched in the previous chapter provides us with a helpful starting point for theological reflection on the issue. In this chapter I explore how a contemporary Mennonite confession of faith can be considered to be in important ways in the spirit of Marpeck. I then move on to consider the complexity of thinking theologically about community engagement in a time in which the "sacred" keeps reappearing in what we generally think of as a secular/pluralist political and constitutional order such as Australia. Out of this complexity I suggest that Christians have good theological reasons for supporting a secular/pluralist political order after Christendom. Though I develop my argument specifically in the Australian context, I invite readers from other nations to take a fresh look at their own context in the light of my argument about theology, secularity, and pluralism in Australia.

Community engagement in the spirit of Marpeck

In sketching a contemporary theology of community engagement in the spirit of Marpeck, I have chosen as a starting point a recent confession by Mennonite Churches in Canada and the United States that picks up the tension between engagement in seeking the welfare of the city, while maintaining our faithful identity as disciples of Jesus. In a statement that allows us to recognize both the possibilities and limitations of such involvement, we encounter the theological commitments of Mennonites in North America that share a family resemblance to those expressed by Marpeck.

The *Confession of Faith in a Mennonite Perspective* was finalized in 1995 by the Mennonite Churches of the United States and Canada, and serves as a guide to contemporary belief and practice of churches with roots in the Anabaptist tradition.[1] There are a number of articles in the *Confession* that are relevant in varying degrees to the issue at hand, including Article 17, "Discipleship and the Christian Life"; Article 20, "Truth and the Avoidance of Oaths"; Article 22, "Peace, Justice and Nonresistance"; and Article 24, "The Reign of God." These articles provide the broader theological framework within which Article 23, "The Church's Relation to Government and Society," on which I am going to focus, should be read. Here is Article 23.

> We believe that the church is God's "holy nation," called to give full allegiance to Christ its head and to witness to all nations about God's saving love.
>
> The church is the spiritual, social, and political body that gives its allegiance to God alone. As citizens of God's kingdom, we trust in the power of God's love for our defense. The church knows no geographical boundaries and needs no violence for its protection. The only Christian nation is the church of Jesus Christ, made up of people from every tribe and nation, called to witness to God's glory.
>
> In contrast to the church, governing authorities of the world have been instituted by God for maintaining order in societies. Such governments and other human institutions as servants of God are called to act justly and provide order. But like all such institutions, nations tend to demand total allegiance. They then become idolatrous and rebellious against the will of God. Even at its best, a government cannot act completely according to the justice of God because no nation, except the church, confesses Christ's rule as its foundation.
>
> As Christians we are to respect those in authority and to pray for all people, including those in government, that they also may be saved and come to the knowledge of the truth. We may participate in government or other institutions of society only in ways that do not violate the love and holiness taught by Christ and do not compromise our loyalty to Christ. We witness to the nations by being that "city on a hill" which demonstrates the way of Christ. We also witness by being ambassadors for Christ, calling the nations (and all persons and institutions) to

---

1. Mennonite Church USA, *Confession of Faith in a Mennonite Perspective*.

move toward justice, peace, and compassion for all people. In so doing, we seek the welfare of the city to which God has sent us.

We understand that Christ, by his death and resurrection, has won victory over the powers, including all governments. Because we confess that Jesus Christ has been exalted as Lord of lords, we recognize no other authority's claims as ultimate.[2]

Article 23 is substantially in tune with Marpeck's theological critique of Christendom. The key theological elements of a stance of community engagement consistent with post-Christendom in the Confession are:

- The church is not limited by geographical boundaries and does not require violence for its protection and ordering.
- The church does not recognize the claim of government as having an ultimate authority over against the call to faithfulness to the way of Christ.
- Governments exist to govern justly and provide order but if they demand total allegiance, they become idolatrous.
- Government as an institution is fallible, and should be subject to critique and nonviolent resistance by the church.
- Christians are called to respect authority and pray for all people, including those in government.
- Christians may participate in government only in ways that do not violate the love and holiness taught by Christ, and do not compromise our loyalty to Christ.
- Christians are called to witness to the nations by demonstrating the way of Christ, honestly confessing their failure to do so, and by being ambassadors for Christ, in calling the nations (and all persons and institutions) to move toward justice, peace, and compassion for all people, seeking the welfare of the city to which God has sent us.

Participation in government is limited by the requirement that such participation does not violate the call to love, and maintain holiness in our discipleship, or compromise our primary loyalty to Christ. The tension in Marpeck's theology is recognizably present but is clearly less stringently expressed.

The call for the church to demonstrate in its own life the way of Christ, and by advocacy and example call nations toward justice, peace, and compassion for all people, is the most difficult element in this Article, in

2. Mennonite Church USA, *Confession of Faith in a Mennonite Perspective*.

the context of massive failures by the churches with regard to sexual abuse and their response to it. The current failure has been public, shaming, and heartbreaking. It's not hidden away in history, like many of the previous failures in Christendom. It's here, it's now, and the pain is pressing in upon us. So how do we acknowledge the call to the church? In what spirit can we respond to it? Is the gap between the normativity of the call and the reality on the ground too big for us to be able to confess the call to the church, as it is phrased here, in good conscience? I am deeply convicted that we need to find a way of speaking about the fallibility and the sinfulness of the church as a human institution, while acknowledging the call to the church to manifest the presence of Christ here and now. I am now highly allergic to theological claims about the character of the church that implicitly place it above "outside" critique and self-critique.

How might we reword the article to emphasize the calling of the church to a continued confession of failure, in turning yet again toward the light? William Stringfellow is helpful here with his observation on the temptation of the church to become preoccupied with the maintenance and preservation of its institutional life. When this becomes the driving force everything else will be sacrificed, and in that sacrifice the church loses its essential identity and freedom. The institution becomes an idol that will claim the sacrifice of the most vulnerable, those who are on the margins, those who are outside the markers of purity laid down by orthodoxy.[3]

There is a continuing temptation for the church in its account of community engagement to instinctively return to the triumphalist rhetoric from Christendom. This theological triumphalism can surface even in the Confession of a minority church such as the Mennonites, which has sought to take up in its practices the ethos of peacemaking and embody a stance of greater humility. The habits of Christendom are hard to break, even and perhaps particularly when we turn to the task of providing theological accounts of who we are and what we are doing. The church, in so far as it is an institution set up and run by human beings, will remain fallible and fall short of its calling. Bonhoeffer's call to the church to take account of its failures serves as a reminder of the dangers when it loses its ability to be reflective and make the necessary continuing turn to repentance. A contemporary test for assessing theological claims about the character of the church is to ask: How would this claim look and sound to someone who has been damaged by sexual abuse by a member of the church, and has been further abused by the leadership of a church who have sought to cover up that abuse? There are other analogous test questions that I could suggest

---

3. Stringfellow, *Free in Obedience*, 95–96.

relating to church failures with regard to race and sexuality, but this one example should make the point for those who have ears to hear.

Marpeck in a time of the "secular"

Community engagement after Christendom is taking place in a complex and shifting context. That's why I have focused the discussion that follows on community engagement after Christendom in Australia, though I suspect that the dynamics that I identify are likely to be observable across the UK and its former colonies. In unpacking the complexity of life beyond Christendom, I will explore the manifestations of the "secular" and the "sacred," and how the "secular" might be understood as having a theological grounding. If those proposals sound paradoxical, stay with me while I try to unpack them.

I have already noted in the attitudes of church leaders in Australia a nostalgia for Christendom, accompanied by a failure to recognize that getting beyond Christendom might be a good thing for the church. Much of the lament by church leadership fails to recognize that using the term "secular," with regard to the political constitutional settlement in Australia in the context of post-Christendom, does not mean either the disappearance of the "sacred" from politics or community life, or the ruling out of a role for the churches and church-related agencies in public life. Of this I will have more to say in a moment. In the meantime, I want to emphasize the apparent paradox that the "secular" can take on the characteristics of the "sacred," while the "sacred" can migrate across the boundaries of institutions and infiltrate diverse parts of our culture. Indeed, it is possible to describe the "secular" as being theologically warranted, if we understand that a Christian critique of Christendom can implicitly desacralize the state and institutions of government. Understood in this way the "secular," that is to say pluralist forms of political order, are consistent with a post-Christendom approach to community engagement by the church and its agencies. So what does that means in the Australian political and constitutional context?

The "sacred" as a form of civil religion in Australia

The continuing presence of the Christendom mindset in the churches in Australia and the call to break from at least some elements of that past was nicely captured by the late Les Murray, one of Australia's most distinguished poets. Christianity "is no longer On Top in Australia, though a great majority of Australians continue to believe in God. The experience is probably a salutary one for us. The time for ecclesiolatry, the worship of the visible church instead of God is past. We're [to] no longer indulge our bad habits of boring people, bullying them and backing up respectability; we're no longer in a position to call on the law to do for us what we should be doing by inspiration and example."[4]

Tim Winton, the Australian novelist, himself a Christian with self-confessed Anabaptist tendencies, offers us a slightly more nuanced reading of the place of Christianity in Australia. Winton observes that his fellow Australians remain uncomfortable and at times angry with public expressions of Christian faith.

> We're pretty good at maintaining a secular public space and that's worth celebrating but we're a bit tin-eared about matters of religion and anxious about using terms like "sacred." This strikes me as a bit ironic because we live in the most spiritually potent continent imaginable. . . . The recent recommissioning and deliberate resacralization of the Gallipoli myth is telling because it suggests a spiritual vacuum. . . . Anzac has been coarsened by the politics of nostalgic regression. It's close to becoming the sort of nationalist death cult we revile when it appears in other places.[5]

The migration of the "sacred" into a form of civil religion in a "secular" society is manifested in the celebration of Anzac Day, the commemoration of a spectacular military failure resulting from the invasion at Gallipoli during World War I. The dawn service in Canberra on April 25 each year displays the migration of the sacred into culture and politics in a striking way. The sense of place and occasion, in the open air outside the Australian National War Memorial, where the central national celebration is held, contributes to this. A typical pre-dawn setting of gray scudding clouds, an air of quiet and reverent expectancy, the lone bugle call and the occasional harsh cry of sulphur crested cockatoos provides an appropriate atmosphere for "worship," for that is what now takes place with crowds of up to 100,000 "worshippers" present (pre-COVID). The language and structure of the liturgy makes the transition from Christian worship to a liturgy of the state seamless. The language of the dawn service gains its moral force and its liturgical claim to the assent of the worshippers from its appeal to the theme of sacrifice. The Anzacs, the Australian and New Zealand soldiers involved in the invasion, sacrificed their lives, we are told, so that we might have a free society. The application of the logic of this moral appeal to our gratitude

---

4. Murray, *The Quality of Sprawl*, 44–45.
5. Winton, *Island Home*, 220.

for the benefits of this sacrifice was extended both implicitly and explicitly to all those who had died during other subsequent episodes of warfare in which Australians have engaged.

This claim to the communal benefits of sacrifice is a powerful one, grounded in an emotionally charged narrative. It is an appeal to us to respond with a lived-out response of gratitude in the way we shape our lives as Australian citizens. The classic text for the Anzac Day service is: "Greater love has no man than this, than a man should lay down his life for his friends" (John 15:13). This text if examined in context will not stand up to the way it is used, that is to appeal to the authority of Jesus to justify war. The death of civilians is never brought into the equation. The biblical citation is preceded by the command by Jesus to love others as he has loved the disciples. The laying down of lives to which we are called, in the pattern of Jesus, is a response to the sacrifice of one who refused to take up the sword against his enemies. It has nothing to do with taking up arms to destroy the enemy. To raise a question as to whether the use of language of sacrifice in war was at odds with the Christian gospel would be shocking in the extreme, a signal that the sacred, that which cannot be challenged, is present. To ask the question as to which gods were the lives of those who died in war offered up as a sacrifice would similarly be un-Australian. The participation by Christian churches in this ongoing engagement with a Christendom mentality is particularly interesting. Defense force chaplains, who play a significant role in these celebrations, are deeply entangled with this peculiarly Australian form of civil religion.

The "sacred" does not disappear, as assumed in narratives of secularization; rather it migrates, and percolates through porous cultural boundaries in a manner frequently unrecognized by the Christian churches, who share with their cultural opponents a fixation with the simplified form of the secularization narrative. The state, the author and beneficiary of the worship of Anzac Day celebrations, takes on the aura of the "sacred." This may seem counterintuitive. Isn't the state "secular" and therefore detached from the "sacred"? Here we have to stop and consider the meaning of the "secular" in a post-Christendom context.

Secularity and pluralism

In thinking about the character of the "secular," I suggest we stop using a frame of reference in which the "secular" is taken to refer to a simplified form of secularization theory, a sociological process that results in the inevitable disappearance of "religion" from public life. We should think about the "secular" rather as the context in which Christians can coordinate with non-Christians in the pursuit of penultimate goods, and in so doing construct a common life, that while not being dominated by the church, or enforced by the state in a Christendom relationship, remains open to the transcendent. In progressing this discussion of the "secular" and coordinating it with a theological perspective, the following way of framing the issues by Luke Bretherton is helpful.

> [T]he secular is that which is not eternity. What is secular can be open to and transfigured in eternity, but its primary point of focus is the things of this age rather than the age to come. The demarcation of the current age as secular is a Christian innovation that breaks open divisions between sacred and profane. If something is secular it can be both sacred and profane ... concerned with both the immanent and transcendent, able to participate simultaneously in both the penultimate and the ultimate.[6]

This account of the secular is about keeping the public space open, available to widespread participation, and therefore desacralized. To put it another way, the secular is a positive space of human freedom gifted to us by God. I will use the term "secular" in the remainder of this chapter with this range of reference. The political requirements of a post-Christendom context expressed here are consistent with the position taken by Marpeck. Simon Barrow in the UK context captures much of Marpeck's "anticipation" of post-Christendom in his normative account of a post-Christendom polity in an account of the state that has the following pluralist characteristics:

- The state is not identified with any single religious tradition.
- Church and state are distinct and separate.
- The state can be critically challenged from the perspective of civil society, and can be lobbied and witnessed to by faith and non-faith interests alike.
- The state is seen in relation to necessary limits.
- The government tries to be neutral on religion.
- Law and justice are not identical.
- State violence is questioned and resisted.[7]

---

6. Bretherton, *Christ and the Common Life*, 231.
7. Barrow, "Redeeming Religion in the Public Sphere."

Government in a plural society requires maintaining a level playing field in public life without endorsing one faith or ideology, or excluding others, rather than taking an ideological anti-Christian, or more generally anti-religious, stance. Barrow observes that the "term 'plural society' may be more helpful than 'secular society' here, because it avoids confusing secularity as an inclusive virtue with ideological secularism (a rejection or critique of religion) and secularisation (a contested theory about the disappearance of religion in society)."[8]

In a secular/pluralist state, churches and other nongovernment organizations "seek to exercise a beneficial, questioning influence in society as a whole—without seeking to grasp state power or privilege for themselves. . . . The idea that the role of public institutions is to maintain a level playing field . . . requires the concomitant idea that the state should not sanction or benefit any one faith or ideology . . . [that] government should be 'neutral' towards religion, or that the state should be 'secular.' If so, the 'neutrality' required is of a positive kind, not simply a prohibitive one."[9]

A Christian "secularity"?

Let me make the claim I have been developing here even more explicit. Secularity as an inclusive virtue can be embraced by the Christian community as theologically warranted. Ian Barns in his discussion of the Australian context recommends that liberal institutions in the public sphere should be defended in terms of a theologically grounded secularity. Christians should be committed to defending key features of the secular polity, including the separation of church and state, the rule of law, freedom of speech, and the protection of civil rights, all not as a matter of defending privileges left over from Christendom or as a way of shoring up the position of the church in an era of numerical decline and cultural marginalization. Constantine, in other words, needs to be disavowed firmly and without any reserve as part of the Christian journey beyond a comfortable role in the established order. For our own theological reasons, Christians should, Barns argues, "be particularly concerned about the accountability and transparency of secular government, requiring that governments honour their responsibilities to maintain the infrastructure of civic life with equity and justice."[10]

---

8. Barrow, "Redeeming Religion in the Public Sphere."
9. Barrow, "Redeeming Religion in the Public Sphere."
10. Barns, "Representing Jesus," 2.

A secular/pluralist settlement in Australia

Having canvassed a theological basis for a secular/pluralist political order that churches should be seeking to advance as a normative project after Christendom, I now want to explore a little more closely how this engages with the Australian reality in terms of the constitutional provisions governing church and state.[11] This background is particularly relevant in understanding Australian government engagement with church-related agencies in the narratives of community engagement in the following chapters.

Australia has developed pluralist/secular relationship between religion and the state in a political culture that has deep roots in colonial history. The Australian tradition of pluralism is one in which political and cultural institutions have pragmatically tried to encourage acceptance of difference without a widely debated ideological, or theological, underpinning. Since the early colonial period Australians have insisted that they share the same rights and freedoms, whatever their denominational adherence, or lack thereof. The acceptance of difference that we find in the Australian constitution, I must quickly note, has substantial limitations. Following the European invasion, the rights of the First Nations in Australia, including right of original occupancy, were not recognized in any treaty and have only recently received a limited judicial recognition, beginning with the Mabo case where the High Court recognized that a group of Torres Strait islanders held legal title to their land. This remains a major item of unfinished business in the pursuit of a genuinely pluralist political order.[12]

To fully embrace a pluralist/secular political order and accept the "anticipation" offered by Marpeck would require acceptance by churches of a form of political engagement that willingly accepts, if not actually celebrates, both pluralism and the secular character of the political order. On the other side of the equation, governments in Australia, particularly those of the center-right in political affiliation, have not yet given up the temptation to retreat to a Christendom mentality, in attempting to use the churches as a source of both social cohesion and electoral advantage.

The Australian Constitution is particularly relevant here. Section 116 of the Australian Constitution states: "The Commonwealth shall not make any law for establishing any religion, or for imposing any religious

---

11. For an account of pluralism comparing the US, England, Netherlands, Australia, and Germany, see Monsma and Soper, *The Challenge of Pluralism*. US readers may find this helpful for its account of the constitutional differences between Australia and the US.

12. For an informed and accessible historical discussion, see Reynolds, *Truth-Telling*, 13–109.

observance, or for prohibiting the free exercise of any religion, and no religious test shall be required as a qualification for any office or public trust under the Commonwealth."[13] Under this provision the Commonwealth government shall not:

- Give preference to any religion or recognize any denomination as the official religion of the Commonwealth.
- Require anyone to worship or to worship in a particular way.
- Prevent or impede citizens from exercising their religion.
- Place a religious test on any position in the public service or the federal parliament.

Compared to the US, there has been relatively little litigation on these issues. A total of seven cases has been heard in the High Court on Section 116, in a little over a century. The argument about whether the Australian constitution provided for an American-style separation of church and state has been "firmly rejected by a clear majority of the High Court in the so-called DOGS case of 1981, while the suggestion that its provisions should apply to the States . . . was rejected almost as clearly when it was put to the Australian people in a 1988 referendum."[14] The High Court in the 1981 case ruled that the Australian government could fund religious education, provided it did not discriminate between religions in such funding. The Australian constitutional settlement then is not one of separation, with regard to funding of education, welfare, and health activities conducted by church-related bodies, but of equitable entanglement.[15]

A very public debate around these questions of church engagement in politics was provoked in 2006 that brings out the theological issues quite clearly. The occasion for this was the publication of an article on faith and politics by Kevin Rudd, who was to serve as Prime Minister of Australia from 2007 to 2010, and then for a short period again in 2013. Rudd's contribution to public theology resulted in headlines in mainstream media and engaged the attention of contributors to the opinion pages of the daily papers. An account of some key themes in Rudd's argument brings us back into contact with Marpeck's "anticipation" of a pluralist/secular political order. Rudd's theological account of faith and politic's relationship was both secular and

13. Australia, *Constitution*, S116.

14. Hogan, "Worrying About Religion." For an accessible discussion of the Australian constitutional settlement that deals with an Australian habit of importing US controversies over the relationship of church and state into Australia, see Frame, *Church and State*.

15. Kaye, *Colonial Religion*, 195.

pluralist. Commencing with an account of Bonhoeffer's life and theology, Rudd drew particular attention to his *Ethics* and *Letters and Papers from Prison*. At the core of his argument is Bonhoeffer's insistence that the church stands in the middle of the village, the public space at the center of human life, not at the boundaries, at the places where human powers give out. Rudd referenced in making his case a famous passage from Bonhoeffer. "We have for one learned to see the great events of world history from below, from the perspective of the outcast, the suspects, the maltreated, the powerless, the reviled—in short from the perspective of those who suffer." Bonhoeffer's political theology is therefore one of a dissenting church that speaks the truth to the state and does so by giving voice to the voiceless.[16]

Rudd noted the post-Christendom context in Australia. "In some respects, therefore, Christianity at last within Western societies, may be returning to the minority position it occupied in the earliest centuries of its existence."[17] Given that the gospel is both spiritual and social in character, he argued, and, if it is a social gospel, and consequentially at least partially a political gospel, then it follows that Christians must engage with policy issues from within an informed Christian ethical framework. Rudd clearly had in view a secular-pluralist framework in which the churches legitimately engage in politics, without any claim to being "in control." While a Christian perspective on any given contemporary policy issue may not prevail in Australia, it "must, nonetheless, be argued. And once heard it must be weighed, together with other arguments from different philosophical traditions in a fully contestable secular polity. A Christian perspective, informed by a social gospel or Christian socialist tradition, should not be rejected contemptuously by secular politicians as if these views are an unwelcome intrusion into the political sphere."[18] A pluralist/secular political order, according to Rudd, is consistent with Christian engagement in the political realm, but not consistent with either Christian domination as by right, the Christendom assumption, nor is it consistent with the exclusion of religious voices from the debate, the religiously secular approach. He simultaneously argued against both religious voices that are concerned about maintaining Australia as a "Christian" country and a viewpoint that requires the exclusion of "religious" voices from public debate. This debate has been relitigated more recently around the issue of whether the Pentecostal church involvement of the current Prime

---

16. Bonhoeffer, *Letters and Papers*, 17.
17. Rudd, "Faith in Politics," 25.
18. Rudd, "Faith in Politics," 27.

Minister Scott Morrison is consistent with the Australian secular political settlement.[19]

Before moving on

Up to now I have been exploring resources first from Scripture, and then from the life and theology of Pilgrim Marpeck, to help us reimagine community engagement after Christendom, pushing back against the pressures of habit and nostalgia. I now turn to the question of what we can learn from recent experience of such engagement by taking a look at what is happening on the ground now. What are the risks and possibilities associated with such engagement in Australia as we transition beyond Christendom?

In undertaking this exercise, I have told some stories of engagement that caught my attention. Of these a couple of the stories are cautionary tales, while others provide inspiration and encouragement. None are intended as examples that demand blind imitation, but are offered to demonstrate possibilities and ground theological commitments in day-to-day institutional reality. They are shared to highlight the nitty-gritty character of such engagement. Some highlight the importance of responding to the prodding of the Spirit in response to the demands of the moment, while others record faithful patience in working with limited resources over the long term. All of them, however, point to the need to reflect critically and take our theological bearings on whether, and how, to engage with the state.

---

19. The popular discussion on Scott Morrison's Pentecostalism can be accessed easily through any search engine. The theologian and sociologist Paul Tyson has provided a thoughtful analysis in "Mr Morrison's ACC address."

Part III

Community Engagement on the Way Out of Christendom

8

The Risks of Contracting

Community engagement, while an imperative deeply engrained within the Christian movement, has a variety of risks associated with it. In Christendom, the association of the church with the state in the use of violence, was at odds with the teaching of Jesus. After-Christendom engagement with the state may carry with it more subtle risks. In this chapter I report on the risks for churches and church-related agencies that have arisen from contracting with government in Australia, and how that engagement has resulted in some church-related agencies becoming extensions of the state, while paying attention to how theology assisted other agencies to retain a focus on their mission.

Beginning in the 1980s, governments across the English-speaking world began shifting to contracting as their preferred technology for funding and managing welfare and human services, whether undertaken by nonprofit or for-profit providers. In Australia, from the very beginning of the shift to contracting, questions were raised, not only about the impact on the delivery of the services, but also about the way the power relationship with government could reshape the agencies. One obvious lever that a government has in the contracting relationship is financial. If an agency is heavily dependent on government contracts, it is vulnerable to changes in government policy, including cancellation of the program. If the government decides not to continue a program, and withdraws funding, under most circumstances there is little an individual agency can do about it. Or, to take another example, if the government changes the provisions of a contract to direct an agency to deliver services in a way that is in conflict with its mission and values, the agency faces the choice of either withdrawing from delivering the program with the consequent risk to its viability, or continuing to deliver the program while compromising on its mission and values.

The power governments exercise through contracts with church-related agencies can also lead to a reshaping of such agencies in quite subtle and not always immediately obtrusive ways. Constant changes in reporting requirements can distort an agency's organizational culture. Management attention becomes focused on reporting, and away from actually providing services to those people they are supposed to be assisting. This is likely to happen where the government focuses on using the contract as a way of micromanaging policy. A government that proceeds down this path will end up deploying a "command and control" form of contracting, where the attention of both the government and the agency shifts from the services that are supposed to be provided to reporting and documentation. Reductions in the quality and responsiveness of service delivery may also result. The increase in costs associated with increasing obligations, and reporting requirements, may drive agencies towards a more bureaucratic style of operation at odds with their founding people-centered mission commitments.

The cumulative impact of these processes on an agency can be thought of as a form of internal, or institutional, secularization, as opposed to the secularization at a societal level. In church-related agencies the presence of this form of secularization may be found in what are not always clearly articulated conflicts between ecclesial and corporate leadership, as the agency shifts from being a mission-based organization to an institution with a managerial culture not too different from that of a government bureaucracy. Agencies that get caught up in these processes risk reenacting a shadow form of Christendom. By this I mean that agencies can become entangled with and reshaped by government, and as a subordinate partner become detached from their original purposes, identity, and rationale.

In identifying the risks of contracting, I have so far focused on the state operating in its bureaucratic mode. The philosopher Alasdair McIntyre suggests that we need to think of the current nation-state as having two distinct and quite different characters and modes of operation. The nation-state is "a dangerous and unmanageable institution, presenting itself on the one hand as a bureaucratic supplier of goods and services, which is always about to, but never actually does, give its clients value for money, and on the other as a repository of sacred values, which from time to time invites one to lay down one's life on its behalf."[1] This means that in some areas of policy and service delivery the state can be bureaucratic, focused on issues of process in

---

1. MacIntyre, "A Partial Response to My Critics," 303.

The Risks of Contracting

a way that gives it a "secular" character. In other areas of operation, the state can manifest itself as a bearer of sacred claims. In its bureaucratic mode it delivers services to the population with variable levels of equity and effectiveness, frequently occluding from view the situation of the poorest and the most marginal in the population, who are being left behind.

The state displays its sacral character in the unchallengeable exercise of power and authority within a specified territory that reaches to matters of life and death, inclusion and exclusion. Citizenship, even in supposedly "secular" countries, has become tied to symbols and rituals that express and reinforce the devotion of individuals to the nation-state. The state, through the liturgies of civil religion, can take on a manifestly sacred character in which citizens may be called upon to kill, or be killed, on its behalf. I illustrated this process in my account of Anzac Day in the previous chapter. Church-related agencies contracting with the state operating in its sacral mode face risks that are harder to manage and are less predictable than those arising from bureaucratic processes.

The stories of contracting that follow illustrate the ways church-related agencies can become extensions of the state in both its sacral and bureaucratic modes. In other words, they can reenact a form of Christendom in which they become both entangled with and subordinate to the state. The accounts draw on extended interviews with managers and agency leadership, as well as on publicly available government documentation and news reports. As much as is possible my accounts are in the words of agency leadership, as they reflected on their involvement in the contracting process.

Employment services contracting

My first examples of the impact of contracting on church-related agencies in Australia relate to the use of contracting to provide employment services.[2] The shift to contracting of employment services in Australia began in 1996, following the election of the Liberal National Party Coalition to government at the federal level. The newly elected government replaced the existing government-run labor market programs with a fully contestable quasi-market in which both nonprofit and for-profit providers competed for contracts to deliver employment services. These contracts were managed by the Australian government department responsible for policy and implementation of employment services. The Commonwealth Employment Service (CES), a public service agency that had previously provided employment services,

---

2. My sketch of the policy changes draws on Fowkes, "Rethinking Australia's Employment Services."

was restructured into a government-owned corporation, Employment National. The corporation sought to distance itself from its public service origins, operating in a way that mimicked for-profit providers.[3]

The proffered justification by the government for the policy shift to contracting was that improved performance would be achieved through payment for results within a competitive environment. Assistance to job seekers was to be client-driven, not program-driven. The stated policy intent was that contracted agencies would have maximum flexibility in deciding how to assist people to get into employment.[4] The Job Network, as the contracting framework was called, was, according to the government, about more than improving efficiency and effectiveness through market competition. The Minister for Employment and Workplace Relations stated that underlying the policy was a "conviction that community-based agencies are better equipped than bureaucracies to deliver 'pastoral care,' avoid treating unemployed people as faces in a queue or numbers in a file, and foster the web of personal engagements which unemployed people have often lost . . ."[5] Undoubtedly a worthy sentiment, that was not borne out by what actually happened, as will become clear in the course of this chapter.

The first Request for Tender to deliver employment services under this contracting framework in 1997 was nothing less than a rush for cash by nonprofit agencies and private providers. The tender attracted over one thousand organizations bidding for a share of the $1.7 billion contract.[6] Contracts were won by a mix of for-profit and nonprofit providers, along with Employment National, the corporatized government agency.[7] Each subsequent round of contracting was accompanied by government policy changes, including adjustments to the services to be delivered, changed conditions applied to job seekers, along with amendments to the fee structure. There was a continuing reduction in the number of successful contracted organizations. The agencies with employment services contracts dropped from 306 agencies in 1998 to forty-four in 2015.[8]

---

3. Considine, *Enterprising States*, 176.
4. Vanstone, "Reforming Employment Assistance."
5. Abbott, "Against the Prodigal State," 38.
6. Considine, *Enterprising States*, 135.
7. Fowkes, "Rethinking Australia's Employment Services," 5.
8. Gallet, "Christian Mission or an Unholy Alliance," 51.

The Risks of Contracting

Salvation Army Employment Plus

In exploring the impact of contracting on church-related agencies in the employment services sector, my first story involves the rise of Salvation Army Employment Plus. This nonprofit agency was set up in 1996 by the Salvation Army in Australia, in response to the shift in government policy on employment services, and was run completely separately from the other Salvation Army social welfare activities. The impact of contracting on the agency can be easily traced out, as it only delivered employment services. In telling the story of the agency, and its experience of contracting to deliver employment services, I draw largely on a personal interview with Wilma Gallet, a Salvationist and former public servant in the Commonwealth Employment Service, who was CEO of Employment Plus during its establishment and early years. Her account of the decision-making in response to the changes in contracting for employment services enables me to draw a direct comparison with decision-making by the Catholic agencies with regard to their involvement in employment services contracting, on which I report later in this chapter.

In preparing for the first round of employment service contracting, the Salvation Army was uncertain as to how wide their tender should be, given that they had little experience in contracting for welfare and human services. The Army's previous involvement in dealing with government in social welfare was largely through grants and needs-based funding, where the Army designed programs to meet identified needs, and then negotiated the funding with government. The approach of the Army to tendering was not done with a really strong conviction that it should be involved in this particular program. The attitude as reported by Gallet was that "if we win something, we'll trial it, we'll try and be 'salt and light,' ... do it with compassion, with justice, respect and dignity."[9] To the Salvation Army's surprise, Employment Plus won everything that it tendered for, seventy sites across Australia, around 6 percent of the total contract, despite the Army having regarded their bid as being something of an ambit claim. In translation, that meant they bid high to ensure that they weren't going to run up a loss that would have to be met from other agency funds. The time frame for implementation of the contract, though, was very tight.

On January 16, 1998 the Army was given the contract offer by the government, to be kept in confidence until the Minister made the announcement in February. The offices in each area where they would deliver services had to be open by May. The Army struggled with the question of whether to

---

9. Gallet interview.

accept the contract but decided to give it a go and see what happened during the first eighteen-month contract period.

The Australian Government Minister responsible for employment services launched the Job Network as a national program at the Employment Plus head office, at that stage co-located with the Salvation Army Drug and Alcohol Rehab Service. Wilma Gallet remembered the occasion vividly for the slightly surreal clash of the political, the Christian penumbra of Army culture, and the media circus. "We made sure there were lots of uniforms present, and I remember the Commissioner, after he did his speech, he prayed. Of course, we all bowed our heads as he was praying, and all the major media were there, and they started to pack up during the prayer . . . I can remember a couple of staff saying, 'Sshh, we're praying.'"[10] The response of the media from a largely secular culture can be easily imagined.

After the initial public controversy over the shift to contracting and the abolition of the Commonwealth Employment Service had died down, the Army received an unanticipated good run of favorable publicity over its participation in the program. According to Wilma, the media apparently "saw the Salvation Army as being different, being involved in employment services for the right reasons, to help disadvantaged unemployed people. The journalists would say things like, well, these private agencies, they're only in it for profit, but not you, you're here to help people."[11]

The majority of the staff hired by Employment Plus had originally worked as public servants in the CES. There was a concern that with this staff profile the agency would be pulled towards a bureaucratic process-oriented culture. In attempting to counteract this, and to communicate the history and identity of the Army to the staff, Gallet bought every site in the agency a copy of *In Darkest England and the Way Out*, written by the founder of the Salvation Army William Booth. It was promoted as a really exciting story about the Salvation Army's founding and its Christian commitments. A concerted effort was made by Wilma to get the staff familiar with and engaged by the story. John Cleary, a noted radio presenter in public broadcasting, himself a Salvationist, would come and talk to staff about the historical heritage that had shaped the Salvation Army, and its theology of social holiness. The message the agency was attempting to convey was that "the only reason we're involved in this is because unemployment has a devastating impact on the lives of individuals, their families and their communities, and because we care for vulnerable people, . . . rather than being the ambulance at the bottom of the cliff, we can be the fence at the top where

---

10. Gallet interview.
11. Gallet interview.

The Risks of Contracting

we can try and help them get a job, so they don't fall into abject poverty and hopelessness."[12]

The program requirements of the employment services program in the first round of contracting were very loosely specified. The government didn't mandate what agencies should spend the money on to get people into employment. All that mattered was the contracting agencies got the results, through moving people back into work. The term "black box contracting" is an appropriate description of this approach. You don't care what happens in the process as long as you get the results. Employment Plus, despite what Wilma described as a flexible and innovative approach to spending plenty of money to help people into jobs, in fact finished the initial contract period with a financial surplus. This flexible approach to delivering a government program wasn't going to last very long given that the substantials risks to the government of unfavorable publicity if anything went awry.

The early financial success of Employment Plus was a source of embarrassment, given that the Army was going out every year to the public on a national basis with its Red Shield Appeal seeking support for its charitable work. To deal with this problem, and to build a greater connection with the Army out in the community, with the surplus from the program Employment Plus created a program called Mission Partnering. This involved approaching Salvation Army citadels, the local congregations, with the message that while the task of Employment Plus was to help people get a job, these people have other needs and Employment Plus would help fund local projects identified by the citadel.

At the end of the first contract period, Gallet suggested to the Employment Plus Board that they didn't have to tender again, to which the Board said, "Don't be silly, Wilma," or words to that effect.[13] At this stage staying with the program looked like it was a reasonable decision. Contracting was not causing any great problems for the agency and Employment Plus was helping people into jobs. Success seemed to beget success. Employment Plus became a much larger presence in the second-round tender for employment services, ending up with a contract worth about $150 million.

There were however signs, in Wilma's view, that a shift in the agency from a mission-driven approach towards a business or managerial mindset shaped by the second round of contracting had begun. "[W]e moved into these really smart corporate offices, I could feel it changing . . . It was becoming much more commercial, and people would talk about an industry, rather than a sector. . . . I knew that public servants would try and turn us

12. Gallet interview.
13. Gallet interview.

into an arm of government. So, I used to make all these edicts such as [in] the language we use, we will talk about service, we'll never use the word 'business.'"[14] Along with these changes, the positive media response to the involvement of the Army, and other Christian agencies in employment service contracting, started to shift after the second tender round in 2000. The media began asking questions like "Why are these Christian groups in it? Are they here because they want to proselytize? How are Muslim job seekers going to get a fair go?"[15]

After the first contract period, even though there was still flexibility in the contract provisions, Gallet felt that change was in the wind to move employment service agencies more directly under government control. This was apparent initially through government instructions under the contracts with regard to branding. Agencies "started getting edicts from the Department that we had to put their brand on our buildings. Prior to that we were the Salvation Army Employment Plus, . . . [but] now we had to put Job Network signage in the building . . ."[16]

Bureaucratic colonization of agencies undertaking employment services contracting also became apparent in the information technology (IT) area, unintentionally kicked along by an Employment Plus initiative. Initially government policy was not to provide an IT software system for contractors. Given its size and financial capacity Employment Plus went ahead and developed its own IT system, an initiative that could not be matched by the smaller providers who then agitated with the Department of Employment and Workplace Relations for them to be placed on a level playing field. Eventually the Department developed a computer system called the Employment Services Model, which ended up totally driving service delivery by agencies. "The computer will tell you when you've got to see people, if somebody doesn't turn up you put in a 'did not attend,' that message goes to Centrelink, they lose their benefit. So, the computer has become very pervasive."[17]

The next step towards a more controlling form of contract came in 2003 with a change in the funding model, along with, you guessed it, a change in the title of the program to the Active Participation Model. The funding change accompanying the change in program title was to prove significant. Prior to this, Job Network agencies were paid a substantial upfront fee when an unemployed person connected with the agency. Agencies

14. Gallet interview.
15. Gallet interview.
16. Gallet interview.
17. Gallet interview.

The Risks of Contracting

spent a lot of this money on activities aimed at overcoming barriers to job readiness or paid for training courses for job seekers. Under the new policy, up-front payments from the government for signing people with the agency were significantly reduced, and the balance of the funds were placed into what was termed a Job Seeker Account. Any funding that agencies wanted to spend on clients would come from this account. The policy intent was to ensure that agencies were spending the money to support job seekers and help them overcome barriers to getting a job. Under this policy, contracted agencies could not simply bank the surplus from the initial payment in their own accounts. If the money held by the government in a Job Seeker Account wasn't spent by an agency it would go back into consolidated revenue. Problems arose, however, because a request by the agency to spend the money for the benefit of the job seeker had to be approved by the Department. The result of this change was not surprising.

> With that came a whole lot of red tape around what you could buy or what you couldn't buy . . . You also started to see some corporate malpractice . . . Instead of spending the money directly on job seekers, what companies would do is they would say well we're going to give them psychological services, we're going to pay for psychologists. But instead of paying that organization over there, $120 an hour, they would hire their own psychologists, they would charge the job seeker account $120, but of course it would only cost them $60, so they would pocket the [other] $60. . . . As providers started to develop workarounds to maximize their profit, the Department responded by tightening the rules.[18]

This gaming of the system by agencies generated an increase in the rules under the contract governing what agencies could do, and a decrease in agency flexibility in responding to the individual needs of the people they were trying to serve. So, what had started out as a "black box" form of contracting, within less than a decade had evolved into a "command and control" model. Program delivery became increasingly uniform across all agencies, whether they were for-profit or nonprofit. Innovation in ways of helping people find jobs with its accompanying risk of failure, was being squeezed out. The 2003 contract round also saw another shift towards government control over agency activity. Previously, there was customized assistance for the long-term unemployed, people who had been unemployed for twelve months or more, or who were deemed to be at risk or vulnerable. The contract now stipulated that you had to see these people every fortnight.

18. Gallet interview.

The tightening of contract requirements meant increasing bureaucratic control by the Department. Every time the media discovered an apparent or possible scam, or the department identified gaming of the system by agencies to maximize their revenue in the face of the government squeeze on the payments made under the contract, the rules were tightened further. That, in turn, placed greater pressure on agencies to comply with the rules, which took more of the agencies' time, and cost them more in financial terms with the risk of inadvertent breaches of the increased number of rules generating yet further controls by the Department in an ongoing spiral.

A study undertaken in 2011 for Jobs Australia, the peak body for employment services agencies contracting with government, estimated that there were at that stage three thousand pages of government guidelines, and that employment consultants within agencies spent 50 percent of their time with any one job seeker in administering and complying with these requirements, within a framework of 144 outcome fee types and associated special claims. The introduction of private and community sector agencies driven by a market mechanism had been supposed to lead to the policy nirvana of innovation and flexibility in service provision. The result was almost exactly the opposite. In the shape of an increasingly complex, overengineered program, with agencies becoming increasingly risk-averse, and doing the same thing for everyone seeking employment, despite the difference in people's circumstances.

One dimension of complexity arose from an intention to provide better information to help unemployed people choose which agency they would register with lead to further gaming of the system by agencies. The Star Rating system was developed, a complex algorithm providing a comparative rating of the contracted agencies, ranging from five stars at the top down to one star. It was designed to help unemployed people identify the best Job Network members in terms of achieving job outcomes, by enabling comparisons between organizations across regions, labor market conditions, and the characteristics of the job seekers they assist. One significant factor in that assessment was the degree of disadvantage of the job seeker.

> If a job seeker had multiple disadvantages, you'd get more brownie points when they got a job. . . . When a provider links with that person, over time it will be revealed that they've got drug and alcohol issues . . . So, the providers were allowed to change the classification, and incidentally not only does that give you higher star ratings if the job seeker is classified as very disadvantaged you also receive higher fee payments. . . . Department of Education, Employment and Workplace Relations would in their performance monitoring just do a scan of the

number of people that were being reclassified, and suddenly they saw this spike in the number of people being reclassified so when they started to dig, they realized these people were being reclassified on no evidence.[19]

As I noted previously, when Job Network commenced a substantial proportion of the staff in Employment Plus had had experience working in the CES, and many of them proved to be interested in doing case management and working with people holistically. The next generation of staff was not experienced in working with people with complex needs, including drug and alcohol or mental health issues, and were not equipped to deal with the complexity manifested in client behavior.

The shift to a controlling form of contracting impacted strongly on Employment Plus, reducing its ability to undertake its employment services on a self-sustaining basis, particularly given an increasing presence of for-profits bent on maximizing their economic performance by focusing on employable job seekers. The Army was finding it increasingly difficult to generate profits from this program to plough back into supporting the needier, more vulnerable, less income-generating clients. The paradox of the evolution of contracting policy as viewed through the experience of Employment Plus over a decade was that the government "created bureaucracies within non-profit agencies that were far more excessive than the bureaucracy that they sought to replace."[20]

The Salvation Army nonetheless remained involved in delivering employment services, and as of 2020 were one of the last of the nonprofit agencies to win contracts in a sector increasingly occupied by for-profit agencies who earned their money by moving job-ready people into employment while ignoring people with multiple needs. It is difficult to see what the rationale for the continued involvement by the Salvation Army in this sector is, given that the contracting regime increasingly directed attention away from the needs of the most vulnerable, long-term unemployed who had multiple barriers to entry to employment. As an agency set up for a specific purpose, Employment Plus did not have any historic linkages to the Salvation Army at a local level in the way that many of the Army's other welfare activities did. The Army's participation in employment services seemed to have developed a momentum of its own. There was little evidence of agonizing within the agency over how continued involvement in providing an increasingly market-driven and bureaucratically shaped

19. Gallet interview.
20. Gallet interview.

service met the aspirations of the Salvation Army to see the unemployed as a whole person including body, mind, and spirit.

Catholic welfare agencies in employment services contracting

I now turn to look at the approach to employment services of Catholic diocesan welfare agencies where theology, in the form of Catholic Social Teaching, played a role in shaping decisions about whether and to what extent diocesan welfare agencies would become involved in contracting for employment services. The governance of Catholic social welfare agencies is also an important element in the story of the extent to which agencies did or didn't get involved in this form of contracting. The story I have to tell draws on interviews with management at the national coordinating level, and directors of diocesan Catholic welfare agencies.

Catholic diocesan social welfare agencies in Australia are independent of one another. Each has its own governing council, with the final say about their operation resting in the hands of the diocesan bishop, who may, or may not, be actively engaged with the agency. This diocesan governance arrangement presented problems for the engagement by Catholic social welfare agencies in bidding for programs that were contracted out at a national level. To overcome some of the difficulties for diocesan agencies contracting at a national level, a national governance arrangement was set up to manage the interests of smaller and regional diocesan agencies, while respecting their individual diocesan mandate. The Catholic Church in Australia already had a national coordination body for welfare services, Catholic Social Services Australia (CSSA), with the responsibility for advocacy and liaison with the Australian government. To manage contracting relationships with the Australian government the CSSA established CSSA Ltd., a company limited by guarantee to manage employment service contracts with the Australian government. CSSA Ltd. was involved in the first round of Job Network contracting in 1998, and won a small contract with sites scattered geographically across several states. It then won a larger number of contracts in round two.

The role for the agency in holding a national contract on behalf of diocesan welfare agencies was to ensure the maintenance of standards around mission and identity as well as service provision. It was also responsible for ensuring coordination across those agencies, as well as offering the opportunity to expand contracts by having a single point of contracting. Phil Murray, at that stage National Manager for Employment Services in CSSA and a former public servant, explained that "we had to make sure that the agencies were complying with the contractual obligations... [and] that they were performing at a good level. If they didn't perform, we were going to lose the contract... We had a provider agreement with the agencies to deliver those services... We also had the ongoing responsibilities for liaising with the Department to keep across things that were happening."[21]

CSSA Ltd. was also responsible for advocacy in employment services, a brief that reached much deeper into policy and program implementation than the public lobbying with which the term is frequently associated. This was not just a matter of liaising with the Department, but an engagement which tried to influence the policy whether at the micro or implementation level. CSSA was "also involved in trying to influence the construction of the program, so that we would interpret how the program was going in the light of Catholic Social Teaching in particular. And where we saw a conflict between what the Church thought was a good thing, and what the contract was doing, we would make representations to the government direct, and the Department as well, to try and get some changes."[22]

The CSSA Ltd. was managing two main employment service contracts in the early rounds. The first contracts were for Job Network and its successor, Jobs Services Australia (JSA) for mainstream employment services. Only about a quarter of the agencies in the Catholic network were involved in these contracts. The other contract was for the Personal Support Program (PSP), which was much more popular with Catholic agencies. Almost every diocesan agency in the national network delivered PSP. The significance of the theological commitment prioritizing serving the most marginal is in the community is demonstrated in the relative popularity of these programs. The contract for the mainstream Job Network involved tension between some elements of what it required compared with some Catholic agencies' understanding of their role and mission. The Catholic welfare system "had its beginnings in the family services area, in orphanages and the core of their services are counseling services.... While the agencies were very comfortable working with particularly disadvantaged job seekers, because that's their core business, they weren't very comfortable often dealing with job-ready job seekers or those that were less disadvantaged... They thought the most disadvantaged were their main priority.... PSP was very popular, because it was largely about counseling [the] most disadvantaged job seekers."[23]

21. Murray interview.
22. Murray interview.
23. Murray interview.

The Catholic identity of the agencies and their mission was articulated with specific reference to Catholic Social Teaching, as a benchmark for assessing both program priorities and the way programs were delivered. There was concern that the cultural impact of contracting on organizational culture could be profound given that the reliance on weekly performance reporting had the potential to create a culture that lost a focus on the individual dignity of the person coming through the door of the agency. As the employment services contracting changed and became more complex, involving more compliance obligations for procedure and documentation, it reduced the ability of agencies to deliver the program in a way that respected individual dignity in the manner required by church teaching. These developments rather narrowed the scope for the kind of counseling and help these agencies were used to providing as part of a more flexible approach to meeting the needs of individuals.

Another point of tension between agencies and government policy was the tightening of activity test arrangements for people on allowances. There was a clash between this policy and the way agencies interpreted the teaching of the church. "The Work for the Dole program was actually banned at one stage by what was then the Catholic Social Welfare Commission and it recommended that agencies didn't do Work for the Dole and only one or two ever did. . . . The activity test was another part of that whole thing that they were never really comfortable with. They didn't like the idea of having to report clients for breaches. They wanted to help them, not cause them some harm."[24]

The increasing controls on the program had a substantial impact on Catholic agencies. "A bigger proportion of their time was going into policing the procedures and making sure it was all okay and checking all sorts of things on an ongoing basis."[25] When new Ministers responsible for employment services moved into the portfolio, CSSA Ltd. would try to explain the problems that were being created with the emerging "command and control" contracting. While Ministers initially responded to these briefings, somehow not a lot of progress was ever made. The bureaucracy itself seemed to be a driving force in preventing progress. "They'll try to reduce some of the red tape, but within twelve months it's gone even further than it was before. They pulled back one step and take another two steps in the other direction . . . The bureaucracy is risk-averse . . . They're the key advisors to the government and they make the arguments . . . There's always evidence

24. Murray interview.
25. Murray interview.

of abuse in these programs that can be found, and they keep closing doors to try and reduce it."[26]

One source of risk aversion was that government was faced with the demand for an equitable service for job seekers, and allowing innovation created the possibility that some job seekers will get better personal outcomes than others. "The government want to see innovation, but they don't want to see failures. They can't afford to see failures for the clients. Otherwise, the government looks stupid or that it's doing lousy things with the unemployed."[27] Employment services contracts were particularly horrendous in terms of their overbearing bureaucratic and administrative nature and represented probably the peak of government micromanagement and reach into contracting organizations.

Peter Sellwood, Director of Centacare Brisbane, in an explanation of why his agency had become involved and then decided to withdraw from employment services, highlighted the tensions between mission objectives and financial incentives. The agency was not in the first contract round because it was not sure there was a role for it given its understanding of the agency's mission, shaped as it was by Catholic Social Teaching. However, because CSSA Ltd. wanted to do a national contract, Centacare Brisbane cooperated by participating in the second contract to give a strong Queensland presence. Peter Sellwood thought that the experience of the agency of the second round was positive. "We decided it was good work. It was actually generating a surplus that we could use in other operations. . . . We were happy to expand as we only had one location. In 2004 we became four sites and then again in 2007 and 2010 we grew. We finished up with about a dozen sites after the 2010 contract."[28]

Despite this initial success, in Sellwood's view, over time employment services contracting took on a character at odds with Centacare's identity and mission given Catholic Social Teaching's view of the individual and their place in society. Their involvement was very much based on "the dignity and respect that comes from being part of work and therefore being part of the community. The workplace is very much a community and if you're excluded from that then you're excluded from a whole range of things."[29] Sellwood drew attention to emerging policy language that was deeply at odds with his own ethical and theological commitments. The Department wanted to focus on people as just a pool of unemployed people that were

---

26. Murray interview.
27. Murray interview.
28. Sellwood interview.
29. Sellwood interview.

solely an economic problem, rather than a social and human problem. Referring to the "stock of unemployed" was offensive to him. Sellwood recalled that when he was unemployed and between jobs, "I didn't see myself as 'stock', I saw myself as someone that needed a job, who wanted a job and could offer something to an employer."[30]

Because the payment system for the contracts increasingly focused attention on moving people into jobs, there was no incentive for agencies to put resources into helping people with multiple hurdles to overcome before they could find work. Centacare was focused on working with the individual in ways that were about more than sticking them into a job, but in so doing was faced with up-front costs with a low likelihood of getting a payment for successful job placement in anything but the long term. At times delivering the program became a process of meeting contract and reporting requirements rather than providing a service for people. Sellwood noted that the star ratings were an example of the axiom that what gets measured is what matters. If your star ratings were not where you needed them to be to maintain your contract, you focused on them with the result that you could "take your eye off the ball in terms of the delivery of mission."[31] The result of these pressures was that the agency would lose sight of its mission because it was simply focusing on throughput.

Even with PSP, a program much more closely aligned with the mission of Catholic agencies, the same process of mission distortion became evident. PSP "became very outcomes-focused again, outcomes determined by the Department, not outcomes determined by us, and the clients we worked with.... We weren't living out any mission because we were just a processing arm of government.... There was no capacity for us to sit and work with a client and try and deal with the range of issues that might be confronting them, it was just get them in a job or you won't get paid.... we had to be real about who we [were] and what we wanted to do and therefore we exited."[32] Over time agencies were just processing people through a program whether it was relevant to them or not, and losing their capacity to express their mission in serving the actual needs of marginal people. This view of employment services contracting was widely shared. The Australian Council of Social Service (ACOSS) concluded that providers had been responsive to signals from the government as purchaser to achieve quick employment outcomes at low costs. Innovations and responsiveness to the unemployed were prevented by a structure of contracting that pushed providers towards

30. Sellwood interview.
31. Sellwood interview.
32. Sellwood interview.

implementing standardized services that were not responsive to individual job seeker needs, while creating high administrative burdens by providers.

Administrative and compliance demands placed upon contractors, accompanied by increased government monitoring and the increased regulation, destroyed agencies' ability to furnish the flexible and tailored support necessary to improve the employment outcomes of long-term unemployed and difficult-to-place job seekers. The stated original policy intent was to enable agencies to display innovation and draw on the specific value resources arising from their "nongovernment" and mission-shaped character. The experience of agencies contracting for employment services tracked closely the outcomes predicted by the sociological theory of institutional behavior. There was a slow grinding away of agencies' commitment to mission and a refocusing of their attention on meeting reporting requirements and shaping their behavior in preparation for the next round of contracts. Agencies became an extension of government through evolving to take on the bureaucratic form of the government delivery agencies they had replaced.

With the best of intentions

Having illustrated how bureaucratic processes can turn church-related agencies into extensions of the state, I now turn to what happens when the state operates in its sacral mode. Becoming an extension of the state in the story I have to tell happened to the Salvation Army at warp speed compared to the process of bureaucratic colonization and mission attrition in agencies that contracted to deliver employment services. The context is one in which the Australian government went full bore in both rhetoric and policy terms in claiming to uphold the integrity of national borders against people characterized as dangerous strangers, that is to say, refugees and asylum seekers. The consequences of contracting with government in this context were confronting and painful, not only for asylum seekers who the agency was supposed to be serving, but also the Salvation Army as an institution, and the staff working for the Army in delivering the contract.

The story begins in late 2012 when the Australian Labor Government announced that it was letting a contract for the provision of welfare and support services for offshore processing centers for asylum seekers. The offshore processing centers were on Manus Island, a province of Papua New Guinea, and Nauru, a small island state in the Pacific, 1,300 kilometers northeast of the Solomon Islands.[33] Both are remote locations that are difficult for the media to access, a not-insignificant benefit from the government's point

33. Doherty, "A Short History of Nauru."

of view. The contract ran from February 2013 to January 2014 and was valued at $94.6 m.[34] The welfare and support services for asylum seekers that were to be provided included educational and recreational opportunities, facilitating English classes, access to gym facilities and computers, and the organization of excursions and cultural events. All this seems at first glance to be quite straightforward, just the sort of activity that would be entirely appropriate for a church-related agency to engage in.

When you look more closely at the background to the policy of offshore processing, which eventually became a policy of long-term detention, the participation by the Salvation Army became problematic. The Australian government had decided to resume offshore processing of asylum seekers arriving in Australia by boat, largely from Indonesia. This decision was taken after failed attempts by the government to set up offshore arrangements for handling asylum seekers with Malaysia and Timor-Leste. The stated reasons for offshore processing included removing the financial incentive for people smuggling, preventing people from risking their lives on dangerous sea voyages, and more generally to protect the integrity of Australia's borders. Offshore processing was stated to be a short-term solution, while a longer-term regional framework for dealing with asylum seekers was developed. The latter never eventuated. Nearly a decade later, the problems created by that failure have not been resolved

The story of how and why the Salvation Army agreed to contract with the Australian government to provide humanitarian services for asylum seekers in offshore locations at Manus Island and Nauru, and what happened in trying to deliver on that contract, illustrates the risks of contracting with a government operating in its sacral mode. The government justified its policy as being in defense of Australian borders. It was a bearer of the sacred trust in upholding the sovereignty of Australia, and when sovereignty is at stake anything goes. In telling the story I draw heavily on interviews with government relations officers of the Salvation Army, reports from news agencies, staff who participated in the program, and evidence given to parliamentary committees.

Following the announcement by the Australian government on the renewal of offshore processing, the Salvation Army took the initiative. The Army wrote to the office of the Minister for Immigration, offering to provide services for asylum seekers and reminding the Minister that it had been involved working on the Australian mainland with asylum seekers in community detention. The Army was up front in acknowledging that it did not support the policy of offshore processing but suggested that nevertheless if

---

34. Laughland and Jabour, "Salvation Army Humanitarian Work."

The Risks of Contracting

there was anything that they could do to help out to just let them know. The Army was confident that it could deliver the required services. It was not clear whether in making the offer the Army was aware of exactly how tight the timetable to start delivery of services would be. The response to the offer by the government was swift. According to Major Brad Halse, Manager of Government Relations for the Southern Command of the Salvation Army, "The Government jumped down the phone just about and arranged a meeting within days to say, . . . 'Okay, we are getting people on the ground very quickly, we're sending people to Nauru. What can you do?'"[35]

Major Halse insisted that, while the Army didn't agree with the asylum seeker policy, it took the view that if the government was going to proceed with the policy anyway the relevant question for the Army was, what was the next best thing for the asylum seekers? It was a political reality. It was going to happen. What should the Army do in this situation? "The view of the Salvation Army at that time . . . was to have a group of people highly committed to maximize the very best out of a bad option for people so we felt that the church should be involved in that. . . . That did bring with it constraints on not only the Salvation Army, on employees, but anybody, you know, working there, [who] was not meant to speak either whilst they're employed or even post-employment."[36] The tension in negotiating the agreement around issues of limitations on the Army's ability to publicly comment on what was happening offshore is pretty clear in Major Halse's explanation. "There was a memorandum of understanding at that stage rather than a formal contract. Everything was being done on the run. . . . The final shape of the contract and the restrictions in it was far less than what was originally mooted. . . . There were things where we just said, 'Well, we can't work on this basis.'"[37] Whatever restrictions on public communication the Army may have rejected during the negotiations, the result was a very restrictive agreement that proved to be a source of conflict of conscience for staff. The imperative for urgent implementation left very little time for detailed consideration by the Salvation Army of the issues involved in undertaking the contract and weighing up the assessment of the extent of possible conflict with its mission statement, let alone for any detailed implementation planning.

> The urgency of this thing, the speed with which it's happened, certainly framed our executive decision-making process . . . We don't really like to work like that, but it was always the principle

35. Halse interview.
36. Halse interview.
37. Halse interview.

> that "Well, you know, here's a great need. There are people being sent there and nobody's really there to be able to look after their welfare needs, basic education, support," things like that and, you know, the overriding biblical principle for us is, "Well, there's a human need and can we meet it, do we have the resources, do we have a level of experience and expertise?" . . . We were sending some pretty young adults up there who were highly motivated in terms of social justice but [with] little, relatively speaking, life experience.[38]

While the emphasis by the Army in agreeing to enter the contract was on trying to improve the situation of those in need, the Army continued to affirm its opposition to offshore processing of asylum seekers. That in-principle opposition did not seem to present a problem for the government. Major Paul Moulds, Director, Social Mission and Resources, of the Salvation Army in Australia, in evidence to the Joint Parliamentary Committee in December 2012, stated why the Salvation Army was engaged in providing services for asylum seekers held offshore. It is worth quoting his evidence at length in the light of what subsequently transpired.

> The only reason the Salvation Army is there is because we care deeply for the plight and the situation of the asylum seekers and believe our presence can make and is making a difference. The Salvation Army has made it quite clear in a number of statements that it is opposed to offshore processing. On 2 September this year the Salvation Army joined other Christian churches in issuing a joint statement of concern about the potential consequences of this new policy on the mental health and wellbeing of asylum seekers seeking protection from persecution. . . .
>
> The Salvation Army has experienced working with asylum seekers both in mainland detention centres and in providing contracted services to the federal government in community detention. Who would be best placed to provide asylum seekers with the best possible support and services during this challenging period of their lives? A security company? A facilities management provider? Or an organisation that brings to this task over a century of experience and skill in working with distressed, vulnerable and marginalised people and boundless amounts of faith, hope and love. We have no choice to do this work. This is who we are; it is our DNA.
>
> Since that time, we have been publicly attacked for this decision by some individuals and organisations. We have been

---

38. Halse interview.

accused of being an agent of the government, providing legitimacy to the government's asylum seeker policies, of doing this for monetary purposes, of being complicit in the detention and mistreatment of asylum seekers. We have responded with a simple response: if not us, who will do this task? Salvationists have always been people of action. The Salvation Army's calling is not just to engage in debate and discussion but to stand with and work alongside people who are suffering and vulnerable. I again reiterate that our presence in the regional processing centres in Nauru and Manus Island does not mean we support the policy of offshore processing, just as our presence serving tea and coffee and providing encouragement to our front-line troops in World War I and World War II did not mean we support war or violence. It is perfectly reasonable to object to a government policy but still be fully engaged in providing humanitarian assistance to those affected by the policy. This is the situation the Salvation Army is in and we will stay the course as long as our support is wanted and needed by the asylum seekers.... It continues to be costly to our organisation but, as I said, we will stay as long as we can make a difference to the people we serve.[39]

The questions rhetorically asked by Major Moulds about who else would undertake the contract if the Salvation Army did not was ironically prophetic. The next contractor for delivering human services after the Salvation Army was Save the Children, a humanitarian charity. The contract after that was delivered by a security company, and then a facilities management provider, all for-profit companies as nonprofit agencies had decided not to be associated with a policy that was clearly indefensible from a human rights point of view. The Army viewed the situation at the time as one in which it saw the opportunity to provide support and services to very vulnerable people. The Army's anticipation of how the power relationship with the government would work was not fulfilled. The Army staff delivering the humanitarian services became identified with the refugees by the security staff and were themselves vulnerable to psychological pressure and suffered obstruction from the security services in carrying out their responsibilities. The staff working offshore ended up identifying with the powerless in their own experience of powerlessness to provide adequate and appropriate support to the asylum seekers.

The decision as the Army saw it involved a conflict between the principle of opposing the policy, and the needs of very vulnerable people. Reflecting on his experience as a Salvation Army worker on Nauru, Mark

39. Moulds, Migration Legislation Amendment.

Isaacs highlighted the difficulty of the role of the Army in carrying out this contract, and the tension of providing humanitarian support to asylum seekers in a detention center. The center was established to deter desperate people from seeking protection by subjecting them to intentionally cruel conditions.

> The contradictory nature of the Salvation Army's position meant they were damned by the government if they assisted the asylum seekers, and damned by their staff if they didn't. Despite this the employees of the Salvation Army . . . showed utmost care for the asylum seekers we worked with and implemented a wide range of programs that alleviated some of the mental pressure placed upon these people. This justified the need for a humanitarian organisation to act as a service provider within detention centres . . . Although the original motives of the Salvation Army were admirable, the implementation of the "Nauru mission" suffered due to inexperience, poor preparation, and the Salvation Army's inability to defend the asylum seekers' human rights and handle government pressure.[40]

There were significant issues arising from the expedited implementation. Screening of workers for skills and maturity, along with appropriate briefing and preparation, were clearly almost nonexistent in the first round of staff placements.[41] The rushed implementation of the policy was bound to have resulted in substantial difficulties for whoever took the contract. The evidence on the recruiting and briefing of staff from recruits for the first round of staffing by the Army suggests that it was under very high pressure from the government to get people there regardless of the level of preparation.

The experience of subsequent humanitarian agencies in offshore contracting, and their apparent inability to defend in any meaningful way the human rights of detainees, raises a question mark over Isaacs's assessment of how much the Army's failure in preparation contributed to the level of oppression of the asylum seekers. While the failure in preparation was real enough and had consequences for both the inmates and the staff, the experience of staff and inmates under later contractors was not that different. The policy logic of offshore deterrence and its inhumane implementation would have swamped even the best planning by contractors.

The decision of the Salvation Army to undertake this contract, and the results of their participation, should be assessed against their understanding

---

40. Isaacs, "The Salvos on Nauru."
41. Isaacs, *The Undesirables*, 8; Isaacs, "Salvo Detention Workers."

The Risks of Contracting

of their mission and identity. The Salvation Army, as an international movement, certainly considers itself as an evangelical part of the universal Christian church, with a mission to preach the gospel of Jesus Christ and to meet human needs in his name without discrimination. The Army describes its work as being about transforming lives, caring for people, making disciples, and reforming society. Starting from the recognition that God is always at work in the world, the Army affirms that it values human dignity, justice, hope, compassion, and community. This statement of mission is hard to reconcile with the reality of what happened in the offshore processing centers. The Army was deeply implicated in a government policy that resulted in the destruction of human health and the mental well-being of inmates. The Australian government refused to apply human rights standards to the processing of refugees and asylum seekers. The damage to people in offshore processing centers extended beyond the asylum seekers and refugees to the staff carrying out the contract, many of whom reported experiencing post-traumatic stress syndrome following their tour of duty.

Criticism of the Salvation Army for participating in the contract came from a variety of commentators, including many from outside the church, who raised questions about the consistency of undertaking of the contract with the Army's commitments and mission and of the hypocrisy of participating in a program that they were opposed to.[42] The Army defended its participation, noting that it "has supported and endorsed the comments made by Amnesty International and the recent UNHRC report. We recognise conditions are harsh, and any comments that could be considered as 'defending conditions' were simply truthful answers to questions regarding the adequacy of food and water. Our staff are working hard every day to give every asylum seeker access to education, vocational training, recreational and social activities that will make the time awaiting the resolution of their asylum claims more meaningful and useful."[43] During the term of the contract, whistleblowing by Salvation Army staff about the conditions and operation of the offshore processing centers was reported by the ABC investigative Four Corners television program.[44] The incoming coalition government did not provide any reasons why the contract with the Salvation Army was not renewed and the contract awarded to another provider. There was a strong suspicion that the whistleblowing by staff on the conditions being experienced by asylum seekers was behind the decision.

---

42. Haigh, "The Salvation Army Is a Branch of Government"; *New Matilda*, "Nauru staff condemn cruel conditions."
43. Haigh, "Salvos Lose Moral Compass."
44. ABC, "No Advantage."

In taking up the contract the Army was caught up in being associated with implementing the logic of the Australian government's policy of deterrence. Refugees and asylum seekers were going to be held in detention in offshore processing centers, not because they had done anything wrong, but to try and prevent other people from seeking asylum. The logic of deterrence was that by causing cruelty in penalizing asylum seekers, the lives of other would-be asylum seekers would be saved. If the state, as it clearly does, is prepared to call for the sacrifice of its own members to ensure its survival during war, should we be surprised if it was prepared to treat inhumanely and carelessly those who are not its members, refugees and asylum seekers? The perception was created by the Australian government that these strangers were a threat to its national borders and its sovereignty. Asylum seeking was treated here as a threat to sovereignty, a threat to that which is most sacred about the nation's existence, and a response analogous to a state of war was therefore required to meet that threat. Given the creation of a perception of threat by asylum seekers to the nation-state, a challenge to what is most "sacred," the essential human character of asylum seekers as children of God, their rights and their vulnerability, was ignored in the way they are treated. The militarization of the language surrounding the practices of offshore detention provides striking evidence of this process.

There was always a wide gap between the official rhetoric of providing appropriate facilities and care for asylum seekers, and the abusive reality of detention as a policy in defense of the sacredness of the Australian nation. This inevitably resulted in a harsher treatment of those imprisoned, even when this was not specifically spelled out in the policy. The Army was committed to a humanitarian role in delivering services but found itself squeezed in actual practice between that commitment and the underlying government logic of deterrence and detention. The reality on the ground in the detention centers was that staff had little success in asserting their humanitarian role against the logic of imprisonment and detention on which the camps operated.

Paradoxically, the very public failure of the Army opened up the reality of government policy to public view, to an extent, and in a manner, that might not otherwise have been the case. The staff employed by the Army ended up accompanying the refugees at least in their experience of powerlessness, in their feelings of frustration at their failure to make a substantive difference, and by the way the logic of imprisonment bore down on them and constrained them in their relationship with the asylum seekers, along with their frustration and grief over the impact on the asylum seekers. It made the relationship between staff delivering humanitarian services and the other contracted staff enforcing the detention tense and adversarial.

The Risks of Contracting

The humanitarian staff became second-order victims of the policy that they were associated with administering.

The Salvation Army justified their "realism" in entering into the contract on the basis that they were accepting an electoral mandate by the government to proceed with the offshore detention policy. This I would argue was not being "realistic" enough. The Army viewed government policy making and implementation as though it was dealing with normal bureaucratic processes, when it was actually dealing with the state operating in a sacral mode. The Army by accepting the contract became implicated in implementing a humanly destructive policy. Official reports released since then have documented the severe impact on the health and well-being of asylum seekers of offshore processing.[45] A subsequent contractor for the provision of offshore human services, Save the Children, had a similar experience to the Army, in having a tense relationship with the government, and facing whistleblowing on conditions in detention, by their staff who were working in the offshore processing centers. Chief Executive of Save the Children Paul Ronalds was of the view that the agency had been treated "as a 'scapegoat' and 'easy target' by both Australian and Nauruan governments."[46] The evidence is clear that any agency delivering humanitarian services was never going to be able to deliver the contract in a way that reflected their commitment to a mission framed in humanitarian or theological terms.

The Salvation Army displayed a lack of awareness of this punitive dimension of the policy environment into which it was stepping. It understood itself to be committed to a humanitarian role in delivering services but got squeezed between a commitment that was central to its identity and the underlying abusive policy logic of deterrence and detention. Staff in offshore processing camps had little success in asserting that humanitarian role against the logic of imprisonment and detention. The institutional environment created by government policy was one in which abuse of both asylum seekers and staff providing humanitarian services became normalized. The management of the contract by the Australian government was undertaken in a way that enabled it to obfuscate its responsibility for the impact of the policy assessed against humanitarian and human rights criteria, by ignoring reports from accountability agencies such as the Australian National Audit Office and the Australian Human Rights Commission.[47]

The Salvation Army, and its successors in contracting for the delivery of humanitarian services, became an extension of the state in its

---

45. Australian Human Rights Commission, *The Forgotten Children*.
46. Ronalds, "Exclusive Interview."
47. Gleeson, *Offshore*, 94–197.

implementation of a policy of punitive detention. The experience of the Salvation Army in contracting with the Australian government for the delivery of offshore humanitarian services for asylum seekers was characterized by conflict between its mission commitments and a government policy that exported the conflict into the agency itself. In telling this story I have tried to fairly represent the tension that was clearly experienced by the Army in making its decision to participate in the contract. I have thought a good deal about this episode. The decision to participate was clearly an agonized one taken with the best of intentions, but with a severe underestimation of the risks involved and the dynamics of Australia government policy. A theologically informed assessment of the evil that can arise from institutional behavior driven by a commitment to the sacred and institutional self-preservation may have been a helpful exercise as part of the decision-making process.

Becoming an extension of the state

In this chapter I have sketched two distinct forces operating to drive church-related agencies into becoming extensions of the state, as a result of engaging in government contracting. In respect of employment services, the forces generated by contracting to push agencies into becoming an extension of the state were subtle and took time to become apparent. A combination of bureaucratic and economic pressures slowly and imperceptibly wore away the commitments of agencies to careful and patient human service, and to linking the people they were serving more effectively with the community. Reflection on the guiding theological commitments of an agency in the context of critical engagement with the reality of an agency's mission might have been helpful in assisting in decision-making about whether to engage in a specific contract or in resisting those pressures in the context of delivering services under a contract. Catholic Social Teaching provided a standard for informing decisions on contracting by at least some Catholic church welfare agencies.

Shifting to consider contracting by church-related agencies with the state operating in its sacral mode, the experience of the Salvation Army in their involvement with offshore processing of asylum seekers is extremely edifying under examination. The sacred when it migrates into government policy making, and this is clearly the case with respect to asylum seekers and refugees, has a very nasty logic and has had severe impacts on service providers and their staff as well as those they were intending to serve. The potential range of services to which this process applies is admittedly not large. Beyond support for refugees and asylum seekers, only contracting for human services that relate to security and defense comes to mind. Should church-related agencies become involved in contracting with government to provide these services? The detailed circumstances certainly need to be assessed on a case-by-case basis, along with careful thought about taking care of the people who will be delivering such contracts where high levels of moral and emotional stress are attached. In the following chapters I will explore a number of differing responses by Christian agencies and movements to the plight of refugees arriving in Australia that did not involve contracting with the government. I will also suggest an alternative logic of compassion and hospitality.

9

Advocacy: Challenging Government while Exiting Christendom

The strand in the tradition of Israel that held that kingship was not necessarily a good idea, and indeed that it would have devastating impacts on the life of the community, opens up a theological basis for advocacy against any exercise of power that is detrimental to community well-being and human flourishing. Even though Israel insisted on having a monarchy, the prophets never treated the kings and their exercise of power as being beyond question and divinely authorized judgment. If Israel was going to choose against all the advice to have a monarchy, God was going to provide the prophet as the necessary antibody to the tendency of the monarchy to arrogate divine status and unquestioned power to itself.

Advocacy by the Christian movement after Christendom has its theological roots in this position of prophetic critique of governing power. It stands as an activity that is analogous to that of the prophets, of bringing a theologically grounded, charismatically authorized challenge to any exercise of power that is destructive of human and community well-being. Such advocacy is a form of community engagement that can take diverse forms, beyond written and spoken speech, including prayer and nonviolent protest as a way of speaking truth to those in positions of power.

The two very different stories that I tell in this chapter suggest something of the range of possibilities of advocacy. The first story is about insider advocacy. By this I mean advocacy in which the advocates have reasonably direct access to decisionmakers, whether they be politicians or public servants. Here effective advocacy in a fairly traditional mode by national coordinating agencies of various churches became possible because of some unanticipated consequences of the shift to contracting by government in

Australia. In this case relationships of trust, friendship, and shared commitments between the staff and boards of denominational national coordinating agencies made advocacy possible, against the grain of a neoliberal contracting environment. The second story is about outsider advocacy in the form of a nonviolent challenge to government by an informal movement of Christian activists under the title of Love Makes a Way (LMAW). The activities of LMAW, calling for the release of children of asylum seekers from detention, and the subsequent Sanctuary initiative by churches in Australia, demonstrated the potential of advocacy grounded in a spirituality of nonviolent resistance, that in this case was shaped by the heritage of the civil rights movement. The counterintuitive element of this advocacy was that the unashamed character of its appeal to explicitly Christian narratives and practices was central to engaging the attention, and substantial involvement, of significant elements of the wider Australian community.

Contracting and insider advocacy

I discussed some of the risks of the shift to contracting by church-related agencies in the previous chapter. The shift to contracting with NFPs for the delivery of social welfare and human services in Australia from 1996 onwards was also criticized for its potential to restrict agencies' freedom to advocate against government policy. The general assumption was that increased contracting with government would lead church-related welfare agencies to become extremely cautious about public expressions of disagreement with government policy, and would dampen if not prevent advocacy by them. An individual agency, contracting with an 800-pound gorilla in the form of a large government agency, would certainly seem to be at a disadvantage in terms of relative power. As it turned out, advocacy by church-related agencies was not silenced by contracting. Some episodes of advocacy by denominational social welfare national coordinating bodies during the period of 2006 to 2008 suggest that the shift to contracting had some unexpected consequences that facilitated insider advocacy. The story about how this happened is based on interviews with agency CEOs and board members of church-related social welfare agencies, as well as media reports from the period.

What the initial intuition about the power relationship arising from the shift to contracting squashing advocacy didn't take account of were the systemic effects of the shift to contracting. At a systemic level, the shift to contracting led to a partial rebalancing in the power relationship between denominational coordinating agencies, at least in the short term. The impact of contracting at a systemic, or sector, level took the following form: the large amount of government funding going through church-related agencies across the country as the result of contracting made it necessary for denominations to develop the capability at a national level to better coordinate and manage engagement by their agencies with government around welfare policy and contracting. The denominational welfare coordinating bodies weren't directly funded by government and were structurally separate from their member agencies who were delivering the contracted services. The funding flowing through the sector from contracts meant that national coordinating bodies were able to fund increased coordination activities at least partly by agency membership and contract management fees. When combined with funds from denominational stakeholders, this enabled the development of national bodies that could engage much more effectively with governments than had been the case previously. The independence of the national coordinating agencies from government contracting enabled informed and resourced policy advocacy.

Within a decade of the shift to contracting that began in the last decade of the twentieth century, the Anglican, Uniting, and Catholic national welfare coordinating agencies all had established national coordinating offices in Canberra. While these peak bodies were not large in absolute terms, the total staffing was more than double at the time that of the Australian Council of Social Service (ACOSS), the national peak body for the welfare sector. The mission statements of the three national peak denominational welfare agencies spell out the linkage with their respective churches and associated theological commitments.

The strategic goals of Anglicare Australia representing Anglican agencies, most of which are diocesan and involved in delivering a wide range of family and children's welfare services, were:

- To influence social and economic influence across Australia with a strong prophetic voice informed by research and the practical experience of the network, and called to speak out for those most disadvantaged.

- To enable the potential, strength, and sustainability of the members, ensuring that they have the capacity to serve the needs of all Australians with dignity, respect, and care.

- To create a network whose members challenge, support ,and lead each other in the development of social services and the people and communities with whom they work.

- To recognize and celebrate the Anglican faith-based inspiration of their work.[1]

Catholic Social Services Australia (CSSA), a Commission of the Australian Catholic Bishops Conference, represented both diocesan and non-diocesan welfare agencies involved mainly in family and children's services, with an increasing element during the period of advocacy in employment services. "CSSA envisages a fairer, more inclusive Australian society that reflects and supports the dignity, equality and participation of all people. Our Mission: CSSA advances the social service ministry which is integral to the Mission of the Catholic Church in Australia."[2]

The UnitingCare Australia (UCA) network stated that its mission was to express God's love for all people through the Uniting Church's commitment to supporting individuals, families, and communities through advocacy and the enhancement of community service provision. UCA's key roles are to:

- Encourage theological reflection on the Church's community services work.
- Advocate to government and within the Church and community those policies and practices that enhance the dignity of people, especially those who are most disadvantaged and marginalized.
- Enable exchange of information across Synods and Uniting Church service providers.
- Seek to enhance the quality of community service provision by the Uniting Church.
- Represent the views of the Uniting Church service providers to governments.
- Work as appropriate with other churches and peak organizations in the community services sector.[3]

These church-related coordinating agencies undertook network support, research, and advocacy on social welfare policy at a national level. Advocacy involved not only taking up the debate on policy in the public sphere, but also working to influence policy in less public spaces such as Senate committees and private meetings with public servants and politicians. The other player in this story of advocacy was the Salvation Army,

---

1. Anglicare Australia, *Strategic Plan, 2014*.
2. Catholic Social Services Australia, *Annual Report, 2013–4*, i.
3. UnitingCare Australia, *Mandate*.

which has a significant presence across social welfare and human services sectors in Australia. It differs from the major denominations in that its advocacy and contract management is located within the Army structure rather than in a separate coordinating body.

Advocacy as saying "no" to government contracts

The Coalition LNP government in its 2006–2007 budget introduced a measure entitled *Welfare to Work—financial case management for income support recipients*. The program was designed around nonprofit organizations contracting with the government to carry out financial management support for those income support recipients who had been excluded from receiving social security benefits. The people involved in the program were those who had been excluded from receiving benefits for periods of up to eight weeks as a result of their failure to meet the job search requirements associated with receiving income support. The process of cutting people off income support was because they had breached the requirements of the employment service program under which they were being financially supported.

The program was to be available to recipients who had children, or other vulnerable dependents, or who were themselves considered exceptionally vulnerable, to enable the payment of essential services. Centrelink, the government agency responsible for making income support payments, would use the funding to contract nongovernment organizations to establish the level of required assistance on a week-by-week basis. The program provided $17.1m over five years for agencies to carry out financial management support.

Frank Quinlan, at the time CEO of CSSA, was a key player in generating the critical response from the church peak bodies to this policy proposal.

> The government of the day introduced a policy which meant that people who were in breach of their mutual obligations requirements would be excluded from any benefits, any payments for eight weeks. . . . Catholic Social Services quite quickly and immediately crystallized on a position that we weren't going to be participants in that sort of a contract arrangement. And in discussions with other church providers and others . . . it quickly became apparent that there was a fair sense of agreement around the idea that organizations operating from our perspective really ought not participate in a contract like that, which was quite

a radical proposition ... but [it] gathered a head of steam quite quickly.[4]

The public criticism of the policy, and the accompanying refusal by church-related agencies to contract with the government to deliver the program, was reported in a steady stream of media commentary over the next few months. The church-related agencies that eventually boycotted the program included agencies affiliated with CSSA, most member agencies of Anglicare Australia and UnitingCare Australia, as well as the Salvation Army, Mission Australia, and Hillsong, a large Pentecostal church in Sydney. This was an impressive united front, as none of the peak bodies leading the charge against the program had any way of enforcing a decision to boycott the program on their members. Indeed, several major agencies who participated in the boycott were not members of the church-related peak welfare bodies.

The boycott emerged against an extended background of uneasiness and debate among agencies right across the welfare sector about government policy. As I noted in the discussion on employment services in chapter 8, Catholic welfare agencies had already been debating whether, and to what extent, they should be involved in contracting in the employment services sector. The Financial Case Management Program proved to be just one step too far. The program was judged by the church agencies to be unduly harsh. The church-related agencies didn't want to be seen as administrators policing harsh government policy and as acting as nothing more than extensions of the state. Agencies thought that these types of measures would likely spill over into other areas of social welfare delivery and would compromise a broader moral commitment by agencies to people who were some of the most vulnerable and marginalized Australians.

The then-Minister for Human Services in the Australian government responded to the boycott by the church agencies by accusing the Catholic Church of pulling a "political stunt," and of walking away from society's most vulnerable. The right to pull "political stunts" apparently was reserved to the Minister. The accusation that agencies were walking away from society's most vulnerable carried little weight coming from a government that had displayed a willingness to place more and more requirements on the unemployed to receive less and less by way of income support, a trend that has continued up to the date of writing this book. The Opposition in turn predictably described the government's policy as "extreme and incompetent."

The few nonprofit agencies that finally agreed to participate in the program were mostly small and very few were linked to the major

4. Quinlan interview.

denominational networks. The government consequently had to deliver the bulk of the program directly through Centrelink, the Australian government agency responsible for managing a range of social security payments. This was a more costly proposition for the government than the original proposal as there were increased costs associated with employing public servants rather than contracting with nonprofit agencies. It should be acknowledged that the decision by agencies not to accept contracts under this program did not result in a loss of funding by them. Agencies simply passed up an opportunity to expand the size of their operations. Even this decision, though, is not one that would have been predicted by an assumption that agencies would be driven solely by economic self-interest.

The very public advocacy by church-related agencies manifested through the boycott and the accompanying public debate had an interesting impact on the relationship of agencies with the government. The Coalition government was as per the Minister's comment "quite cranky" about the boycott by the agencies. The Coalition government blamed the boycott on the churches as the key stakeholders in the agencies. In this they were mistaken. The decisions on the boycott were driven very much by leadership of the agencies who brought the church leaders along with them. Frank Quinlan, who was in charge of the CSSA at the time, thought that it was quite an important moment in the relationship between the church-related agencies and government.

> I think they were caught a little unawares . . . They expected most of the organizations to be quite acquiescent, and to just take on the contracts. So, I think it forced a bit of a rethink of some of their approach, which was helpful. . . . For those of us that were engaged in that, it was something of an awakening of a sense of political power that goes with the strength of being a major provider . . . It helped us to realize that that it is in fact a complex interrelationship, and just as large organizations can start to become dependent on governments, governments can start to become dependent on large organizations.[5]

While this is the only case of a public boycott by church-related agencies in Australia of a government program that was put out for contract, the boycott and the associated advocacy had a number of noticeable results. The first was a recognition by agencies that in the early years of contracting they had let themselves become involved in a rush for cash in their response to government contracting and that this had led to mission drift. Subsequently many agencies began using a template shaped by their mission

5. Quinlan interview.

commitments as a central element in decision-making on whether or not they would bid for specific contracts. The second was that the shock of the boycott brought some of the potential of the systemic impact of the shift to contracting into focus. The Australian government realized it had become very dependent on agencies and that their acquiescence in its policy initiatives could not always be taken for granted. On the other side, the denominational coordinating agencies realized that they actually had a degree of leverage in their relationship with government. The relationships among the coordinating agencies mediated through their leadership played a leading role in an informal networking decision process that led to the boycott.

The Major Church Providers: network advocacy

The effectiveness of the boycott and the subsequent government response was the trigger for more intentional cooperative activity by the denominational peak welfare bodies, under the rubric of the Major Church Providers (MCP), as a way of prosecuting that cooperation into the future. Significantly the agencies did not set up the MCP as a legally constituted body separate from the denominational agencies. Through this arrangement Anglicare Australia, CSSA, and UnitingCare Australia, along with the Salvation Army, have cooperated in a range of policy, research, and advocacy activities. The MCP has worked on the basis of personal friendship and collegial connections of the church-related peak welfare bodies. This approach stands in stark contrast to the contractual culture that is now shaping the welfare sector generally. In an important sense this has been a truly "countercultural" approach by the church-related coordinating agencies.

The MCP has operated through regular collegial contact amongst the chairs of the denominational agencies and the Salvation Army. Major Brad Halse from the Salvation Army noted that meetings of the MCP were fairly informal and not always full minuted.[6] The cooperation extended beyond the CEOs of the coordinating agencies to the boards. Fr. Joe Caddy, as chair of the CSSA board at the time, reported that he met with the national chairs of the other peak bodies twice a year for about three or four years.[7] The relationships and trust between the agency CEOs Caddy thought was critical to the functioning of the MCP, a view confirmed by Lin Hatfield-Dodds, then CEO of UnitingCare Australia, in her description of cooperation during the period from 2006 to 2008. "At the national level, we're all talking with each

6. Halse interview.
7. Caddy interview.

other, we meet regularly. We don't have a formalized structure . . . When things come up, the first thing we do is get on the phone, get together, and reflect theologically."[8]

Tension in the relationship between the church-related peak bodies and the peak welfare body ACOSS also encouraged a cooperative approach by the denominational coordinating agencies to draw together their shared weight on issues on which they wished to advocate. Rev. Ray Cleary, formerly CEO of Anglicare Victoria and a board member of Anglicare Australia, noted this as one of the reasons for the use of the MCP for advocacy by the denominational coordinating agencies. "You had a number of . . . so-called trendy lefties in the sector who actually saw the church as too powerful and setting the scene too much and [they] wanted to do something different."[9]

Policy advocacy remained the focus of MCP. Frank Quinlan, then running CSSA, observed that MCP "really arose out of an eagerness for those organizations . . . to express an identity that was unique, and that was linked to church. So, in a sense to differentiate ourselves from the vast field of often quite excellent service providers operating in that space . . . we felt it was important for us to be able to say, by use of that sort of connection to the Church . . ."[10] John Warhurst, then a professor in politics at the Australian National University and a member of the CSSA board, observed that the MCP "was also driven by a feeling that there were artificial barriers between the denominations and the separate churches. . . . They had a lot to learn from one another . . . They had a lot in common . . . They wanted the voices in the church heard and they felt that it would benefit all of them at the advocacy level."[11] The importance of informal contacts and connections built the relationships between senior people in the peak agencies. This was demonstrated by invitations to speak at each other's conferences and finding opportunities to work cooperatively.

> If you wanted to make a submission [and] you didn't have the resources in your single denominational area, you would task someone from one of the agencies to effectively work on behalf of all the agencies . . . One of the ones that I remember was the whole question of salary levels within the social services sector . . . It was from the Uniting Church on that occasion that a lot of the research and advocacy work was . . . feeding information into the CEOs of the religious group. . . . The religious

---

8. Hatfield-Dodds interview.
9. Quinlan interview.
10. Quinlan interview.
11. Warhurst interview.

faith-based organizations didn't want to be outflanked by the non-faith based organizations because they thought they had a particular voice to put forward.[12]

According to the Rev. Ray Cleary, cooperation around big issues came out of regular meetings between CEOs of Catholic Social Service and Anglicare and the Uniting Church, along with the relevant management staff members in charge of government relations from the Southern Territory of the Salvation Army.

> The church agencies needed to find a way or a mechanism of meeting or talking with each other. Not to be exclusive but to actually say, well, what is going on here? Why are we being sidelined? The other reason I think is because many of us who were in church-based agencies began to say, look, there must be things that historically we did in common that we should be doing again. . . . We started meeting up over dinner. A very good way of doing it; we found that we had a lot in common.[13]

The concern to articulate the distinctive voice of the church-related welfare agencies was also voiced by Lin Hatfield-Dodds. "In our thinking there was real value for a particular faith-based voice and it's not a proselytizing voice, but it is a very clear value-driven, fearless voice."[14] The key question, as Rt. Rev. Chris Jones, chair of the board of Anglicare Australia, said, was in knowing when to bring the MCP partnership into operation. It "has had, at different times, an important role to play. . . . It's something that we need to keep ticking over and roll out when I think there's a big issue that it's worth us actually being able to work on together because we do have a shared set of values . . . It gets rolled out when it's useful, but it's kept in the background when it's not."[15] Such assessment took into account the diversity of views of the members within each of the denominational coordinating agencies, as well as the diversity between the coordinating agencies given their differing ecclesial and theological backgrounds. The cooperation through the MCP points to a wider network of connections and stakeholders in the mainstream denominations, who share a deep commitment to social justice, to be able to speak together arising out of the substantial investment they have in the Australian community.

- 12. Warhurst interview.
- 13. Cleary interview.
- 14. Hatfield-Dodds interview.
- 15. Jones interview.

> Part of the effectiveness and frankly the charm for each of us I think of the Major Church Providers group, is it is informal and flexible enough to be very agile, so in the early years . . . we'd meet however many times over lunch or coffee in our offices. . . . That's been really helpful for all of us to understand not just each other's networks, but each other's churches, because then you know what's possible in terms of agility and response . . . There's a high, high degree of trust and it's a very effective group.[16]

Advocacy during the Global Financial Crisis, 2008

In contrast to the public advocacy that took place in the Financial Management program boycott, an example of behind-the-scenes advocacy can be found in the contribution by the MCP to Australian government policy-making during the Global Financial Crisis (GFC). I do not attempt here to provide an overall account of the policy-making process by the Australian government related to the GFC, but rather put on the record the role of this network in that policy process as seen by key players from the church-related peak agencies.

In the period between the boycott over the Financial Management contract and the GFC there had been a change of government at the national level with the election of the Australian Labor Party. This political development opened the door for the MCP to take a more active role in advocacy. In November 2008 the MCP agencies gathered some of their major member agencies involved in service delivery at Parliament House in Canberra to participate in a summit on the impact of the GFC on social services. After that summit, and in light of the deliberations that followed, they prepared a report that offered a number of recommendations to government. The agencies reported that "there was a looming and impending crisis for people who were perhaps the least prepared to ride out the global financial crisis. And as government was setting its policy around how it would respond to the global financial crisis, we acted together . . . to encourage them to take specific measures around ensuring that people who were least [well off] were somewhat protected."[17] Lin Hatfield-Dodds explained how the advocacy process worked from there.

> We then had a joint Parliamentary Forum . . . There were a series of Labor ministers that came, we had a senior advisor from the

---

16. Hatfield-Dodds interview.
17. Quinlan interview.

Advocacy

Prime Minister's office ... We had in the room about thirty of our CEOs from around Australia who spoke ... The GFC was biting in the communities ... We were saying "There's a firestorm coming" so our message to government was, you need to pour some more resources into these kinds of things—financial counseling, emergency relief, family crisis work—but most critically, government, we need you to talk to Australia's financial institutions. ... People are going to default on their mortgage payments, [and] if all the people we think are going to default, default, the welfare net's broken, we can't hold it.[18]

Beyond drawing information from the agency membership networks to inform government, the MCP took an active role in pushing for a package of responses. On the basis of both on-the-ground information and moral claims, the MCP pushed the case for a substantial response. The outcomes were "$50 million for financial counseling and an oversight group for the stimulus spend in that area. ... It was called the community response task force; there would have been about twelve or fifteen of us appointed to it and we used to meet about every four or six weeks. We'd meet with Deputy Prime Minister Gillard, Minister Macklin, and Parliamentary Secretary Ursula Stevens ... and then a bunch of deputy secretaries ... All of us were there because we had the capability to make decisions stick in our network."[19]

Joint advocacy by the MCP worked when there were strongly shared values by the coordinating agencies. It required sensitivity amongst the leadership to those policy areas where there would be tensions within and between the coordinating agencies, given the diversity of views of the members of each of the coordinating agencies, as well as the diversity in ecclesial and theological backgrounds. It was felt by the participants to be important for the mainstream churches with a shared deep commitment to social justice to be able to speak together where they had a shared understanding given their substantial investment in the Australian community. This insider advocacy was one that was marked by both a degree of closeness between churches, their agencies, and government that carried with it memories of Christendom but was at the same time marked by a degree of tension with government.

This policy advocacy worked through both bureaucratic and political channels. What the peak bodies brought to the table was information on emerging trends in areas of community vulnerability, information that was

18. Hatfield-Dodds interview.
19. Hatfield-Dodds interview.

specific and policy-relevant, accompanied by an ability through member agencies to implement specific programs quickly at a grassroots level. Contracting with government by agencies did not prevent policy advocacy by church-related agencies and may have enhanced it in certain respects. Leadership in church-related agencies chose the conditions under which agencies applied their tactics in the advocacy process. The peak agencies drew on their connection to key stakeholders in the Christian churches and on trust and shared theological understandings of the basis on which their partners in other agencies were acting. This advocacy as community engagement was driven by the agencies as an expression of their Christian witness, rather than acting as an extension of the state. In an era characterized by formal contracts shaped by asymmetry of power, the operation of MCP was based on trust, collegial relationships, and agreement on shared moral priorities shaped by shared articulation of Christian traditions of seeking community well-being and the common good.

Outsider advocacy on behalf of asylum seekers

It's easy to confine our thinking about advocacy to insider advocacy, submitting reports to inquiries, organizing interviews with politicians, doing press releases, organizing public support as the basis for influencing government. The story about advocacy that I have just told fits that mold precisely. This pattern of advocacy both drew on the past while leaning at moments in the boycott towards a future in which there would be an increasing distance between churches and government. Other forms of advocacy carry with them clearer evidence of the shift beyond Christendom that does not assume a close connection with government—rather the reverse. In illustrating what outside advocacy looks like I turn to Love Makes a Way (LMAW) and the subsequent Sanctuary campaign. This was advocacy that didn't have much organizational structure and involved nonviolent and respectful confrontation with government. It was advocacy of a type not often seen and even less reported on in Australia, in its intentional nonviolent discipline and unapologetically explicitly religious, mostly Christian character.

LMAW emerged as a movement of Christians seeking an end to one particular dimension of Australia's inhumane asylum seeker policies, working through the medium of prayer and nonviolent action. It facilitated civil disobedience as a public witness to the injustice of Australia's asylum seeker policies, calling for specific changes to that policy.[20] To challenge Australia's inhumane asylum seeker policies, LMAW was convinced that Christians

20. Love Makes a Way website.

could not rely on anger, hate, or propaganda, but must seek to speak the truth in a spirit of nonviolent love, according to the teachings of Christ. The actions themselves, as well as the outcomes sought, were self-consciously and intentionally grounded directly in the Christian faith, specifically the teaching and practice of Jesus.[21]

The advocacy took the form of a campaign seeking the release of children from offshore detention, and their return to the Australian mainland. This was followed by community generated action, the Sanctuary campaign, to ensure that the children and their parents were not returned to Nauru after medical treatment in Australia. Both LMAW and the Sanctuary campaign represent forms of advocacy that are consistent with the more marginal place of the church in the political structure of Australian society after Christendom. They involved forms of critical Christian engagement with government that have not previously been common in Australia. I acknowledge at the outset of the story my friendship with several of the people who were central to sparking the movement, my participation as a media contact person in an LMAW action in Canberra, and that I participated with my wife in rallies in Canberra in support of the Sanctuary campaign.

The political and policy context

The background to this advocacy action was the Australian government's shift in August 2012 to the use of offshore detention on Manus Island and Nauru to keep asylum seekers who had arrived in Australia by boat from being processed as refugees on the Australian mainland. I have already discussed the contracting process for the provision of offshore humanitarian services undertaken in support of this policy. The following account of the way this policy was implemented demonstrates the obduracy of the government as a background to the choice of a confrontational form of advocacy by LMAW.

The Australian government announced that from that date (August 2012) no asylum seeker arriving by boat in Australia would ever be resettled, as a deterrent to the dangers of boat travel. Since that date successive Australian governments have continued to state that no refugees sent to offshore detention in either Nauru or PNG would ever settle in Australia. Those recognized as refugees could remain in Nauru or PNG on either a temporary or a permanent basis, although integration prospects with regard to employment and citizenship are practically nonexistent in both

---

21. Anslow, "Asylum Seekers and Love Makes a Way," and McKenna, "Easter Made Me Do It!"

countries. Paths to settlement in any other countries for asylum seekers whose claims for refugee status were recognized have proved to be virtually nonexistent. The Australian government has continued to reject an offer from New Zealand to settle a number of refugees there on the grounds that once they are permanent New Zealand residents they may travel to and settle in Australia. A very small number of refugees have been relocated from Nauru to Cambodia under an agreement with Australia, for which the Cambodian Government received $55m, though none have remained there on a permanent basis. The United States has resettled close to a thousand refugees from Nauru and PNG in return for Australia accepting refugees from Central America. A further group of male refugees from Manus Island are being resettled in Canada under its community resettlement provisions, through funds raised by support groups in Australia and Canada. This latter initiative is the result of community action in both Australia and Canada to raise the funds, find sponsors, and do all the necessary paperwork.

Advocacy for children

Having organized the offshore settlement program, the Australian government has been extremely reluctant to allow people located on either Manus Island or Nauru to be brought to Australia for any reason, even emergency medical treatment. People have been flown to Taiwan for treatment to avoid bringing them to Australia. In 2014 there was growing concern amongst Australians, including significant numbers in churches, at the conditions being experienced by refugees in the offshore camps and particularly the situation of children. Information about the treatment of asylum seekers was being shared by whistleblowers from the Salvation Army and then Save the Children, both of which had been working in the offshore humanitarian support program. The Australian government's policy of indefinite offshore detention, and the living conditions inside the Manus Island and Nauru detention centers, had at that time already been condemned by the United Nations High Commissioner for Refugees (UNHCR), Amnesty International, Human Rights Watch, the Australian Medical Association, the Australian Psychological Society, and a wide range of refugee and international law experts in Australia.

There was a blockage on the normal possibilities for political advocacy to bring policy change through engaging with either of the two major political parties. Both parties—the Liberal National Party and the Australian Labor Party—were in lockstep on the policy for handling asylum seekers offshore. Party discipline on this issue was tight. The only political party with representation in the federal parliament that publicly opposed mandatory offshore detention were the Greens, who had strong representation in the Senate but had little policy leverage in the lower house of parliament where they only had one member. They were limited to using their position in the Senate to obtain information through Senate inquiries and question time.

Focusing an advocacy campaign specifically on the situation of refugee children in the way that LMAW did had both a moral and theological underpinning, as well as a pragmatic rationale. The campaign was focused on the situation of children, who because of their extreme vulnerability had a high priority claim in both humanitarian and theological terms for care and support. The pragmatic rationale was that a campaign focused on children would be an easier case to make to the broader Australian community than one addressed at having asylum seekers as a whole released from offshore detention. The other reality was that children brought to Australia for any reason would be accompanied by their families.

Love Makes a Way

LMAW was a spontaneous response by a small group of Christians that generated this advocacy action. The theological influences shaping the LMAW approach were diverse, though the civil rights movement in the United States, particularly the Nashville civil rights movement and its initiator Rev. James Lawson, was a critical influence. LMAW started its public advocacy in March 2014. At that date there were 1,138 children in immigration detention centers, both onshore and offshore. By that stage there were already well-documented reports on the deleterious effects on the health and well-being of children of prolonged and indefinite detention. LMAW intended to create a crisis in the community that would force a confrontation around the human impact of offshore detention. In the background the horror of offshore detention more broadly had been highlighted by the murder of Reza Barati, a twenty-three-year-old Iranian man, on February 18, 2014, inside the Australian detention center on Manus Island. The story of how the campaign began has achieved a semi-legendary status. According to the version of events recorded on the LMAW website, it all started in a pub.

> In a pub in Paddington, Sydney, three friends started gathering together to discuss what they could do about the cruelty being inflicted on people seeking asylum in Australia. Matt, Josh and Justin had no idea that their conversations at the Paddington Arms would develop into an idea that would snowball into Love

Makes a Way. Early on they invited their friend Jody to join them, and together they planned what was intended to be a one-off nonviolent direct action in the office of then-Immigration Minister Scott Morrison. They invited their friends Kate, Dan, Jaxon, Jarrod, Donna and Miriam to join them, and on 21 March 2014 the first Love Makes a Way action took place. The mainstream and social media response was beyond any of the group's expectations. This level of publicity was repeated when a second action happened a few weeks later in Perth, this time with a number of Christian clergy. Before they knew it Christians from all over Australia started to ask how to get involved, and they realised LMAW was more than a one-off thing.[22]

Now meeting with friends in a pub is a quintessentially Australian activity. Nothing could be more natural. That such a meeting would involve planning pray-ins in parliamentary offices does not fit neatly into common images of what people get together in pubs to do. Nor does this narrative sit easily with the normal perceptions of Australian Christians as politically conservative killjoys. So informal was the beginning of the movement that the initiators of the action only decided on the hashtag #lovemakesaway ten minutes before they walked in to commence the pray-in.

On March 21, 2014 the first LMAW action, involving a group of eight Christians, took place. Several of those involved had undertaken training in nonviolent direct action and the event was shaped by an awareness of and deep affinity with the Christian grounding of the civil rights movement in the United States. Five of the people in the sit-in were arrested. Once news of the event spread, requests came from across the country about how to get involved, so the initiators started the LMAW Facebook group. Hundreds liked the Facebook page in the first twenty-four hours. The hundreds then turned into thousands.

The response from both the mainstream and social media was far beyond expectations. A similar level of publicity was generated by a second action weeks later in Perth, this time involving clergy. Christians from all over Australia began asking how they could get involved. LMAW became, as they say, a "thing." It seems to have touched a nerve across the Australian Christian community. Many Australian Christians were frustrated and angered by the suffering of refugees and felt that there was a need for action grounded in their faith commitments. The response came from the grassroots, not through institutional church structures. The movement had a degree of freedom and spontaneity characteristic of the Spirit at work.

22. See the Love Makes a Way website.

ADVOCACY

How did LMAW spread?

LMAW actions spread not as a result of any strategic planning, or top-down institutional direction, but by groups of Christians in local areas responding spontaneously to news of the protests and contacting the initiators to find out how they could get involved. Training was provided by the initiators in the theology and praxis of engagement for interested regional groups who then planned the local action. Jarrod McKenna, Matt Anslow, and Justin Whelan, from among the first participants, began training people in regional locations who were wanting to participate in nonviolent direct action with LMAW.[23] In the brief training sessions they drew heavily on the experience of the Nashville civil rights movement and emphasized the need for a strong commitment to the practices of nonviolence and spiritual discipline by those participating. The preparation involved a community-building approach emphasizing reflection on what people are bringing to the action in terms of skills and experience, and recognition of personal limits of individuals on the extent of their engagement. The workshops affirmed the gifts and accountability of those participating.

News about LMAW spread along networks of friendship and connection through a range of churches, and across normal lines of theological affiliation. In Sydney, for example, leaders in the Anglican Church normally regarded as theologically and socially conservative spoke up on the issue and supported the action, and members of Hillsong, a Pentecostal megachurch, participated. Other lines of connection ran through TEAR Australia, a Christian aid and development agency with significant links to evangelical churches, and the Anabaptist Association of Australia and New Zealand (AAANZ). Justin Whelan, one of the initiators of LMAW, published the following statement online about the advocacy:

> There is overwhelming evidence that detention beyond a limited period is a "factory for mental illness," self-harm and suicide attempts, especially among children. We know this but do it anyway. The deliberate and wilful infliction of mental injury on innocent children for the purpose of deterring others from seeking our protection is bipartisan policy. This is a scandal. More than that: it is evil. And as Gandhi once said, "non-co-operation with evil is as much a duty as co-operation with good." This principle drove us to engage in nonviolent civil disobedience—the purposeful and peaceful act of breaking the law and accepting the consequences in order to arouse the conscience of the nation over this injustice. History has shown that such

23. Bastian, "Love Makes a Way."

actions can be powerful. The US civil rights movement is just one example in which civil disobedience played a key role in sparking a movement to end injustice.

Our group was made up of committed Christians from Catholic, Uniting, Quaker, Churches of Christ and Hillsong churches. Like Scott Morrison, we follow Jesus—someone who himself was a refugee. We try to heed the call to love our neighbours as ourselves, to stand up for the oppressed, and to welcome the stranger. Because of that shared faith, we decided to conduct the sit-in in the form of a prayer vigil. We prayed for Mr. Morrison, we prayed for our nation. Mostly we prayed for asylum seekers locked up in conditions described as "inhumane" and "a violation of the prohibition against torture," with a particular focus on the children who are the most vulnerable victims of this horrible tragedy.[24]

LMAW advocacy

LMAW advocacy took the form of peaceful sit-ins in the electoral offices of parliamentarians. The action normally commenced around the time the electoral office opened in the morning. These offices are usually located in shopping centers or in commercial office space. The people who were participating, usually numbering around six to eight, often though not always including ministers in clerical apparel, would enter the office and request to speak to the member of parliament about the release of children from detention, noting that they did not intend to leave till they had that conversation and a commitment to the children's release. What normally followed was that the office was shut by the staff to any further members of the public and the member of parliament never appeared during the course of the day, though there were a few exceptions to that rule. The people inside the office typically devoted the next few hours to meditation, prayer, and singing hymns.

Those supporting the pray-in outside on the street marked the presence of the sit-in with banners, conducted their own liturgy, and sought to engage passers-by in discussion. They also responded to media inquiries, and occasionally entered into conversation with offices involved in parliamentary security. At closing time, the police would usually be called in. On some occasions people conducting the sit-in were simply evicted from the

24. Whelan, "Why I prayed for Asylum Seekers." Matt Anslow, one of the initiators of LMAW, laid out a theological underpinning of this action in "Prayer as a Weapon."

office. On other occasions people were arrested, and less frequently the arrest was followed by a summons to appear in a magistrates' court. The police clearly found the process of arresting clergy and religious demonstrators disconcerting. Arresting the dean of an Anglican cathedral in a rural city was not something they had ever had to do before. While the treatment by police of people participating in the LMAW events was normally respectful, there was one substantial exception. On December 12, 2014, a female priest and a mother with her infant were among eight people strip-searched and charged with trespass following a peaceful sit-in at the Foreign Minister's electorate office in Perth. Simultaneous sit-ins on December 12 saw fifty-three Christian leaders arrested or forcibly removed from electorate offices of Government MPs across Australia.

During 2014 there were twenty-two nonviolent civil disobedience actions under the auspices of LMAW. The media appeal of the advocacy actions was substantial and assisted in ensuring that the violence being done to people seeking asylum in Australia remained continually in the public eye. These actions included a bipartisan sit-in in May 2014 in the offices of both the then-Prime Minister Tony Abbott and Opposition Leader Bill Shorten. A National Day of Action on December 20, 2014 included seven simultaneous action in six cities. In 2015, a group of forty priests, nuns, Christian leaders, pastors, ministers, and a former Catholic bishop staged a protest in Parliament House, occupying the foyer and singing hymns. The Moderator of the Uniting Church in Australia and a former Uniting Church president took part in these direct actions. In 2016 there were fifty-six vigils conducted in a week around Australia at the offices of MPs and Senators. Some people chained themselves to the Prime Minister's residence, Kirribilli House. In this week of actions 300 risked arrest and 250 people were actually arrested.[25]

Matt Anslow, discussing this form of advocacy noted that "non-violent direct action is about dramatization. It's a way of unearthing the tension that exists but that people want to keep quiet. If you dramatize it people can't ignore the tension."[26] LMAW kept maintaining the tension with the assistance of Christians continuing to emerge to participate in this witness. When the Nauru files that documented the ill treatment of refugees and asylum seekers in offshore detention were leaked, volunteers did ten-hour public readings of the files. Some people chained themselves to Kirribilli House, the Prime Minister's residence overlooking Sydney Harbor.

---

25. Bastian, "Love Makes a Way."
26. Bastian, "Love Makes a Way."

The theological justification for civil disobedience involves an acknowledgment of the state and its responsibilities, while taking peaceful action that acknowledges that there are higher claims than those of the state that may call for a response.[27] As I noted previously, people participating in the sit-ins were not always arrested and where they were arrested charges were often dropped at the discretion of the police. On the few occasions when the police placed the matters before the court the magistrates often dismissed the charges. There was an apparent reluctance by authorities to push enforcement of the letter of the law too hard for fear of generating even more publicity in the media. The willingness to accept arrest by people normally regarded as respectable resulted in a note of unease, a tension manifested in the way police approached enforcement against trespassing, the usual charge against those participating in the sit-ins. The paradox noted by people in the movement was the stark contrast between the treatment of the protestors and that received by asylum seekers in detention.

The theological stance of LMAW was that in all their actions they did not seek to demonize the people responsible for these policies, whether as members of parliament or the people carrying out the detention. The intention of the demonstrators was to invite those they were confronting with the call to a better way, with the promise that they would support them in this. The intention beyond the release of children was to seek to change public attitudes, primarily but not exclusively within the church, to inspire people to take bold actions that witness to God's love for all people. Anglican priest Chris Bedding, who was involved in the LMAW activity in Perth, made the connection between advocacy and the motivation of the group in an opinion piece on the ABC website.

> We didn't start with sit-ins of course. We're far too polite. There have been letters and discreet conversations, petitions and talkfests, research projects, rallies in the streets and sermons. We've fed and clothed and housed asylum seekers that few care about, and we've argued for more foreign aid and better regional partnerships. We've offered our facilities and homes to provide a more humane living environment, and we've harnessed our media machine to advocate for common decency. For more than a decade, since the dehumanizing began, we've been on the case. We actually enjoy this work, that's how daggy we are. Yet political leaders of every stripe have laughed and have not given us so much as an "amen". That was unwise. Because now we're all fired up. Cranky Christians aren't going to burn your office down. We're going to come and sit-in it and pray. And awkwardly sing.

27. Broughton, "What Action should Christians Take?"

And we'll be super polite and thank the staff as the police take us away. Then we'll show up to court in mismatched suits and make friends with the bailiffs. If you fine us, we'll pay on time. And we'll pray like crazy.[28]

From the very beginning those who initiated the LMAW action were conscious that they were outsiders to the political process. They were explicit about how their Christian commitments shaped their advocacy, its goal and its methods, and the language of advocacy that they used. LMAW attracted a good deal of interest from activists outside the churches because of the willingness of Christian leaders to be arrested for advocating for a cause which had no material benefit for the church as an institution.

How successful was this advocacy? Over time most of the children on Nauru were gradually shifted to onshore detention in Australia. LMAW was undoubtedly one of the influences in building community pressure on the government, though the Australian government never admitted that it was responding to public pressure, or that the advocacy was justified. There was also some success in developing support within the church for the plight of asylum seekers. This in turn lead to a "Sanctuary" movement, in which community activity was directed at ensuring that children who had been brought to Australia for medical treatment were not subsequently sent back to Nauru.

Advocacy for "Sanctuary"

By 2016, coincident with LMAW activity over the previous two years, a significant number of children had been brought to mainland Australia for medical treatment. The threat by Australian government agencies to transfer children back to Nauru after medical treatment set off a community movement to provide sanctuary for the children and their families. The movement involved cooperation between churches and secular progressive activist organizations to try to prevent the children from being taken back to offshore detention. The Sanctuary campaign began on February 4, 2016, one day after a High Court decision that ruled there was no legal basis that would prevent the Australian government from returning asylum seekers to Nauru following medical treatment in Australia. In response, over 120 churches from nine denominations around Australia offered refugees and asylum seekers at risk of being transferred to Nauru physical protection from removal by Australian authorities through sanctuary in church

---

28. Bedding, "Cranky Christians Against Asylum Seeker Cruelty."

buildings. The offer included provision of food and other necessities, along with a commitment not to hand over asylum seekers and refugees to the authorities. In the event no refugees or asylum seekers actually sought shelter in an Australian church. The offer though was highly publicized.

The Sanctuary initiative was developed by the Australian Churches Refugee Task Force (ACRTF), an umbrella group for churches concerned about the plight of refugees and asylum seekers. The ACRTF, which had previously undertaken more traditional advocacy submission based activities, issued a press release on February 4, 2016 announcing that the St. John's Anglican Cathedral in Brisbane, among other churches, had been declared a place of sanctuary for asylum seekers.[29] The Anglican Dean of Brisbane and the president of the Task Force argued that "there is irrefutable evidence from health and legal experts that the circumstances asylum seekers, especially children, would face if sent back to Nauru are tantamount to state-sanctioned abuse."[30]

On February 17, the Baptist Association of NSW & ACT, a denominational body neither then, nor later, noted for taking an activist stance on social issues, released a briefing document to Baptist churches in New South Wales and the Australian Capital Territory in support of church sanctuary. Two of Australia's largest Catholic healthcare organizations offered to provide medical support to any of the 267 asylum seekers applying for church sanctuary to avoid their forced removal to Nauru, and encouraged other hospital groups to do the same.[31] The churches involved in the sanctuary campaign worked closely with other civil society groups involved in advocating for asylum seekers, particularly the progressive advocacy organization GetUp!, which had a leading role in the campaign. The movement adopted the slogan "Let Them Stay," a clear message and a straightforward demand that the Australian government not return refugees and asylum seekers who had been transferred to mainland Australia to offshore detention facilities.

An analogous movement to the Australian refugee sanctuary initiative as a form of advocacy can be found in the US in the 1980s, when Christian activists and churches organized support for Salvadorian refugees crossing into the US from Mexico. Their efforts to assist the refugees in applying for asylum ran aground on the fact that the US government regarded them as being on the wrong side of the civil war currently proceeding there. The

---

29. Australian Churches Refugee Taskforce, "Cathedrals and Churches around Australia Offer Sanctuary."

30. Farrell, "Churches Offer Sanctuary to Asylum Seekers."

31. St Vincent's Health Australia, "Medical Support to Asylum Seekers."

group then decided to hide the refugees in homes and churches. The sanctuary movement, as it became known, grew over the next decade to include hundreds of organizations in North America providing assistance to refugees from Central America seeking refuge in the US. Whether there was any awareness of this previous US movement in the minds of the Australian Christians who led this initiative is not clear. The common scriptural and moral frame of reference and language is probably not surprising.

The offer to provide sanctuary in church buildings was a statement of an intention to undertake an act of civil disobedience in defiance of Australian law. This statement of willingness to break the law was made publicly as an act of advocacy intended to influence government policy and lead to a change in that policy, which could be undertaken within the framework of existing legislation, though there is no doubt that the campaigners were also seeking to bring about a change in the legislation. Many church groups who were among those offering sanctuary also engaged in training in nonviolent direct action, workshopping ways of protecting refugees and asylum seekers on church grounds should they become at risk of removal by government officials or police. In the event no asylum seekers sought sanctuary in churches, and no church members of groups actually broke the law. The offer of sanctuary with its implied civil disobedience, though this was not the emphasis of the campaign, attracted media attention and aroused wider public sympathy for the plight of refugees and asylum seekers than had been the case up till then.[32]

The combination of the advocacy campaign by church groups in concert with the wider refugee rights movement were effective in halting the transfer of the majority of affected asylum seeker children and their families back to offshore detention. Over time more than half of the refugees and asylum seekers at the center of the protests were released into community detention in Australia, including all the families and children. Eventually all the children on Nauru were returned to Australia. It is hard to disentangle the relative importance of the various elements of the advocacy, but the involvement of the churches was a significant element as the coordinator of the #letthemstay campaign for Get Up! acknowledged. The campaign certainly galvanized a strong response from the Australian public well beyond the membership of the churches who had initiated the activity. Thousands of Australians participated in protests across the country in support of the refugees and asylum seekers. Professional associations and unions joined in the campaign. The Victorian Premier Daniel Andrews offered to provide a haven in the state of Victoria to refugees and asylum seekers at risk of

---

32. Calligeros, "Anglican and Uniting churches offer sanctuary to asylum seekers."

transfer to Nauru in Victoria. He was joined in this by a number of other state premiers.[33]

The Australian government never conceded that it was responding to public advocacy campaigns. However, in 2020 the Cabinet Minister responsible for this policy area proudly announced that there were no children in offshore detention. The fact that the government made this announcement several years after the advocacy effort is testimony to the actual as opposed to the acknowledged impact of the advocacy.

Advocacy after Christendom

In the liberal form of the nation-state the predominant model of relationship offered to the church and church-related agencies is that of partnership, where they serve the nation-state by sustaining its rule as a source of values, and as a contributor to maintenance of social order. The church in this model distinguishes itself from the state, as an individual consumer choice for citizens interested in "religion" as a private activity. Against this it might be helpful to adopt a way of thinking that does not rely on the spatial carving up of society into differing spheres of influence, but rather thinks about the church and Christian action as a vector that complicates matters though advocacy.[34]

These episodes provide insights into alternative forms of advocacy on our way out of Christendom. What was demonstrated in both forms of advocacy reported on in this chapter was the possibility of creating a more complex public space that may bring with it conflict with government policy. In both the boycott of a government contract and the LMAW and Sanctuary demonstrations, there was publicly enacted conflict and discomfort for the government and promotion of informed conversation directed at the common good. In both cases advocacy was driven by community engagement that envisaged rather different possible public outcomes from those that were on offer from the government. Making public space more complex involves intentional intervention by agencies that do not let themselves be contained by either the state or the market, whose activity is informed by a normative moral and social vision. The critique of government policy, implying a limit on the claims of the state, came through interventions grounded in Christian theological traditions and the creation of a social movement. In an era focusing on legal specification and formal contracts both forms of advocacy were not based on any formal organization. The activities operated on trust,

33. Dastyari, "Let the Asylum Seekers Stay," 341.
34. Cavanaugh, *Migrations of the Holy*, 46–68.

Advocacy

on relationships, and on a shared moral vision that found an expression in a trust in the spontaneity of the Spirit in response to the discerned needs of the moment rather the formal demands of a contract and legal obligation.

10

Practicing Hospitality Toward Refugees and Asylum Seekers

In the light of tension between churches and governments in quite a number of countries in recent years, practicing hospitality towards refugees and asylum seekers by churches and church-related agencies may be a quintessentially post-Christendom form of community engagement. Certainly the issue of how we treat refugees and asylum seekers brings to the surface a conflict between the moral commitments of the churches and the policy direction of governments in the US, the UK, and Australia in recent years.

My account in the previous chapter of the advocacy of Love Makes a Way (LMAW) highlighted the opposition of significant elements of the Christian churches to the Australian government's policy towards asylum seekers and refugees, an opposition that was expressed in scriptural language and underpinned by strong theological claims. The efforts of LMAW to advocate on behalf of refugees and asylum seekers was not cost-free to those involved in praying in the offices. They ran the risk of arrest, conviction, and a court record. In this chapter I provide an account of how two church-related agencies, Jesuit Refugee Services Australia (JRSA) and Baptcare, have put their money where their mouth is in providing hospitality for refugees and asylum seekers without government funding, but with the financial support of their church communities. I begin with an account of some theological underpinnings of hospitality. I then provide further details about Australian government policy towards refugees, and how that policy has shaped the church-related agencies' hospitality.

Practicing Hospitality

Fear of the stranger

The context for my theological discussion of hospitality can be best appreciated by lingering for a moment with the theme "fear of the stranger." Recent government policy dealing with refugees and asylum seekers in nations such as the UK, the US, and Australia has been underpinned by a rhetorical strategy of creating fear of the outsider, the stranger, the one who is different, whether that difference is of skin color, ethnicity, or religion. The obsession of Donald Trump during his presidency with building a wall on the Mexican border was justified as necessary to prevent the "hordes" from Central America invading the US. As this example illustrates, the evocation of fear of the stranger by governments is accompanied by the promise, implicitly if not explicitly, to protect the nation's borders, with us as their supposedly vulnerable and fearful citizens against the unspecified but undoubtedly terrible threats to our life and welfare that the strangers pose. Governments having evoked the fear then promise to do "whatever it takes" to "protect" us. This approach is analogous with the modus operandi of the mafia, which creates the fear through raising the threat, and then offering to relieve you of the threat—for a price. The difference is that in this case the price of the promised security will be paid by the vulnerable stranger, the refugee, the asylum seeker, though the taxpayer will also have to stump up the funds for the wall or the detention centers.

Even those of us who intellectually reject this weaponized fear of the stranger can become paralyzed by the political and social environment that it creates. Consider our response to the heartrending photos or video clips of refugees being turned back at border crossings, rescued from overturned boats, or even left to drown. While many of us may glance at these pictures, we may also not look for too long, lest we register too deeply the reality of our shared humanity in refugees' vulnerability and the helpless grief that is evoked within us by the suffering we are witnessing. We don't want to think too long about their likely fate, being detained in camps for perhaps decades with little or no prospect of safe settlement or a secure future for them, or even more poignantly for their children. Those that make it to nations such as Australia or the UK, outside of the trickle sponsored through the UNHCR humanitarian program, will end up struggling to survive on the margins of a society in which they have few rights, uncertain legal status, and little hope for a stable and dignified future. Sometimes however, in the gaze of recognition we register our shared humanity and this generates gestures of hospitality. It is those gestures of hospitality, mediated through church-related agencies, and their motivation, that I will explore in the course of this chapter.

Scriptural accounts of hospitality

Stories from the First Testament (Old Testament) provide the starting point for my theological sketch of the practice of hospitality. The story of Abraham, Sarah, and their three guests, in Genesis 18, is one of the most significant of these stories and is referenced in Hebrews 13:2 with its reminder of the possibility of entertaining angels, or messengers, unawares. This story has a richness and depth that invites substantial reflection, but even a brief reading offers a substantial account of hospitality in which God becomes present in the everyday, in a shared meal, in a moment which delivers a promise for the future. In contrast, there is in the following chapter, Genesis 19, the story of Lot and his visitors, with the appalling demands that are made by the people of Sodom. This story is a salutary reminder of the dangers of offering hospitality to strangers when it cuts across the grain of the expectations of the surrounding community, and where fear and violence drive a community response. Beyond these stories, the First Testament (Old Testament) points us in a direction of widening, not narrowing, the scope of who is to be included within the exercise of our hospitality. Take Deuteronomy 10:19, for example, which suggests in a reference to strangers who were enemies: "you shall also love the stranger, for you were strangers in the land of Egypt." Leviticus 19:34 similarly points to a widening of the range of hospitality beyond the immediacy of family and tribe: "the alien who resides with you shall be to you as the citizen among you; you shall love the alien as yourself, for you were aliens in the land of Egypt: I am the Lord your God."

Concern with hospitality does not disappear when we move to the Second Testament (New Testament). Jesus picks up the theme from the story of Abraham and instructs us that strangers may be God's special envoys to bless or challenge us, a theme that resonates through the Gospels.[1] In various accounts of the ministry of Jesus we are reminded constantly that while he was dependent on hospitality, not least of women for much of his ministry, on occasion he also served as a gracious host. In the course of receiving this hospitality Jesus frequently urged his hosts in parables and general conversation to open their banquets and dinner tables to give priority to the poor and the sick.

The teaching on hospitality in the Gospels is explicit, indeed memorably so. In Matthew 25:31–46 we learn that in providing care and hospitality to the least of these who are members of Jesus' family we are doing it unto Jesus. Though this particular teaching was an injunction to his followers to

---

1. Koenig, *New Testament Hospitality*, 3–4.

provide hospitality to members of the community of disciples, Christians have taken this call to hospitality and applied it much more widely, to bring within its scope those outside our immediate community. In widening the scope of hospitality we find an echo in the injunction of Romans 12:13 to "extend hospitality to strangers." Here again we have an extension of hospitality from the immediate community, the church, to those who are outside.

This drive to extend the scope of our hospitality recurs throughout the Gospels. In Luke 10:25–37, in the parable of the Good Samaritan, Jesus shakes up our imaginative limits about who our neighbor is, to the point of including our ethnic or religious enemy.[2] Or consider Luke 14:12–14: "He said also to the one who had invited him, 'When you give a luncheon or a dinner, do not invite your friends or your brothers or your relatives or rich neighbors, in case they may invite you in return, and you would be repaid. But when you give a banquet, invite the poor, the crippled, the lame, and the blind. And you will be blessed, because they cannot repay you, for you will be repaid at the resurrection of the righteous.'"

With this imperative echoing throughout the Gospels, it is not surprising that the Christian practice of hospitality from its beginning included in its scope the poor and the neediest. This commitment led to the development by churches of a range of hostels, hospices, and hospitals that have survived, and have become part of our wider culture. The origins of these institutions in the Christian churches are not widely recognized, or even remembered, in contemporary society. Their original ethos may now be under threat, becoming more powerfully shaped by technology and the disciplines associated with medicine than by the original theological commitments. Nevertheless, the contribution of the Christian practice of hospitality remains as part of our heritage after Christendom.

The practice of hospitality

Though hospitality in the scriptural stories and injunctions that I have just referenced can appear at first glance to be nonreciprocal in its character, on a closer examination the giving is not just one way. The guest in receiving the hospitality will enter into a relationship that may be transformational for the giver as well as receiver. We can therefore speak of hospitality as being political in that it offers the possibility of conceptualizing and enacting a common life with the "other," with those who are at some level strangers to us or outside of our circle of friendship, at the point at which hospitality

---

2. Marshall in *Compassionate Justice* devotes several chapters to discussing the parable of the Good Samaritan and its significance for public policy.

is exercised.³ Hospitality when we practice it toward the stranger implicitly aims at forging a common world of meaning and action, between the one exercising hospitality and the receiver, while recognizing a continuing difference on each side. Strangers, while presenting us with an opportunity to show our love for God through the exercise of welcome, offer us the possibility of the gift of their presence and the development of a committed relationship between guest and host. Hospitality is a gift of oneself in which we demonstrate that we are someone who can participate in reciprocal relations over time and acknowledge that we are not self-sufficient but need others.

Alasdair MacIntyre helpfully reminds us of another dimension of exercising hospitality to strangers that is particularly relevant when the stranger comes to us in the character of a refugee. Hospitality, he argues, is grounded in the capacity for expressing grief or sorrow over someone's distress that we can potentially understand as our own. The stranger is then included in a communal relationship that extends the bonds and the boundaries of our obligations, characterized by a just generosity.⁴ "Hospitality means letting the stranger remain a stranger while offering acceptance, nonetheless. It means honoring the fact that strangers already have a relationship—rooted in our common humanity—without having to build one on intimate interpersonal knowledge. . . . It means meeting the stranger's needs while allowing him or her simply to be, without attempting to make the stranger over into a modified version of ourselves."⁵ Emotional identification and respectful distance in the practice of hospitality need to be held in tension. Hospitality involves recognition of the stranger by providing an appropriate response to their needs, while at the same time honoring both their shared humanity and the reality of their strangeness to us. This balancing is difficult to achieve when the stranger, in the form of an asylum seeker, presents themselves to those seeking to exercise hospitality respectfully, but in a situation of extreme vulnerability and need.

Refugees and asylum seekers

Before moving on to the policy framework within which churches and their agencies have found themselves offering hospitality to refugees and asylum seekers in Australia, I need to address an issue of terminology. The terms

---

3. Bretherton, *Christ and the Common Life*, 272–79.
4. See Bretherton, *Christ and the Common Life*, 274–75.
5. Palmer, *A Company of Strangers*, 68.

"refugee" and "asylum seeker" are often used interchangeably in casual conversation.

When we come to consider public policy, we need to exercise care in our use of the terms. For the purposes of my discussion in this chapter, where we are dealing with Australian government policy the distinction between the two categories is critical. The term "refugee" refers to people who are forced to leave their homes for many reasons, including conflict and violence. The UN Refugee Convention defines a refugee as: "Any person who owing to a well-founded fear of being persecuted for reasons of race, religion, nationality, membership of a particular social group or political opinion, is outside the country of his/her nationality and is unable, or owing to such fear, is unwilling to avail himself/herself of the protection of that country."[6]

The critical question is whether the claim for protection as a refugee has been accepted by the country in which the claim has been made. Asylum seekers are refugees who have formally sought protection, but whose claim for refugee status has not been finally determined. It therefore includes people whose claim for protection may have had an initial unfavorable assessment but are seeking either an administrative review of that claim or appealing to the courts on the assessment of the claim. A refugee is someone whose claim for protection has been recognized and the asylum seeker is someone whose claim has not yet been settled. Where I refer to both those who have and those who haven't had their claim for protection recognized, I will refer to "refugees and asylum seekers."

Australian government policy on refugees and asylum seekers

Refugee policy has been a deeply contested policy space in Australian politics over the past two decades. The contestation has been between the Liberal National Party (LNP) in power at the national level on the one hand and a motley coalition of advocacy groups, churches, professional organizations, and the Australian Greens political party on the other. Since setting up offshore processing in 2012, supposedly as short-term response, the Labor Party has refused to engage in public debate, let alone advocacy, over the treatment of asylum seekers and refugees, for fear of being attacked by the LNP as being "weak" on protecting the Australian borders and by inference being willing to see harm caused to the Australian community. Within the national parliament only the Greens and some independents

6. Refugee Council of Australia, "Who is a Refugee?"

have consistently challenged government policy. With the ALP in opposition, but largely missing in action on the issue, the Australian government has been able to deliver a harsh and punitive policy on refugees and asylum seekers with little reason to change course. It has responded to criticism with large dollops of fear, abuse of the critics, and maximum quantities of secrecy lubricated with exorbitant amounts of budget expenditure.

The central plank of the current Australian government policy on asylum seekers has been that from August 13, 2012, any person arriving in Australia by sea without a valid visa has been liable to removal to Manus Island (a province of Papua New Guinea) or offshore to the island of Nauru, for processing, even if they applied for asylum immediately upon arrival in Australia. They would not be able to settle in Australia, even if their claim for asylum was recognized. Not all of the asylum seekers who arrived by boat during 2013 to 2014 were actually sent offshore. Opprobrium was heaped on refugees and asylum seekers by the government as being terrible people who had "jumped" a nonexistent "refugee queue." The Australian government has consistently referred to asylum seekers arriving without a valid visa as "illegal maritime arrivals." However, even if they are found to have a valid claim for protection as a refugee, as most do, they cannot apply for permanent protection in Australia. They can only apply for a three-year Temporary Protection Visa (TPV) or a five-year Safe-Haven Enterprise Visa (SHEV). The latter is a visa that offers an exceedingly uncertain path towards a longer-term visa with the possibility of eventually receiving permanent residence in Australia. While these visa holders are permitted to work and study in Australia, they must continue to reapply every time the visa lapses. They have no long-term certainty about their future. Before the pandemic shutdown of international travel, a continuing flow of people arriving in Australia by air with a legal visa were able to make a claim for protection. With the government downgrading the public service capacity to manage processing of claims, everyone has had to wait increasing periods for their applications to be processed, and decisions made on their claim for protection or renewal of visas.

"Cruel and inhumane": onshore immigration detention in Australia

To understand fully the horror of Australian government policy on refugees, against which church-related agencies have become engaged in providing hospitality, we need to not only take account of offshore processing of refugees, but also the onshore detention of asylum seekers in Australia. While years of campaigning have made the plight of asylum seekers stranded in offshore detention on Manus Island and Nauru visible to the Australian community, and reduced the numbers held there, the cruel and inhumane character of the Australian mandatory onshore immigration detention system is much less well known and has becoming increasingly hidden from view. As of May 31, 2019 there were 1,270 people in onshore immigration detention. The average period of time these people had been held in detention by the end of 2020 had reached 503 days. Detention centers have taken on over the past decade an increasing resemblance to prisons in their style of operation, management, and the treatment of those held in detention.

Mandatory detention of refugees was introduced by the Labor government in 1992, with the length of detention capped at 273 days. In 1994 the government removed the time limit on detention of refugees.[7] Provided a person is detained for a lawful purpose, there is now no time limit on detention, and a person could be detained there for the term of their natural life. The High Court of Australia has found that mandatory indefinite detention is not unconstitutional—this despite the fact that it could be in breach of Australia's international human rights obligations. Provisions of human rights treaties even when Australia has ratified them are not directly enforceable in Australia, unless they have been incorporated into domestic law. Australia has no human rights legislation at a national level or constitutional provision for human rights. The High Court has found that the detention of noncitizens for purposes specified under the Migration Act, that is, to remove them from Australia, to determine their visa application, or to determine whether to allow them to make a valid visa application, must be pursued and carried into effect as soon as "reasonably practical" if the detention is to be lawful. This limitation in practice has proved to be of little effect in restricting the time people are kept in detention by the Australian government. Convicted criminals have more rights under Australian law than asylum seekers. The imprisonment of criminals is undertaken under a transparent judicial process, which takes account of individual circumstances in sentencing, issues a defined sentence, and has a process for appeal. Even though people seeking asylum have committed no crime, they may be subject to mandatory and potentially indefinite detention. Australia's onshore mandatory detention system is cruel and inhumane. It is killing people, spiritually as well as physically.

Accompanying these draconian legal provisions unrestrained by any effective legal supervision are the substantial discretionary powers of the Minister for Immigration, referred to as the "God" powers, that can

7. Manne, "Australia's Uniquely Harsh Asylum Seeker Policy."

determine whether or not detainees will be released into the community while their claims are assessed.[8] The exercise of ministerial power is not transparent and has a highly arbitrary character to it. The death of Abdul Aziz, a twenty-three-year-old Afghani asylum seeker, provides a brief glimpse into this horror. Abdul, who had arrived in Australia as an unaccompanied minor in 2013, died suddenly late on a Friday night in July 2019, at the detention facility where he was being held. People living in the same unit were in shock after watching staff from the contractor who manages the center, and then medical staff, attempt and fail to resuscitate him. Another asylum seeker collapsed watching the attempt to revive Abdul and was hospitalized the same night. On the following Sunday, another Afghani man in the detention center attempted self-immolation and was saved from hurting himself more seriously by his roommate. The man who had collapsed on Friday night was rehospitalized after another collapse.[9]

The coroner's office was the first Australian official to make contact with Aziz's family. It was five days after Abdul died before someone from the Australian government called to offer condolences. Abdul's family asked the coroner not to do an autopsy. They just wanted him back as "the Australian government killed him [and] we don't need any tests." The findings of the Australian Human Rights Commission (AHRC) report in 2017 into onshore detention was that the operation of the system was unlike similar operations any other liberal democracy, with regard to the length of time for which people were held. "Australia's system of mandatory immigration detention—combined with ministerial guidelines that preclude the consideration of community alternatives to detention for certain groups—continues to result in people being detained when there is no valid justification for their ongoing detention under international law."[10]

Hospitality to asylum seekers in detention

Against that background it should not be surprising that exercising hospitality towards those in onshore detention facilities is not only difficult but has been made more so in recent years. The Australian government has gradually turned onshore detention of refugees and asylum seekers into a form of punitive incarceration. Exercising hospitality to those in detention is increasingly hard to do. Those who are the recipients of these gestures of human contact are mostly not in a position to give voice to their experience.

8. McAdam and Chong, *Refugee Rights and Policy Wrongs*, 94–113.
9. Holt, "A Final Goodbye to Abdul."
10. Davidson, "Australia's Onshore Immigration Detention."

Practicing Hospitality

Those doing the visiting have reasons not to tell us much of the story because of the risks to their ability to continue visiting and the need to maintain the privacy and safety of those they are visiting. The management of the detention centers is making it more and more difficult for visitors to be present with asylum seekers as fellow human beings and to assure the detainees that they are valued and not completely forgotten. Despite all this, visitors shine a ray of light on a system that is getting progressively darker in its increasingly hostile response to any display of the virtue of compassion as an expression of hospitality. The exercise of hospitality in these circumstances is limited but all the more significant when seen against the background of systematic government cruelty.

Visitation as a form of hospitality has been undertaken by the Jesuit Refugee Service Australia (JRSA), which has been involved with sisters from two Catholic religious orders in visitation to detention centers over recent decades. The Jesuit Refugee Service is an international Catholic organization founded in 1980 as a work of the Society of Jesus (the Jesuits), inspired by the compassion and love of Jesus for the poor and excluded. JRSA is the Australian arm of this international body with a mission of accompanying, serving, and advocating for refugees and people seeking asylum and other forcibly displaced people within Australia. I'll say more about the wider work of hospitality of this organization a bit later in this chapter. For the moment I will focus on their work in visiting asylum seekers and refugees held in detention within Australia.

The JRSA Immigration Detention Centers program involves providing pastoral care in detention centers, care shaped by an ethos of accompaniment. JRSA accompanies asylum seekers as a way of confirming that they have not been forgotten and that they are welcomed and affirmed as fellow human beings, despite being held behind electric fences in facilities that are often and increasingly deliberately located in remote parts of Australia. The JRSA staff and volunteers along with visitors from partner organizations, the Catholic religious orders, the Sisters of Mercy and the Sisters of Charity, regularly visit centers on the Australian mainland. The visitors provide assistance by meeting some of the refugees' basic practical needs, taking them on excursions when permitted, conducting weekly religious services, ensuring that their psychosocial needs are being met, and most importantly, making themselves available should asylum seekers simply need to talk.

Many visitors have been exercising this form of hospitality and presence with JRSA over several years. They listen to the detainees and their presence helps to assure people that they are important, and that there are people who care for them. This exercise of hospitality has taken a number of forms over the journey. One visiting group takes musical instruments into detention, enabling people to share songs or learn how to play. Another group has banded together to visit regularly and purchases items such as warm jumpers for all those who need them. They all share in common a spirit of volunteerism and a commitment to fostering a welcoming and inclusive community. They see people in detention as human beings, not "noncitizens," "prisoners," or "unlawful arrivals." As one visitor described it, they do "little things for lots of people."[11]

In reporting on this visitation, I have drawn on a report based on a survey of visitors to detention that, without identifying the visitors, gives some sense of the nature of hospitality that they have been offering. In 2019 Jesuit Social Services spoke confidentially to regular volunteer visitors to immigration detention facilities across Australia about what was happening to the visitation program. The CEO of that agency, Julie Edwards, who prepared a report based on the interviews, noted that the institutional environment in detention centers is one in which the rules and regulations applicable to visiting people in detention are often opaque, constantly changing, and overly restrictive. The world of the detention center is one that shares much in common with Kafka's novels, in which power is exercised in an arbitrary and dehumanizing way, against visitors as much as it is against detainees. Many avenues of the exercise of hospitality by visitors have been systematically shut down over recent years.

> In the past, many visitors would bring homemade or specially sourced food to share with people in detention. This was important on several levels, including that culturally appropriate food "helped people overcome the feeling of homesickness and added more diversity to the limited food options available in detention." It was also a gesture of sharing and generosity on the part of visitors and helped as a bonding experience. At present, however, any food brought for people in detention must be sealed and packed, with a visible expiry date. This means items such as fruit and homemade foods are effectively prohibited. People detained are also not permitted to take food out of the visitor's area—meaning any food brought in must be consumed during the visit. "I used to make a point of cooking food from the [person's] homeland," a detention visitor said. "But now I can't."[12]

Two further anecdotes from the report capture the abusive antihuman character, not only of the rules and regulations limiting the possibilities to

11. Jesuit Social Services, "The Harsh Reality," 2.
12. Jesuit Social Services, "The Harsh Reality," 2.

exercise hospitality towards asylum seekers, but their actual administration. Each of these anecdotes is shocking in the way it reveal the abuse built into both the rules and their administration.

"In Melbourne, items including blank sheets of paper, Christmas cards and a walking stick belonging to a visitor were denied. One visitor told us that they were made to individually unwrap Ferrero Rocher chocolates before taking them inside. Another explained: 'One guy requested a watch. He was given permission to get it. He got the watch—then other guards came and took it away from him.'"[13] The second story is even more heartbreaking. Even an attempt to provide an English language book to help a young man in detention advance his language skills was ultimately rebuffed. "He was not allowed to take it back to his living area as it had to go through the correct process," recalls his visitor. "I told the young man to get the form and get it filled in. Next week he explained he couldn't fill in the form and they wouldn't help him. I asked for a copy of the form so I could help him [but] this was not allowed. After about six weeks he gave up and said, 'I don't want to learn.'"[14]

In the face of this bureaucratic obstruction and Kafkaesque implementation of detention, efforts by visitors to exercise hospitality would seem in human terms to be quixotic. Yet on a reading of the call to hospitality in Scripture they are totally appropriate. There is after all nothing in the Scripture that qualifies the call to provide hospitality by the need for us to make an assessment about its likely success or effectiveness. However, there have been times previously when the activity has had an impact in modifying policy in a less inhumane direction.

The history of participation in visitation in the early 2000s is revealing. This visitation over a long period underpinned advocacy by JRSA that led to the Australian government's decision in October 2010 to release unaccompanied minors into the community as an alternative to detention. JRSA lobbied for and then piloted a residential program in the community to support this group of detainees on their release. Following the success of the pilot program it was expanded by the government. The Jesuit Social Services' Community Detention Program was delivered in partnership with Red Cross, MacKillop Family Services, and Catholic Care. The program provided "accommodation and case management support to people placed in community detention while their immigration status is being determined. Support is provided to young people (under 18) and vulnerable adults and families in need of a safe and caring living environment. The aim is to enable

---

13. Edwards, "Visitors to Australia's Onshore Detention Centres."
14. Edwards, "Visitors to Australia's Onshore Detention Centres."

people to improve their physical and mental health, reduce isolation and provide people with a safe and supportive environment to live in while they await an outcome on their visa status. Where possible we aim to assist people to transition into independent community life."[15]

This advocacy was an important factor that led to the release of a large number of asylum seekers into the wider community. Around 30,000 asylum seekers who arrived in Australia by boat between August 13, 2012 and January 1, 2014 were not removed to Manus Island and Nauru. While the situation of these people when they were released into the community was an improvement on their life in detention, the improvement was only relative. People in this group were barred by the government from making an application for protection for up to four years after arriving in Australia and most were prevented from working, studying, or volunteering. They received financial support at that stage that was less than the totally inadequate unemployment benefit. Since 2015, they have been allowed to make application for protections as their asylum claims are being assessed through a so-called "fast-track process" that has very limited procedural safeguards, certainly less than in the process that is still available to those who arrive with valid visas. Even if their claim as a refugee entitled to protection is accepted, they will only receive a SHEV or a TPV visa. They have to apply for renewal of these visas every three years with no certainty that they will be granted. If anything goes wrong during their application, say they are late lodging it, they may become a nonperson so far as the government is concerned.

Asylum seekers in the community

Asylum seekers and refugees who are resident in the community in Australia, while better off than those in either offshore or onshore detention, face substantial hurdles to even "getting by," let alone living a dignified human life. Asylum seekers face the reality of both economic insecurity and uncertainty about whether and when their claim for protection will be accepted, and whether even with recognition of the claim there will be a pathway towards a secure future in Australia, or anywhere else for that matter. The government's recent policy of withdrawing even minimal financial benefits from asylum seekers and refugees is designed to drive them into returning home given the lack of opportunities for resettlement in a third country. Most of them have strong fears about returning to their homeland and continue to struggle on in a situation of economic and social insecurity.

15. Jesuit Refugee Services Australia, "Settlement and Community Building."

Practicing Hospitality

Even those people who arrive in Australia on a valid visa and claim protection are faced with an increasing level of insecurity. They are now waiting for up to four years to have their claim for protection heard and assessed. If unsuccessful in their claim at the first instance they face a further period of waiting of up to two years to have an appeal heard by the Administrative Appeals Tribunal (AAT), with similar delays before they receive a hearing in the courts if they choose to seek judicial review of the AAT decision. If they succeed in the courts, they are likely to be referred back to the AAT for rehearing of their claim with further long subsequent delays. In this situation it can be difficult for such families to do more than tread water, at the best gaining access to low paid, casual work to pay the bills. They will generally have the right to work but have no access to Australian government financial support such as unemployment benefits or child allowances.

Support by the Australian government for people seeking asylum previously was provided through the Status Review Support Services (SRSS) program. The program provided a basic living allowance, casework support, and access to torture and trauma counseling. The level of financial support was limited, just below that available to those on unemployment payment. From 2018 the Australian government began moving asylum seekers off SRSS. Any new applicants for protection, those arriving in Australia on valid visas, faced highly restrictive eligibility criteria to access SRSS. People currently on this payment were "exited" from it if they were deemed "job ready." Pregnant women, families with young children, and survivors of torture who did not meet the heightened vulnerability criteria to continue receiving the SRSS payment were placed at risk of not having any form of income to pay rent, pay for prescriptions, or even get enough food for each day. This policy is effectively, if not explicitly, designed to discourage asylum seekers from staying in Australia long enough to have their claims for protection assessed.[16] Asylum seekers waiting to have their claims for protection assessed can have difficulty finding work because of their lack of permanent resident status. Those who have found employment are usually working in casual, low paid jobs, typically in construction, cleaning, hospitality, aged care, and childcare. Advocacy by community support groups has helped in some cases to make the pathway to employment a bit easier.

With the arrival of the COVID-19 pandemic, income support for unemployed Australians was doubled for a six-month period. Asylum seekers remained ineligible for any unemployment payment, let alone the supplementary payment if they lost their jobs. They remained without access to any form of Australian government income support. Some of the

16. Refugee Council of Australia, "How Cuts to Support."

states and territories stepped in and made emergency funding available for agencies supporting asylum seekers who had lost employment or were on reduced hours of work. This was the case even though none of the asylum seekers could have left Australia even if they wanted to because of the shutdown of international air travel. The Australian government policy towards asylum seekers has essentially been "You are not welcome, go away. We won't assist you in any way whatever." This view has not been shared by many in the Australian community, including many congregations and church-related agencies. Their response has been to do what they could to exercise hospitality to these strangers in the face of deliberate government neglect. The extent of this informal hospitality is hard to determine. In my role as president of a community nonprofit support organization in Canberra I am aware of congregations, some of whom are struggling financially, that have given generously and consistently to support our organization. I am also aware of many individual Christians who have opened up their homes to asylum seekers.

Community hospitality

In addition to the visitation of people in detention that I discussed earlier, the release of large numbers of asylum seekers into the community JRSA has extended its hospitality to accompanying people where they are. JRSA offers dignity and hope through a range of practical support in the western suburbs of Sydney. The withdrawal of government support that I discussed above has shaped the JRSA expressions of hospitality. These activities now include providing emergency assistance, temporary shelter, a food bank, professional casework, community activities, assistance in job seeking, legal advice, and a project to empower women seeking asylum. To give you an idea of the scale of their activities, JRSA during 2019 helped some 3,700 people.

An ethos of hospitality does not have a fixed agenda, as is the case in a contracted government program where an agency is constrained as to how it can respond and what it is allowed to do for people who walk through the door. Increased pressure on emergency services, such as facilitating access to food and finance to meet the immediate needs of asylum seekers, was the result of them being dropped off the SRSS and left to find work for themselves. The slow compounding of the experience of uncertainty, rejection, and destitution leading to a loss of hope and the accompanying deterioration of peoples' physical and mental health has continued as a result of the combination of government policy and the increasing delays in the assessment of applications.

Originally asylum seekers were released into the community on a payment less than the unemployment allowance, itself totally inadequate to support a family. During this period, they were not allowed to work, study, or volunteer with charitable bodies. Only in the last three years has this group of asylum seekers been allowed to seek employment. Many families who picked up the limited opportunities that were available and managed to take care of themselves displayed substantial resilience despite the uncertainty that they had been living with. While the local economy was reasonably strong and there was a ready availability of low paid, low skilled casual work many people continued to support themselves to the extent that it was possible. For many families there was a profound shame in seeking assistance and it was only requested and reluctantly accepted when people had reached an extremity of need.

In the face of this reality, developing a community of welcome and belonging remained a key priority for JRSA. In creating community JRSA has provided many opportunities for people seeking asylum. Refugees exercise leadership roles and display skills and talents through a wide variety of programs including Cooking Together, Play with English, the Community Garden, the Homework Club, the Men's Group, and many holidays, festivals, and social events.[17] With the assistance of a grant from the City of Parramatta Council, JRSA also established a Community Garden that provides a welcoming space. The grant enabled JRSA to employ a gardener to help coordinate and maintain the garden, as well as to pass on skills and draw upon the strengths and knowledge of asylum seekers and the community in helping in the garden each week. Besides providing an opportunity to exercise skills and become involved in growing food and fruit, the garden also performs an important social function by providing a place in which people can experience peace and quiet and has been used for picnics and social functions. Fruit, vegetables, and herbs grown in the garden are used by community cooks and given out to asylum seekers through the JRSA Foodbank program.[18]

Making women welcome has been an ongoing priority issue for JRSA. Their Women's Space in Parramatta, Western Sydney, ran a Finding Safety program with primary prevention activities, workshops, self-advocacy, and key referrals for refugee and asylum-seeking women survivors or those at risk of sexual and gender-based violence. The key objectives of this space

17. Jesuit Refugee Services Australia, *Annual Report 2019*, 9.
18. Jesuit Refugee Services Australia, *Annual Report 2019*, 10.

are to build social networks, provide psychosocial support, help build leadership skills, and facilitate self-empowerment, as well as providing safe, person-centered and non-stigmatizing wraparound services. In 2019, JRSA held many events with various speakers on women's rights and domestic/family violence education, as well as workshops on issues such as work and housing rights. A monthly Peer Support Group fostered support amongst the participating women. In partnership with the Refugee Advice and Casework Service, JRS also established an at-risk women legal clinic in Parramatta, bridging the gap between the domestic violence and refugee/asylum seeker sector while highlighting the issues and the needs of women and girls seeking asylum.[19] Funding has come about equally from local government, church and philanthropic grants, and individual donations.

JRSA on a budget of just over a $1 million per annum has been able to engage public support through donations along with building partnerships with business and community nonprofit organizations as well as engaging local government. While operating with a definite commitment based on Catholic Social Teaching shaped by the Jesuit tradition, it has been able to build its coalition of support from people with strong humanitarian commitments based on a wide variety of religious and secular traditions. The ability of the agency to continue to attract this support despite the damage to the churches from their failures with respect to sexual abuse is based I suspect on its strong record over decades in advocating for and supporting refugees and asylum seekers. In both cases the public response has been based on the record of what agencies have actually done for good or ill. In a pluralist post-Christendom context, partnership building in community engagement is going to critically depend on the public record of an agency rather than on an established location and connection to government. In this case clear distance and indeed opposition to government policy and harnessing resources from the community has been essential.

Baptcare and the Sanctuary project

Another sustained exercise in providing hospitality to asylum seekers is the Sanctuary project established by Baptcare in Melbourne. Baptcare is a community care organization owned by the Baptist Union of Victoria (BUV) that provides a comprehensive range of social welfare and human services across Victoria and Tasmania. The agency has an annual turnover of over $270 million with a significant involvement in aged care.

---

19. Jesuit Refugee Services Australia, *Annual Report 2019*, 12.

Practicing Hospitality

Baptcare has taken an active approach to engaging with Baptist congregations in Victoria to assist them in involvement in meeting local community needs. Baptcare's engagement in providing hospitality for asylum seekers arose from both involvement with local congregations and intentional reflection in identifying an area not covered by the government services that aligned with their mission. The agency has committed significant financial resources independent of government funding to this project of over $800,000 a year. In developing its involvement with asylum seekers and refugees Baptcare has engaged closely with other agencies involved with asylum seekers and with its stakeholder communities in Baptist congregations in the inner city of Melbourne. The agency has focused its expression of hospitality to asylum seekers on providing housing, along with accompanying support services.

The Baptcare Sanctuary program commenced in 2008 when the Brunswick Baptist Church, a congregation in inner metropolitan Melbourne that had been housing people seeking asylum for some years, approached Baptcare seeking to increase the housing available for those seeking refuge who had no income or support. The program that emerged from that collaboration provides supported transitional, free, or low-cost transitional accommodation for asylum seekers living lawfully in the community while awaiting the outcome of their application for a Protection visa. The Sanctuary facilities include one housing twenty-eight men, and the other with forty-six individual bedrooms plus a three-bedroom family unit. The facilities are buildings-adjacent to, and owned by Brunswick and West Preston Baptist Churches, that had become surplus to the congregations' requirements. These are inner city suburbs in Melbourne with relatively good access to public transport.

In addition to providing much needed housing for asylum seekers with limited income, the Sanctuary program aims to improve the psychological well-being of residents by establishing a positive community connection through strengths-based and empowerment models. Residents are supported to secure the best possible outcomes throughout the asylum seeker process, including both those that secure refugee status, and those who are unsuccessful and are subsequently returned to their country of origin. A range of services is provided, including pastoral care, case management, access to support services (medical, legal, counseling, etc.) and the opportunity to participate in a range of social activities. At the time it was set up most of the residents in the Sanctuary program had no right to work and were denied access to Medicare, necessary health services, and welfare support. Most of the residents were wholly reliant on charitable support for their housing, food, and medical costs.[20]

The situation with regard to asylum seekers' entitlement to seek work has changed since the program was established. Support is now provided to help residents seek work, leading to a number of the residents gaining employment, which has assisted them to achieve a degree of independence within the community. Visa processing with all its uncertainties casts a large shadow over the men in the residential accommodation. It has profound effects on their mental health and ability to function. The rate of suicide for asylum seekers is around twenty-six per 100,000 compared to around nine per 100,000 in the general population.[21] Sanctuary is not just a matter of providing accommodation. Creating a welcoming space at these two facilities and includes use of plants in the buildings and gardens that express a stance of life and hope for the future. A critical issue for the Baptcare Sanctuary program for asylum seekers is that it is funded by surpluses from the agency and from community fundraising.[22] No Australian government funds are available for programs such as this that support asylum seekers.

The commitment to support asylum seekers by Baptcare has extended over time. Houses of Hope is an extension of Baptcare's Sanctuary program, which provides an alternative mechanism of transitional accommodation and support to people seeking asylum. It is a community-based response to the critical shortage of housing for people seeking asylum. In partnership with churches and volunteers, Baptcare's Houses of Hope offers safe, suitable, and secure housing to very vulnerable individuals and families who otherwise face homelessness. Residents are able to access basic services as well as pathways to education, employment, and independence through the Sanctuary program. Houses of Hope provides accommodation for forty-six people. Referral partners for this program include most of the nonprofit agencies involved in supporting asylum seekers in the region. Houses of Hope residents' access Baptcare Sanctuary services, including casework, social and spiritual support, and education and employment services.

How does Houses of Hope work? Churches and members of the community offer houses, units, and flats, ideally located close to public transport at no rent, or at a reduced rent. Each tenant is carefully chosen and matched to the accommodation to ensure their suitability. This includes men, women, couples, and families of all ages. Tenants are expected to contribute

20. BaptCare, *People Seeking Asylum*; Brunswick Baptist Church, "BaptCare Sanctuary."

21. Morrison, "Planting Hope."

22. McLean interview.

a discounted rent if they have an income. Volunteers from local churches and the wider community are linked to households to provide practical and social support. Baptcare Sanctuary manages the tenancy arrangements, including furnishing the house and minor maintenance repairs. These houses provide a stable foundation of affordable accommodation and support so that people seeking asylum, often with no government or financial support, are able to access basic services as well as pathways to education, employment, and independence. Houses of Hope gives churches and people who want to help a way to make a meaningful difference to people's lives. Accommodation is currently provided for fifty-seven people through a total of fourteen houses. This is a profound form of hospitality.

The significant dimension that I want to emphasize here beyond the funding that enables the program to continue in opposition to Australian government policy intent is the partnership with local congregations. The two congregations I mentioned earlier see themselves as linked to the Sanctuary program. Brunswick Baptist church expresses its mission in the following terms: "We the people of Brunswick Baptist Church are a multicultural community of embrace grounded in Jesus. Inspired by Paul's vision in Gal 3:28, we journey together as neither Jew or Gentile, citizen or refugee, young or old, gay or straight, healthy or sick, male or female, because we are all one in Christ Jesus."[23] In celebrating ten years of operation in 2018, a longtime member of the Brunswick congregation, Meewon Yang, said at the celebratory dinner: "Our partnership with Baptcare is as strong as ever. Members of our church still come and eat a meal with residents at Sanctuary Brunswick once a month. It is a wonderful way to connect and offer social support."[24]

West Preston Baptist Church provides support to asylum seekers living at Sanctuary through a monthly dinner cooked by a team from the church in the common dining area. They eat dinner with the residents and build friendships with them. The church is involved in delivering food bank supplies to Sanctuary each week and the congregations provide assistance to Sanctuary residents who receive refugee status and then need to find other accommodation.

Sanctuary has been a partnership between local congregations and a large agency with a strong commitment to shape its mission with reference to its Baptist identity, an identity in which tension with government in a Christendom setting has been part of the tradition. The connection between local congregations and an agency with professional skills in initiating and

---

23. Brunswick Baptist Church, Ministries.

24. Baptcare, "Sanctuary Celebrates 10 Years."

developing the Sanctuary program has demonstrated what can be achieved by such a partnership.

In 2014, Tri Nguyen, then minister of Brunswick Baptist Church, along with three asylum seekers, made a pilgrimage from Brunswick Baptist Church to Canberra to deliver a gift to Parliament, a large model of the boat in which he and his father and sister fled Vietnam in 1982. The boat was put on wheels and pulled behind walkers. Tri did it as an expression of thanks to Australia for the gift of refuge, hospitality, and care that he and his family had received as refugees in Australia. The walk raised over $11,000 in funds for Baptcare's Sanctuary facilities in Brunswick and West Preston. No one from the Australian government was willing to receive the boat on their arrival in Canberra. It remains in Canberra waiting for a time when an Australian government will be willing to engage in a recognition of hospitality to asylum seekers.

Hospitality in a conflicted and complex policy space

In the previous chapter I discussed the role of advocacy in making public space more complex and the likelihood of creating conflict with government. The same analysis applies to exercise of hospitality by the community agencies in this chapter. Here the emphasis was on complexity rather than conflict. The message here is that community engagement by churches after Christendom will lean into complexity and conflict, with activity being generated from a community basis rather than the top-down simplification and uniformity of political space characteristic of Christendom.

The insertion of spaces for hospitality towards asylum seekers implies an implicit critique of government policy, and a rejection of the claims of the state to an overarching moral authority. The agencies involved in the narrative in this chapter displayed a commitment to a politics that rejected the effort of the state to clear asylum seekers and refugees from the public space by performing practices of compassion and accompaniment that oppose the logic of fear and deterrence.

What's clear in the accounts in this chapter is that the initiatives were driven by strong mission commitments and enabled by diverse sources of funding. The programs involve performances of compassion that have been developed and funded independent of the Australian government as expressions of the mission of the respective agencies. In the case of JRSA they were able to tap into funding through local and state governments but were not overly dependent upon either of those sources.

Practicing Hospitality

JRSA's activities were placed in the context of a mission that was international in scope and empowered by a commitment to a faith that does justice. The Baptcare initiatives offer a critique of government policy, and a commitment to human community not constrained by a government appeal to fear.

11

Presence on the Margins

Presence as a form of community engagement by institutions entails a relationship of geographical proximity over time. Presence at the human level is about attention, respect, and openness in relationships and carries with it a suggestion of patience, of taking time. Presence requires attentiveness and pushes us towards consideration of our engagement with others. William Stringfellow has drawn our attention to the theological importance of presence. The church as the body of Christ "has a task and mission to the world, not to add to the work of God in Christ, but to claim by the very presence of the Church and its members in the world, the scope, design and style of God's City of Salvation and welcome all into the same."[1] I want to emphasize that presence is about more than doing things for people and solving problems through the power of our access to resources and government authority. Presence requires attention to both people and the community around us.

"On the margins" is a phrase that shapes the stories I have to tell in this chapter. "Margins" is a term that carries a range of meanings and resonances. We talk, for example, of the margins of a book, of writing in but not on the margins. In contrast, we speak of a town or suburb as being on the margins, geographically as well as metaphorically, with reference to its relationship to political and economic power. When we talk about people being marginal, we are suggesting that they are distant from power, or are not effectively connected to the power that can shape their life and future.

The Gospels in their account of the life and death, and the ministry and teaching of Jesus provide an underpinning for a stance of presence with

1. Stringfellow, *Free in Obedience*, 33.

those on the margins. Jesus was continually present with those who were marginal to society, and those who failed to maintain the purity codes. Jesus was notorious for his presence with tax collectors, sinners, and women, and for his attention to them in dialogue and healing. Jesus manifested his presence geographically in his engagement with people in Galilee and Samaria, both areas that were marginal in multiple ways to the religious and political centers of power. Jesus' presence with those on the edges reaches its ultimate in his crucifixion with two criminals, ending his life outside the gate so far as both the Jewish rulers and the Roman imperial power were concerned.

The stories I tell in this chapter are about presence on the margins. The first is about presence as practiced by the Wayside Chapel, a parish mission of the Uniting Church of Australia (UCA) in inner city Sydney. The second story is about how Doveton Baptist Church, a small, struggling congregation on the margins of Melbourne, has been present in service to a community buffeted by the forces of globalization. Both these stories gesture toward some of the cultural and economic forces that are shaping the environment in which community engagement is taking place, as well as bringing into view how post-Christendom engagement might be undertaken.

The Wayside Chapel

The Wayside Chapel is a parish mission of the Uniting Church of Australia (UCA) located in a nightclub and entertainment precinct. Kings Cross, where the mission originated, with its narrow streets and lanes, is squeezed between the Central Business District of Sydney to the west and the highly salubrious upper-class, harbor-side suburbs to the north and east. In the UCA a parish mission such as the Wayside Chapel is a category of church presence in which a congregation is linked to an agency involved in the provision of community services in locations in which a congregation would not be self-supporting.

The Wayside Chapel has a high public profile across the wider Sydney metropolitan area, a profile that has been sustained from its controversial beginning over half a century ago.[2] The mission commenced in 1964 as an initiative of the Rev. Ted Noffs, at that stage a minister in the Methodist Church. Just over a decade later the mission merged with significant elements of the Presbyterian and Congregational churches to become a part of the UCA. The Wayside quickly developed a presence that included, along

---

2. The story I tell here draws on Graham Long's memoir *Love Over Hate*, as well as an extended interview with Graham in early 2014, and material on the history of the mission from the Wayside Chapel website.

with the chapel for worship, a coffee shop and a drop-in and community resource center. A crisis center was opened in 1965 in response to the growing problem of drug addiction, followed by the development in the 1970s of drug education programs. In the late 1990s, the Rev. Ray Richmond and others associated with the Wayside established a Tolerance Room, where people injecting drugs were able to do so in a supervised environment.

Over several decades of controversial involvement Rev. Ted Noffs built a public profile for the Wayside as a place of nonjudgmental compassion manifested through an active engagement with local social problems. The "reverend as a stirrer," that is a clergy person at odds with the ecclesiastical and political establishment, compassionate and a provider of practical support, Ted's public persona proved to be an effective formula for getting the public to open their wallets in support of the Wayside. This model has been followed by a number of clergy in Australia over the years and has proved to be an effective path for community engagement by such clergy. It is a model that has caused headline-averse church leadership considerable discomfort from time to time, to the joy of many others in the community.

By the turn of the century the difficulties of succession for an organization based as the Wayside was on the charisma and profile of its founder were beginning to bite. The mission was operating out of rundown buildings and was in severe financial difficulty with an income of less than $300,000 a year. Ninety percent of that funding came from two recurring grants for social programs from the state government. To increase the degree of difficulty in charting a path for survival, the organization's database of donors was out-of-date. It was costing the Wayside more to mail out an appeal for funds than was returned in the form of donations. It was at this point in June 2004 that the Rev. Graham Long, originally an ordained minister in the Churches of Christ, with experience in both prison ministry and running a welfare agency, was appointed as the General Manager of the Wayside. His appointment to the joint role of CEO/pastor in the mission had to wait the process of his accreditation as a minister by the UCA.

When safety inspectors arrived at the Wayside building shortly after Graham's appointment, they condemned 40 percent of the mission's accommodation. To continue operation the Wayside faced a major rebuild that would cost $8.5 million. In an effort of lobbying that drew on all the Wayside's community profile and public reputation, the mission was successful in gaining one-off capital grants totaling $5m from the state and Australian governments towards the rebuilding. The political goodwill that was harnessed was bipartisan and drew on both local state and federal politicians. The balance of $3.5 million came from fundraising from the public as well as philanthropic bodies. The funding represented a willingness by the public, many without any connection to the churches, to support an institution that was understood to have strong community connections, not because it was a specifically church-related activity. The Wayside finished the rebuilding process debt free. Subsequently Uniting Church's Chapel by the Sea mission at Bondi, close to the famous beach, has been merged with the Wayside Chapel.

Leadership and governance issues

Governance issues are rarely exciting but can be quite important in understanding how an organization operates and the way its mission does or doesn't get implemented. The governance of the Wayside Chapel is critical to understanding the operation of the Wayside Chapel. As a UCA parish mission in NSW the Wayside does not have an independent legal status. The Uniting Church Property Trust in NSW, functioning under the state legislation that set up the Uniting Church in the state, is the legal entity that holds the property of the Wayside and signs the contracts associated with the running of the mission. That legal structure establishes the line of accountability from the CEO of the Wayside to the UCA NSW Synod, as governing body of the church. There is however an important distinction between the formal legal responsibility for property and finance, and the ownership of the vision and the mission of the Wayside.

The board of the Wayside, not the Synod, is at the heart of maintaining the mission and vision elements of its governance and its accountability to the wider community that supplies much of its funding. The importance of this can be seen in the effort by Graham Long, shortly after his appointment as CEO, to gain a new chair and bring a systematic change in board membership so as to develop a board with members who had the necessary skills and access to networks in the business community. A reshaped board from Graham Long's point of view was critical to the task of articulating a vision and raising the funds that would enable them to carry out that vision without being bound by the requirements associated with government contracting. Ian Martin, a senior figure in the finance industry, whom Graham brought on board as chair of the board, and who has only recently retired, formed a close partnership with him. They worked together to get the board membership they needed to engage both the community and the business sector. There was a shared understanding of leadership between Ian and Graham as to how they would operate and their respective responsibilities. In board meetings the chair has respect, "he's not an equal partner, so if we get into a tight squeeze the chair will say here's what we're going to do, and that's what happens."[3]

Having completed the transfer of his accreditation as a minister to the Uniting Church, Graham took up the formal combined title of CEO/pastor for the organization. Somewhat against the grain of the practice in many church-related agencies, Graham held that this combination of management and pastoral leadership was important. "What makes Wayside radical is we hold that together in the one-person ordained minister and CEO. And I understand that all the momentum in the world wants to split those two roles. You end up with a businessperson, often speaking government speak, and with some fool who sings songs on Sunday. And, you know, you've just disempowered both. It's only when you hold that together that there is a creative tension."[4] The role of the CEO/pastor in Graham's understanding is about leadership, upholding the vision of the organization, and setting the philosophical framework. The way that this works is that "anything that's a question of direction will come to me, and I will canvas opinions, but I will make the call; it's my call. It's not a committee call. I'll use my people to milk whatever wisdom is there to be milked, but it's my call."[5]

Graham was of the view that most people working in the Wayside are better than he is in carrying out that mission, though the history of the agency over the past few years suggests that he is being unduly modest about his role in the day-to-day implementation of the mission. The evidence suggests that he has modeled the mission in a way that is powerful and evocative. His storytelling in the weekly newsletter circulated to 15,000 supporters of the Wayside involves reflection on moments of encounter with people at the Wayside that model the ethos. The journey of internalizing these commitments can take staff at the Wayside some years. People apply to work at the agency because they are attracted to the philosophy or have been volunteers and like what they have experienced there. Graham observes that people joining like the chapel's values.

> Our values are no secret, no cowboys, no rush, no complacency and no judges. . . . People are attracted to that and that's what they want to do, but it takes some years actually to unlearn the [surrounding] culture that we're in. And I think realistically you just have to know this is going to be a wrestle, and it's a good wrestle but you'd better be doing the wrestling, or otherwise you'll just create another welfare agency. You can be an arm of

3. Long interview.
4. Long interview.
5. Long interview.

government, and I don't want to be an arm of government. . . . My senior people mostly get it. Our frontline workers are struggling with it, because it's very seductive to live in a world where I'm the expert and you're the client. To overcome that is very difficult, so it's a never-ending battle of trying to show people a better way.[6]

The congregation at the Wayside

As a parish mission the Wayside in its early years had a congregation that met on Sunday morning, but by 2004 the congregation was vanishingly small, a total of only four people. A decade later the congregation has grown to be between forty and sixty people. Of this congregation Graham Long has often commented: "We are not much like a church, which might work for you if you are not much like a Christian."[7] At the end of each service people form a circle and hold hands while Graham pronounces the benediction. It is likely that in this moment of sending out, judges and teachers attending the service would find themselves holding hands with ice addicts and sex workers.

Though the growth of this worshipping community has been less than might have been anticipated, and indeed hoped for by Graham, the congregation is in his view the pumping heart of the place in that it celebrates the Eucharist every week. This has been the practice from the very beginning of the Wayside. Ted Noffs is reported to have said in explaining this that "this was bound to be someone's last week alive."[8] Sadly, given the health status of many of the visitors to the chapel, it becomes the location for memorial services, up to fifty such gatherings in some years. Most of the memorial services are held without a body, or an undertaker, as many of the people concerned die as paupers. On these occasions people attending are encouraged to speak from the heart and for Graham these events are amongst some of the most important activities that are undertaken at the Wayside. The Wayside is also the location for one to two weddings each week, some involving people with family connections with the Wayside, while others involve those who are looking for some spiritual foundation at an important moment in their life. The role of church and worship in the Wayside is linked in building community, and in gathering as church where love is lived out in community.

6. Long interview.
7. Long, *Love Over Hate*, 138.
8. Long, *Love Over Hate*, 141.

Mission

The logo of the Wayside is both striking and challenging. It has a heart sprouting angel wings, with a crown and a banner bearing the motto, "Love over Hate." That's an unusually strong and striking statement to have as an organization's public face to the world. Many mission statements, it has to be said, head towards the safe and the bland. Not so for the Wayside. Love here is understood as being directed at the goal of community while also being the way of achieving its mission. Love is about working "in a collaborative way to invite people out of singular, individual life into the risky and healing place of community. The Wayside's mission is not to fix people, but to love them and be with them, knowing that if they are really met, they'll really move toward health and life."[9] The language, though it is soaked with Christian references, does not draw out the scriptural and theological connections explicitly beyond the reference to the church as community. This distinctive vision evolved out of dialogue between Graham and Ian Martin. Graham reported that "we settled on [an intention] to create a community with no 'us and them,' and we identified isolation and loneliness as our enemy.... Our mission became to meet you rather than fix you.... In a culture of a privatized self, most of what we do to fix people actually alienates them. ... You walk away with a pamphlet, or a program, or a pill, but you're more alone than when you walked in."[10]

This vision of community puts the Wayside into tension with much of both the language and the practice of government welfare programs. The critique of the welfare model is that for most "helping" agencies, whether government or nongovernment, the client is the "problem" and the agency with its program is there to fix them. The person in their radical shared humanity becomes lost and instrumentalized. "Even when that's done from good heart, with good intention, there's a push-away in it, because you will be forever the needy one, and I'll be forever the one with the answers and the skills ... You are important to me because you are a cog in my wheel, and a statistic in my next funding application..."[11]

The Wayside's commitment is to draw people out of isolation to receive compassion and support, whether they have been marginalized by homelessness, mental health issues, or substance abuse. The emphasis is on creating community, on meeting with people, not working on them or processing them through a program. Services are only provided in aid of

---

9. Long interview.
10. Long interview.
11. Long interview.

that goal, not as the central activity of the Wayside. Graham's approach to engagement with its visitors and the language in which it is expressed is something that he has reflected on a good deal. Whether personalism informed by the Christian tradition is the best term for this vision, I am not quite sure, though it certainly leans in that direction. For most helping agencies, whether government or nongovernment, you are treated as "a client." Governments and their welfare agencies now have abandoned even that nod to a nonmarket frame and label all those who approach it for assistance as "consumers" or "customers." The Wayside by contrast has visitors whose presence is welcomed.

Government funding (or not)

In 2014, when I conducted a long interview with Graham, in addition to questions of mission I discussed the significance of being financially independent from government. He observed that over the decade since he began at the Wayside that in addition to the capital investment the operational budget had increased tenfold, to around $3m. Over the same period the proportion of government funding had decreased to 18 percent. Growth in funding has come entirely from nongovernment sources. From two full-time staff in 2004, the mission had increased its staffing to around thirty-six, along with around 600 volunteers. The Wayside, with only 18 percent of its funding coming from government, was an outlier when compared to an average of 70 percent dependence on government funding for Uniting Church agencies across Australia. Graham was clear that the funding strategy of the Wayside's board was to minimize dependence on government funding. Graham explains his philosophy on the issue of whether or not to accept government program funding as follows:

> The two original little subsidies we still have from State Health, and I have to say the senior people who acquit those grants each year have to be a bit bilingual, you know, because the government mission and ours is really quite different. But what we can do honestly is report facts. X number of bodies, X number of showers, X number of referrals, X number . . .—so that's what we report, and I think the government doesn't understand it and couldn't care less about our mission. But they accept the facts of what we do, and for that [there] is a certain amount of money. Well, if we lost those things that would be $300,000 roughly out of a $3M budget now; [it] wouldn't be the end of the world. I wouldn't like to lose it because it's not easy chasing money from

the public, but I could live with[out] it if we lost it. To accept further government funding the program being contracted by the government would have to be an obvious fit with the mission. We don't have the attitude of golly gosh there's something out there, it's a little bit outside of our mission, let's go for it, and if we get it yippee. I don't want to be like a dog that'll beg for any bone. I'd rather do what we do well, and if that means we miss opportunities well that's fine.[12]

One of Graham's key strategies was to harness the public profile, and the history of the Wayside's association with its founder Ted Noffs as the basis for attracting donations from the community at large. Graham reflected that "the Wayside Chapel as a brand was just handed to me on a plate. I think a lot of Sydneysiders, and a lot of people around the country, recognized the brand. . . . It's been ten years of lifting profile and moving supporters from a very old age group to a younger age group."[13] The Wayside has as a matter of policy sought to build up an operational reserve that provides a foundation from which it can invest in its programs and services as well as underwriting operations. The weekly email *The Inner Circle*, which goes out to 15,000 people, is a key vehicle in communicating the message and character of the agency and in appealing for support. It has been read out weekly on ABC Sydney Local Radio for many years.

The Wayside operates a range of services that place dignity, respect, and love at the heart of their approach with programs and spaces that see everyone as a person to be met, not a problem to be solved. The Community Services Centres (CSC), one in Kings Cross and more recently another in Bondi, have been providing community services to members of the eastern suburbs since 1964. CSC staff and volunteers work together, seven days a week, to provide those of the community who are sleeping rough with a safe space and amenities such as showers and emergency clothing, as well as information and referral services for accommodation, legal health, and welfare within the inner city. The CSCs also provide space and activities for the indigenous community, training for youth with access to employment in a restaurant run as a social enterprise and pathways programs back into training and employment, as well as a twilight program of structured activities for people in the neighborhood.

---

12. Long interview.
13. Long interview.

Continuity and change

The overall philosophy and practice of community engagement, and of avoiding a reliance on government programs, has not changed. Two significant developments though have occurred. In July 2016, the UCA's NSW Synod moved responsibility for the governance and operational responsibilities for the Chapel by the Sea and its related operations in Bondi, five kilometers to the east, to the Wayside Chapel. The Chapel by the Sea was established in 1977 and included a worshipping congregation along with a Community Services Centre and the North Bondi Op Shop. This move extended the reach of the Wayside within the region and has provided a location for a social enterprise based around a restaurant to provide training and vocational opportunities for young people who have been on the margins and not otherwise engaged with the community.

The other significant development was that the board announced Pastor Jon Owen as the new joint CEO and Pastor for the Wayside Chapel in March 2018, following the retirement of Graham Long. Jon Owen, who had been the Assistant Pastor at Wayside Chapel, took up the joint role of CEO and Pastor on July 1, 2018.[14] Prior to coming to the Wayside, Jon had spent some twenty years building community in some of the most disadvantaged neighborhoods in Melbourne and Sydney. He was a qualified social worker, and previously a member of Urban Neighbours of Hope (UNOH), a missional order affiliated with Churches of Christ (in Australia and Thailand) and the Baptist Union (in New Zealand). Most recently, Jon and his family had lived in a housing commission suburb in Mount Druitt (Bidwill) in the west of Sydney, a home that was shared with those seeking asylum, refugees, people in recovery, and ex-prisoners.[15]

The appointment of Jon Owen as CEO and Pastor was significant in signaling a commitment by the board to maintaining the current ethos and mission as well as the existing style of leadership and management. Jon's background places him in the same vein of spirituality and community engagement as his predecessor. The appointment was carefully managed, as Jon spent nearly two years as Assistant Pastor before taking over the leadership role from Graham Long.

In exploring the mission of the Wayside as "presence" I have focused on how it has sustained this culture. Stories about its day-to-day operation are worth reading and give texture and depth to its ministry of "presence." Both recent CEO/Pastors Graham Long and Jon Owen have communicated

---

14. Stewart, "Meet the Wayside Chapel's New Pastor."
15. SBS News, "The Pastor Who Opened His Home."

what the Wayside is about by telling stories of listening, presence, and encounter and the impact over time on the lives of those visitors. The stories sometimes are about changes in lives and human flourishing, and often they are about community and connection in the middle of pain and disruption. Most of the stories can be found on the website.[16]

The Wayside has worked hard at maintaining clarity about its mission and identity, building a diversity of funding sources that has enabled independence from government, a governance structure in which the board works to support that strategy, and a leadership that holds the vision and provides guidance on how it is implemented. Behind this is a refusal to operate on the assumption that the state is the first point of call when it comes to resourcing agencies and churches in the task of building community. Through the leadership of Graham Long, the Wayside has emphasized the importance of affirming a common humanity between volunteers, staff, neighbors, and visitors. It has demonstrated an inclusive approach to engagement in the lives of those on the margins while articulating a strong implicit critique of the prevailing institutional culture of welfare agencies. The practice of presence at the Wayside stands in opposition to a utilitarian contract driven approach which looks to funding by government of programs to solve problems.[17]

Doveton Baptist Church

In my second account of "presence with those on the margins," as a form of community engagement after Christendom, I turn to the local community level. In the balance of this chapter, I will report on what such "presence" looks like when lived out by a small congregation, in a community characterized by entrenched economic and social inequality and located on the margins of a major metropolitan area.[18]

Doveton as a marginal community

Doveton is currently an outer suburban community of around 8,000 residents. During the 1950s and 1960s it was built to provide housing for workers in the then expanding industrial plants around Dandenong, an

---

16. Wayside Chapel, "Wayside Stories."

17. Long, *Stories from the Wayside* and *Wayside*.

18. My account of Doveton Baptist Church's community engagement is based on an extended interview with Pastor Paul Lewellyn.

outer urban service and retail center thirty kilometers southeast of the city of Melbourne. Doveton is about twenty minutes by bus from Dandenong, with a further hour's commute by train to the CBD. Despite its proximity to Dandenong, Doveton is in a different local government area, just inside the northern boundary of the formerly semirural city of Casey, whose population center of gravity is in the rapidly expanding commuter belt suburbs to the south. Doveton thus remains both geographically and economically marginal, not only because of its location on the edge of the Melbourne metropolitan area, but also because it is in a local government area with which it has little in common in terms of transport links, community connections, sociological makeup, and economic interests.

The manufacturing boom in Australia that was the rationale for the development of Doveton during the 1950s lasted only two decades. Changes in economic policy, including tariff cuts, and the floating of exchange rates, led to the gradual winding down and eventual closure of most of the manufacturing plants in the region, in the face of import competition during the 1980s and 1990s. This resulted in fewer well-paid and secure jobs in the region. Deteriorating employment conditions and periods of high interest rates led to financial stress and increasing poverty.[19] As a result of the decline of manufacturing and the accompanying casualization of employment, by 2007 Doveton moved into the top forty postcodes in Victoria when measured by an index of socioeconomic disadvantage. The situation has not improved since then. In 2015 Doveton was named as one of the state's top seven "struggle" towns, based on the extent of unemployment, criminal convictions, family violence, and level of education.[20] Despite these indicators of socioeconomic distress, Doveton seems on first appearance to be a peaceful and quiet outer suburban location. The only immediate clue to disadvantage when I got off the bus serving the suburb was that the small suburban shopping center was comprised almost exclusively of opportunity shops and reject stores.

Community infrastructure in Doveton

Equally significant, but not measured by the indices I referred to above, is that Doveton Baptist is one of the very few nonprofit community organizations actually located in Doveton. To engage with government in seeking

---

19. For a detailed discussion of Doveton in the 1990s see Bryson and Winter, *Social Change, Suburban Lives*.

20. Vinson et al., *Dropping Off the Edge*; Bailey, "Doveton a 'Band One' Disadvantaged Suburb"; and Bailey, "An Economy Is Not a Society."

grants, delivering services, and coordinating activities, a community needs organizations with a legal structure, an ability to manage finances, and a capacity to harness volunteers. There are very few groups within Doveton who have the wherewithal to handle relationships with government. While organizations located outside the community can carry out these activities, such a location is likely to reduce their effectiveness in speaking for, and engaging with, the community. The nonprofit organizations in Doveton in 2014 were the Doveton Neighbourhood Centre, the Doveton Baptist Church, and the Holy Family Catholic Church. While the Catholic Church remains a major presence in the community, its activities have largely been confined to the parish school and the various congregations within the parish. The parish still carries with it the scars from a series of priests located there who engaged in sexual abuse up until 1997. Since I did the interview on which this narrative is based, the situation with regard to community organizations has begun to change. By 2020 an Afghani Islamic Centre, a Pentecostal church, and a Samoan church had been established in Doveton. All of these community groups I should note are likely to be considered as marginal so far as middle-class public servants are concerned when looking for community partners. These organizations have the additional disadvantage of being relative newcomers, concerned with establishing themselves and not necessarily outward looking.

Mainstream Christian denominations who pulled out of Doveton during the 1990s seem to have done so on the assumption that people from the suburb could take the bus or a car to Dandenong, or to neighboring middle-class, suburban areas to go to church. The departure however stripped out critical community organizational resources. Doveton Baptist, established in 1964, was the only Protestant church that remained. The church is a member of the Baptist Union of Victoria (BUV), an association of Baptist churches and agencies that provides a variety of support services to affiliated bodies in the state. According to the pastor, Paul Llewellyn, attendance at the Sunday service in 2014 was about seventy people, with church membership numbers in the mid-forties. In the Baptist polity members elect the deacons, who make up the decision-making body for the congregation. Half of the congregation are retirees, or elderly, so gold coins and $5 notes were common in the collection plate. The church did not have a lot of people who would see themselves as being leaders, as most of the congregation comes from lower socioeconomic groups and lack generally organizational experience and self-confidence. Importantly, though, the congregation is comprised of residents of the suburb who share much in common with the community in which they live with respect to both economic vulnerability and social background. The members of the congregation in being present with one another in worship and fellowship provide a space for meeting and the basis for support for a wider community that has few other points of community connection to anchor its life and coordinate activities.

Community engagement

Doveton Baptist has been a hub for community engagement over the past two decades. The church has had dealings with the Shire Council, state, and Australian government departments, as well as with nonprofit community organizations in the region. The infrastructure for handling government funding for community engagement by the congregation was laid with the establishment of the Doveton Baptist Benevolent Society (DBBS) during the late 1990s as an incorporated body separate from the church to carry out welfare activities on its behalf. Originally DBBS depended on personal donations and some funding from the Church. An opportunity shop was set up by the church in the Doveton Shopping Centre in about 2008 to help with funding its activities. Donations to DBBS are tax deductible as opposed to giving to the church, which is not tax deductible and therefore comes from the after-tax income of church members.

There is little funding available from the denomination leve through the Baptist Union of Victoria to support local congregations that are financially struggling. If a local congregation is going to survive it cannot rely on the denomination but has to find the resources itself. The economics of maintaining a congregational presence in a low socioeconomic area like Doveton are difficult. Pastor Paul Lewellyn explained the economics of the congregation.

> The only reason the church can afford a fulltime pastor is that we have opportunity shop income, and because the church was physically larger in its past, we own a number of houses that we now rent out. Now we rent them out at largely below even Doveton market rent, so that it's not a lot, but it still is income. This size church would normally only have a three-day-a-week pastor, and so the fact that I probably do spend two days a week doing community chaplain sort of work.[21]

---

21. Lewellyn interview.

Providing emergency relief

The welfare activities of the DBBS were originally funded through the opportunity shop, until in 2012 it obtained a quarterly grant under the Emergency Relief Program, under a three-year funding agreement with what is now the Australian Government Department of Social Services. The Emergency Relief Program brought in $20,000 per annum for funding a food relief program, where for three days a week volunteers take appointments with people referred from Centrelink or other agencies to provide food vouchers, food from donations, petrol vouchers, and medical prescriptions. On Thursdays there is a free community lunch generally attended by about thirty people and funded by the DBBS in partnership with Cornerstone, a church-run drop-in center in Dandenong. Beyond that activity all the volunteers helping with emergency relief are from the church. Emergency relief is a safety net of sorts for those who have fallen through the cracks of the income support system.

Subsequent to my visit the Australian government required all agencies to apply for new funding agreements for the provision of Emergency Relief, which led to a new involvement by the church with the City of Casey on the funding and management of Emergency Relief funding. The application process was a huge amount of work and left Llewellyn with the impression that the government's aim was to reduce the number of agencies they dealt with directly, as the process was more suited to a regional or even national organization. The outcome of the process was that the congregation was informed that it would not continue to be funded for the provision of Emergency Relief by the Australian government.

However, all was not lost. DDBS then signed a memorandum of understanding with the City of Casey to be their Doveton branch. Under this arrangement DDBS receives $20,000 per annum, as under the previous funding agreement. The bonus of this arrangement is that the City of Casey now handles all of the statistical reporting of emergency relief expenditure to the Department of Social Services. The City of Casey spent over $20,000 in having a new database developed to handle the data uploads and they have provided access to the program to DBBS at no cost. The paperwork for emergency relief for DBBS, apart from the data uploads, has almost disappeared. The annual financial acquittal is a one-page statutory declaration that the funding has been spent appropriately. While the City of Casey retained most of the Australian government emergency relief funding that it had previously received, the neighboring City of Greater Dandenong lost around $480,000. Not surprisingly given their geographical location, DBBS has subsequently seen an increase in help sought from people living in Dandenong. The emergency relief funding has not increased in the ten years that DBC has been receiving it, so they have sought other funding to support their welfare activities.

As Doveton is an identified low socioeconomic community with high needs it has not been difficult for DBBS to obtain grants, and the church has not faced competition for such grants from other organizations within Doveton. DBBS has received funding from Lord Mayors's Feed Melbourne program for several years, three years funding from the Lord Mayor of Melbourne's Charitable Trust, and a grant from Collier's Charitable Trust. The paperwork for these grants is reasonable, but DBBS struggles with the uncertainty of one-year grants, and a wait of up to six months between applying and getting the funds.[22] These problems are common right across frontline agencies in the social services sector.

Community connections

Doveton Baptist has been able to attract funding for a wide variety of community programs that benefit the wider community. Beyond its involvement in providing emergency relief, the DBBS has had a grant each year of around $3,000 from the City of Casey to enable the congregation to organize the annual community carols. The church has organized the carols for the past twenty-five years with assistance at times from other church groups. While Doveton Baptist has been the principal church involved, the community carols event is not in any sense "owned" by the church. As Paul explained, the carols are "held out in public space, and really, we just do all of the organizing and make sure it happens and invite a lot of participation and try to get a good mix in the program there."[23]

While the opportunity shop funding has gone into the church budget at various stages, the church has made its facilities available to the community. The groups using the church facilities included an Alcoholics Anonymous group, two non-English-speaking congregations, a South Sudanese Nuer group, and a Tamil group. Two thirds of the use of church facilities were for community activities. Counting the opportunity shop, Benevolent Society, and church ministry programs, 80 percent of the volunteer effort from the church goes towards programs that engage with people who aren't part of the church.[24]

---

22. Email from Pastor Paul Llewellyn to Douglas Hynd, January 29, 2015.
23. Lewellyn interview.
24. Lewellyn interview.

The church through DDBS also receives a grant for the supported playgroup program, an Australian government program where the money is given to the local councils to distribute for families of general and complex disadvantages. This program exists to cater for the mothers who need more intensive support. Even though the grants from the local council for community activities are smaller than those that were provided for the emergency relief funding from the Australian government, there is a lot more paperwork involved in their applications and acquittals. Beyond the paperwork though there's a human level of networking with the council and this is something that Paul takes to be important in relational as well as pragmatic terms. For the last four years the Council had a prayer to open every Council meeting, an activity that is certainly not typical of local government in Australia. The neighboring Dandenong City Council, for example, doesn't open with a prayer. Paul commented that he had volunteered to be on the roster as a way of building the connection with the Council. "Particularly the first year or so I was on it, they were scratching to get anybody to show any interest. So, I was up there about every month or six weeks . . . It helps them to see a face and see a name, and when the grant applications come around, they're aware of who you are."[25]

Paul began his ministry in Doveton in the middle of a government-funded community development, a neighborhood renewal project that was run through the state government, in partnership with the Council and the Brotherhood of St. Laurence, a major Anglican social welfare agency. There were about a dozen communities across Victoria that were identified and got the funding under this model, in recognition that they were communities who needed support to do community organization. Things that came out of that funding included Australia Day celebrations, the Doveton show, and various competitions building community spirit. When the funding ended and the government services were pulling out, an incorporated body— Doveton Eumemmerring Township Association (DETA)—was formed. The minister of DBC became the treasurer and another church member was on the executive committee. While DETA gets funding to do Australia Day, volunteers from the church did the setting up and packing up. Paul explained that the church's involvement in that initiative grew out of the connections that developed during the neighborhood renewal project.

> What we've seen is that the Neighbourhood Learning Centre people have now come on board and help support us to do the carols. It's part of our standard practice now when we think of a new thing, like, how do we better support asylum seekers, to go

25. Lewellyn interview.

> and seek a partner to do that with. So, I went checking out who's already doing this conversational English, can you come in and provide the training and the resources and the guide? That's the way the church now thinks.[26]

The church at the time of my visit was looking at facilitating further activities in response to identified community needs, working in partnership with local government and specialist service providers.

> What we're looking at starting for this year is conversational English classes for asylum seekers where they can't get access to government-funded English programs ... Our niche will be focusing on some of the young mums from the asylum seeker community ... The aim is to try to get them into the playgroup, and then at the end of playgroup, while we mind the kids, have them have an hour or so of English classes. ... That's something that we've been talking to the City of Casey about, and they're thrilled. ... It was natural for us to go and seek a partner to do that with. So, I went checking out who's already doing this conversational English, can you come in and provide the training and the resources and the guide?[27]

Family violence, social policy, and breaking the silence

All the above activities are perhaps typical of community engagement by congregations in communities such as Doveton. The church's involvement in a program addressing community violence is not so typical. I will devote attention to the experience of this involvement by the church as it brought community engagement, through a partnership with local government, state government, and the Australian government, along with a pastor's network, directly into the church's worship and teaching life.

Promoting Peace in Families Program was a joint initiative of the City of Casey and Cardinia Casey Community Health Service, a state government-funded entity in partnership with the Casey Pastors Network. Funding came from the Australian Government's Attorney-General's National Crime Prevention Program. The Casey City Council at the time of the funding had the highest incidence of domestic violence in its region, taking up half of all police time. The Council employed a couple of part-time workers to get the program underway. Four large churches came on board as the

---

26. Lewellyn interview.
27. Lewellyn interview.

first group to help develop the material for responding. They were churches with multiple pastor teams who could release somebody to work with the council workers, and then ran the program in their churches. In the next round there were only eight churches in the region who were willing to be involved in this four-to-five-week educational program directed at giving survivors of family violence the opportunity to tell their stories within a church context to help educate congregations on the realities of family violence. Paul explained some of the realities of church and class that lay behind the silence that the program was seeking to challenge.

> Churches have a high predominance of older single women in many denominations. Some of them are widows, but a lot of them were divorcees escaping abusive marriages, that they couldn't talk about, it was going to be a stigma just to be divorced and be single, let alone without getting into the dirty laundry of what was going on. . . . If somebody tried to talk about it, they would be effectively punished for bringing up a taboo subject. . . . A lot of people in the church had this fairy-tale belief that it didn't happen to people like them. . . . [but] it's just as prevalent within church groups as it is in the wider community. . . . A middle-class person has more resources to cover up what's going wrong in their life, compared to somebody who lives in Doveton where the neighbors for six houses around will hear about it. The middle class do the quiet war and put the makeup on and then come out and pretend like everything's right. The perpetrator might be an elder in the church and a respected figure that nobody would doubt. So, the whole family violence project was aimed at bringing facts to the congregations so as to really ask them to change their whole worldview about this topic.[28]

When he received the letter from the Council about the program, Paul went to the leadership of the church and reported that they had been invited to participate in this program, noting that the church was already supporting people who were in this situation. The church leadership agreed to participate. The program involved nearly nine months of preparation and training, with Paul taking the responsibility for coordination within the church and involvement with the grant coordinators. It proved to be a very demanding commitment. Doveton Baptist received no direct funding for its activities. The grant covered the training for delivery of the program and the materials, while the funding, and acquittals of the grant, were managed by

28. Lewellyn interview.

an oversight committee, which included representatives from the Council, Casey-Cardinia Health, Victoria Police, and the Casey Pastor's Network.[29] The demands for Paul in representing the church in the organization and running of the program were substantial, given the size of the congregation.

> It meant monthly meetings . . . There was a fair bit of training provided; a lot of the funding went towards those training courses. There was one person in the church who was trained at a certificate-four level, involving four days' training. There was a couple of us who attended two-day training, and then a whole whack who did one-day or half-day training . . . Anybody who was either delivering material or was going to be somebody that people would then disclose to, had to have some level of training. . . . The lady who had done the four-day training was the ultimate person that people would be directed to, but even small group leaders needed training to say well what happens when somebody in my small group starts saying this and being the guide on how to, well, you don't shove them down, the things you don't do, but you don't have to solve it, you're directing them on, tell them to talk to Paul or June. So, it was the thing for the church for a year, because there was all this preparation, training before the whole delivery period.[30]

There were some difficulties with the material provided that reflected both class differences and theological issues, and required some reworking for use by the church. Paul reflected on the extra work that was involved in dealing with those issues. "The Bible study guides were over the top of the heads of a working-class congregation; they were developed by somebody who works in a more middle-class educated environment . . . The sermon materials I very majorly reworked. . . . They were full of 'drop the odd verse in here and there' . . . I'm a much more exegetical preacher: if I'm going to deal with a passage, I want to deal with it authentically. I was reworking the material to the framework that I was comfortable with, without it at all decreasing the impact of the message."[31]

All the churches that went through the program had people coming forward for the first time to report their experience of family violence. The church at Doveton had four or five people who came forward out of a relatively small congregation. "There was one current situation which it wasn't a physical violence, it was more the verbal mental sort of abuse, but basically

---

29. Lewellyn interview.
30. Lewellyn interview.
31. Lewellyn interview.

the program gave the language to the wife in this case to say I know I've not liked it, but I now understand that it's actually illegal, it's that much wrong. It did require the churches to deal with a taboo topic, not just on Sundays in the sermons, but in small groups, for a whole month."[32]

Theology and ministry

In reflecting on community engagement, Paul drew attention to the distinction between the church creating space for community engagement by groups within the church, and the church itself actually owning an activity. He illustrated this by pointing to the difference between Doveton and Heathmont Baptist, a much larger church of around 300 members where he had been previously involved as a member for many years.

> The way programs and ministries happened is if somebody had a bee in their bonnet and a passion for something, sure the church would let them do whatever, but it wouldn't own it as them doing it. So, you had these small groups, isolated small groups, doing their particular passionate thing, which may be an outreach, I mean there was stuff being done trying to reach homeless people. There was stuff done for playgroups: Heathmont Baptist got into playgroups before there were community playgroups, and they had a kindergarten. But there wasn't this sense that the church [as a whole] was doing this.[33]

The situation in Doveton was different. A significant proportion of the congregation live in rental and public housing, and were on Centrelink benefits such as unemployment and disability payments as well as the aged pension. The congregation was typical of the wider community that it was part of. Speaking of the congregation, Paul explained that "we're embedded in a high-needs community; we actually look around us and see the same needs that government, at whatever level, sees in the community. So, there's actually a commonality in purpose and desire."[34]

During 2013 the church had begun to rethink its vision and mission and wondered about whether it should be making distinctions between what it did as church and what it did as DBBS. In the end they just integrated the vision, affirming that it didn't matter what bank account the money came out of, or whether it was funded by a government agency or

---

32. Lewellyn interview.
33. Lewellyn interview.
34. Lewellyn interview.

the church. "It was all our ministry of this faith community, reaching out to its wider community. We see our whole purpose of existence is to be a blessing in whatever way we can, so we're not running programs overtly aimed at building the church numerically. We didn't just do that because of the welfare needs or because we have a Benevolent Society, we do that because that's what Christ has called us to do and be. It is our vision as a church, that the church that exists for its local community to help them in any way we can."[35]

Theology as the primary language for articulating the mission of the Doveton congregation stands in contrast to the terminology of social capital with its inflection towards economic language in describing community engagement. The underlying theological commitment is that the church is engaged in the community because that is what Christ has called the church to do and be. The church exists for its local community and to help in any way that it can. People know where DBC can be found and that it has remained in the community when other organizations have departed. Paul had the following comments on how community engagement relates to evangelism, discipleship, and church membership.

> It is a joy and a blessing when we see people out of those ministries come and engage with us in our little community, and that's happened a little bit, and that's a real encouragement.... We're in the loving-people mindset in whatever opportunity we engage them in, and if that leads to something more, that's terrific ... I believe we are a very welcoming church for people who just walk in the door. We have the advantage of being in a prominent position and being long term. So, there's a lot of people who know who we are and where we are, but it still was worth doing a website, there's people who've come here because they found us on the web, that's the modern age. It's a pretty basic website but it lets them find us and when the service is on, when they get here, they're warmly welcomed. If you're new and you're a visitor and for that first year we'll just love you, but by the end of that we expect you to contribute ... That's sort of the DNA, we're a church of doers, maybe not leaders, but definitely doers, and it's not a comfortable church to be a pewsitter in. We do lose people who obviously don't want church to be a big part of their life, they want it to be just an hour and a half on a Sunday morning and nothing else—long term those people don't stick around. They'll go to a bigger church where they can get lost. We're also not the church who's going to do the best, we're not

---

35. Lewellyn interview.

a programmed service provider for our own congregation. We don't have enough musicians, so we go on recorder music most weeks.[36]

The theme of presence was one that was important in Paul's reflection on ministry and mission in this marginal community.

> I would encourage any church to partner [with] government. They are part of our world, we're here, they're here, we have common purposes, we should engage with them. This is my first church as a pastor, so I've spent many more years not being a pastor than being a pastor. I'm an engineer, but a chemical engineer that's spent many years [in] manufacturing and management. I might have had ideas that I was here for the ministry of the word, the sacrament and pastoral care, but it's also writing grants and acquittals and engaging . . . It doesn't have to be the pastor, but you would need someone with those good administrative skills and business know-how, and a little bit of entrepreneurial [moxie]. You need that mix.[37]

Presence after Christendom

The stories of the Wayside Chapel and Doveton Baptist Church illustrate different forms of community engagement as "presence" with those who are on the margins in the transition beyond Christendom. What is clear from both these stories is that embodying "presence" requires an intentional and patient approach. It not only requires clarity about mission but also attention to questions of finance and governance and careful thought about how a church can facilitate and sustain such presence. For both Wayside and Doveton, there has been a practice of patience that is not focused on quantifiable results, fixing people, or solving problems. It is rather about maintaining a fundamental integrity in the connection between theology and practice at an individual and organizational level. Both stories draw our attention to the importance of the language that we use to describe our activities, in reaching for an inclusive approach to partnering and building community.

---

36. Lewellyn interview.
37. Lewellyn interview.

Epilogue: Lingering with the Beatitudes

I started this book with an argument as to why and how we needed to read Scripture "again," from a location in which churches were no longer "in control," but still implicated in the exercise of power. On the way from there to here, we have read Scripture "otherwise," encountered Pilgram Marpeck's life and theology, and looked at some recent experiences of community engagement in Australia. So, how to draw this exploration of community engagement after Christendom to a close in a way that keeps us looking forward?

Given that I started with reading Scripture "again," it seemed appropriate to conclude by returning to read Scripture "again," this time a reading that provides a guide to the spirit in which we should undertake community engagement as we move forward and continue the transition beyond Christendom. So I devote the Epilogue to a rereading of the Beatitudes (Matt 5:3–12). I acknowledge that this passage is not an immediately obvious starting point as churches across nearly all Christian traditions have read the Beatitudes as a guide to individual spirituality that has no application to church involvement in public policy and community issues. Indeed, it sometimes seems to have had little application to the life of the Christian community. Even when approached as a guide to individual spirituality, it has been generally agreed that the Beatitudes set an unrealistically high standard that can only be met, if at all, by spiritual virtuosi. In Christendom, for example, the Beatitudes were the preserve of religious orders whose members had withdrawn from ordinary life to live separate lives as "super" Christians. Consequently, the Beatitudes have been quarantined from either influencing the church's life in the world or providing a critique of its engagement with political power.

Given that the Beatitudes are presented as deriving directly from Jesus, it's surprising that this element of his teaching has been so narrowly confined in its application, if not largely ignored. Against the grain of this dismissal, I suggest that we should linger with the possibility that the spirit and the priorities of the Beatitudes are antithetical to Christendom. If that is the case, then a rereading of the Beatitudes is precisely what we need now to inform community engagement after Christendom. Such a rereading isn't easy and will require a sustained effort to continue to linger with the Beatitudes, allowing them to reshape our engagement with the communities within which we find ourselves.

The Beatitudes and community engagement

In offering what can only be a beginning to a rereading of the Beatitudes, what follows is no more than some notes scribbled in the margin of this provocative text, as an attempt to help us become attentive to this teaching of Jesus and reflect on how it might bear on us in a situation of being engaged, but not being "in control." In reading the Beatitudes "again," in this context, I have approached them as statements of wisdom that gesture towards a way of life that points towards the transforming reality of the kingdom of God.

In attempting this reading, I want to record a deep debt to two friends who in different ways have inspired me to pay close attention to the Beatitudes and their implications for Christian discipleship in public life. Professor Christopher Marshall over several decades has developed restorative justice as a practice informed by reflection on Scripture that has been shaped by a deep engagement with the Anabaptist tradition. Chris has brought the perspectives of the Jesus' account of the kingdom of God in the Beatitudes, and the parables of Jesus, into public life as ways to move toward shalom.

My other source of encouragement is Dave Andrews, who has not only taught the Beatitudes passionately to anyone who would listen, but has been living them out for several decades through the life of the Waiters Union in the inner suburbs of Brisbane.[1] The Waiters Union is a network of local residents who are committed to developing a sense of community in the locality with their neighbors, including those who are marginalized, and doing so consciously in the radical tradition of Jesus of Nazareth.

The Beatitudes

In the Gospel of Matthew, the Beatitudes are placed at the beginning of the collection of teaching by Jesus that we know as the Sermon on the Mount. While the teaching of the Sermon is addressed to the disciples, the inner

---

1. See Andrews, *Plan Be*.

Epilogue: Lingering with the Beatitudes

circle of Jesus' followers, it wasn't limited strictly to them. According to Matthew, a crowd gathered around to overhear what Jesus is saying.

> Blessed are the poor in spirit, for theirs is the kingdom of heaven.
>
> Blessed are those who mourn, for they will be comforted.
>
> Blessed are the meek, for they will inherit the earth.
>
> Blessed are those who hunger and thirst for righteousness, for they will be filled.
>
> Blessed are the merciful, for they will receive mercy.
>
> Blessed are the pure in heart, for they will see God.
>
> Blessed are the peacemakers, for they will be called children of God.
>
> Blessed are those who are persecuted for righteousness' sake, for theirs is the kingdom of heaven.
>
> Blessed are you when people revile you and persecute you and utter all kinds of evil against you falsely on my account. Rejoice and be glad, for your reward is great in heaven, for in the same way they persecuted the prophets who were before you. (Matt 5:3–11)

This clearly structured block of teaching is easy to memorize. It is a first step in letting the Beatitudes begin to shape your discipleship. In this way it has become part of my daily life over the past decade. Both Jim Forest, a Catholic peace activist, now a member of the Orthodox Church, and Clarence Jordan, a radical Baptist, have expounded the teaching of the Beatitudes through the image of a staircase that takes us one step at a time towards God.[2] There is no doubt that the Beatitudes can be read using that focal image. Given the testimony of two such distinguished witnesses, who am I to argue? But it's not the only way to read the Beatitudes, I would suggest. What I would draw attention to is the intertwining responses that emerge when we pay closer attention to the teaching. Visualize each of the Beatitudes as a colorful thread, that when interwoven with all the others produces a strong, bright braid. The virtues that the Beatitudes call us to turn out to be mutually interlocking and self-reinforcing when intertwined as a way of life.

Each of the wisdom sayings that comprise the Beatitudes, when lived out in conjunction with the others, offers a consistent orientation for our community engagement through the commitments and practices that they invoke. While the sayings are conditional in character, they contain an implicit imperative, a guide to the way we should engage with people and the world consistent with the practice of Jesus.[3] The Beatitudes point

2. Forest, *The Ladder of the Beatitudes*, 2; Jordan, *The Sermon on the Mount*, 8.
3. Stephens, "Mary McKillop," 45–46.

to a range of virtues that have a communal and public focus: humility, empathy, self-restraint, righteousness, mercy, integrity, nonviolence, perseverance.[4] I'll talk about the specific issues expressed in each Beatitude, and the vocabulary in which they are framed, along with providing a brief commentary in which I will include examples of the way each has been, and may be, embodied.

Before I start with a consideration of each wisdom saying, I need to deal with the term "blessed." It's difficult to give a good contemporary translation of the term. For the seventeenth-century translators from the Greek, the term "blessed" meant something consecrated to, or belonging to God, or sharing the life of God. The Hebrew term for "blessed" had the sense of "Oh the good fortune" from the root meaning of to go straight or to advance. Following this line of approach, I suggest that we interpret the term "blessed" as an invocation that one is on the right track or making headway. The Australian vernacular expression "Good on you," with its endorsement of the path you have taken and your effort in taking it, catches something of this sense. We need to keep that range of resonance in mind as we embark on this rereading.

Blessed are the poor in spirit

In his opening statement "Blessed are the poor in spirit for theirs is the kingdom of God," Jesus provides us with a summary of the Beatitudes. The stance of being poor in spirit is one of vulnerability and dependence on God. It also points to a way of engaging with others that does not rely on political, institutional, or cultural power. Humility and modesty are virtues that are central to what it is to be poor in spirit. This is a call to pay attention to others through learning how to listen and to be present with them, rather than asserting ourselves and our view of the world. In taking the stance of the poor in spirit we are opening ourselves to take the perspective on life of those who know they are not in control. From this perspective we can begin to see the world as they do. From this position we can grasp and imagine the possibility of the kingdom of God becoming present as a gift that is not in the control of the powerful of this world.

Bonhoeffer leaned into this Beatitude when he observed in his reflections on the experience of struggle against the Nazi regime: "There remains an experience of incomparable value. We have for once learnt to see the great events of world history from below, from the perspective of the outcast, the

4. Andrews, *Plan Be*, 7.

Epilogue: Lingering with the Beatitudes

suspects, the maltreated, the powerless, the oppressed, the reviled—in short from the perspective of those who suffer."[5]

This invocation carries profound implications for community engagement. Who are those who we need to be paying attention to as we shift our priority from assuming an identity, a location with those who are in power, to those who are on the outside, to those who are marginal? The answer to this will undoubtedly differ between national contexts, though the international resonance of the Black Lives Matter movement suggests that racism is a widely shared reality. Racism is a powerful determinant of who is on the outside across much of the world. In Australia, listening by churches will need to start with the First Nations people who have offered an agenda for justice based on extensive listening and conversation within their own emerging polity. *The Uluru Statement from the Heart* that arose from an extended conversation among First Nations peoples provides an invitation to those of us whose history and identity lies in the colonial settler state to begin listening to this deep conversation about our history and our future, an invitation that sadly has not yet been taken up by the Australian government.[6]

To become poor in spirit then is to open ourselves in vulnerability, to the possibility of receiving the gifts of God's grace and healing in the present moment. In becoming poor in spirit, we may just come to realize that we who are providing social services need to place ourselves alongside those are receiving the services, and in doing so realize that we also need healing and forgiveness. We are all deeply implicated in much of the injustice and destruction that we are concerned with remedying in our advocacy and service.

The orientation of the Beatitudes directs us against the unconscious grain of many church organizations, even those whose commitments are to service of the poor. In bureaucratically structured organizations there is a distinction in status and power between the professionals and the marginal people who are the "subjects" of the programs and services. This is a distinction that the Wayside Chapel has sought to avoid. People are persons to be encountered and engaged, not problems to be fixed. What we have in the Beatitudes is a discipline for exposing the tendency for the church and church-related organizations to drift away from living their values and coming to depend on, and consequently be shaped by, external financial

---

5. Bonhoeffer, *Letters and Papers from Prison*, 17.
6. *The Uluru Statement*.

resources, and their alignment with social and technical power and political influence.[7]

Blessed are those who mourn

"Good on those who mourn, for they shall be comforted" may strike us as somewhat odd, if not downright paradoxical, but let's see where it takes us. If you don't mourn, you can't be comforted. This seems to be the logic of the invocation. This Beatitude seems to refer back to Isaiah 61:1–3, where God's people are mourning over their oppression by their enemies, and the prophet is called to bind up the brokenhearted. This is not just a reference to a personally experienced grief, such as the death of a family member. It deals in its initial reference with the experience of Israel: the invasion and the exile, a trauma that profoundly shaped the national consciousness and theology.

> The spirit of the Lord God is upon me,
>   because the Lord has anointed me;
> he has sent me to bring good news to the oppressed,
>   to bind up the broken hearted,
> to proclaim liberty to the captives,
>   and release to the prisoners;
> to proclaim the year of the Lord's favor,
>   and the day of vengeance of our God;
>   to comfort all who mourn;
> to provide for those who mourn in Zion—
>   to give them a garland instead of ashes,
>   the oil of gladness instead of mourning.

The scope of this invocation is wide. Grieving over injustice—and there was then, and still is currently, a good deal to grieve over—can be expressed as empathy and compassion arising from awareness of the reality of injustice. Anguish over the state of the world, and the apparent triumph of evil, cruelty, and the greedy despoiling of God's good creation, all fall within the scope of such mourning. Lamentation as a form of mourning is the necessary starting point if we are to be comforted, and more than that, to grasp the possibility of a liberation, the experience of freedom from the conditions over which we have been mourning.

To say it one more time: only when our hearts are broken, this Beatitude suggests, will we receive comfort. Paradoxically, in mourning there is

---

7. In *Out and Out,* Andrews develops a therapy for both ourselves and our organizations based on reflection on the Gospels.

Epilogue: Lingering with the Beatitudes

the possibility of receiving the comfort through realizing that the violence that has brought the grieving is not the final word. We can begin to experience, or at least imagine, a future beyond this grief. The importance of mourning has been echoing in Australia through our experience of the year 2020, starting with grief over the impact of climate change in fire and flood as a sign of what is coming even if we begin to take effective action to reduce emissions, and then the disruption and death brought by the pandemic.

The relevance of mourning as the first step in the response of churches and church-related agencies to the sexual abuse scandals should hardly need underlining. We need to mourn for what we in the church have done and failed to do because of our concern with institutional reputation and self-preservation, and the destruction of human lives that followed. Our hearts need to break. Comfort can only come the other side of mourning and joining with those who have been mourning over decades at these failures.

Blessed are the meek

"Blessed are the meek, for they shall inherit the earth." The term "meek" as used in the Beatitudes presents more than one problem for us. Knowing how to respond to this invocation is difficult given the associations that the term has now acquired in our culture of being someone who is easy to walk over and will show no resistance to aggression. We have also come to understand the need for assertion by the vulnerable against the abusers. Against this background, how can we respond to this invocation? The original meaning of the term "meek" was quite different from its current associations with being easily pushed around. Meekness originally was a disciplined gentleness that was both patient and strong. Its original meaning is demonstrated when people are able to hold their ground without the use of violence, to stand firm when they are psychologically and physically under pressure.[8] Reading a number of accounts of the life of the late civil rights activist John Lewis, I was struck by how much his behavior displayed this characteristic in an exemplary way.[9] His ability to absorb violence with deep strength without either retaliation or withdrawal from the nonviolent struggle for justice became legendary.

The civil rights movement provides multiple examples of the power of the practice of meekness, as have several notable "strikes" by indigenous communities in Australia. These strikes typically involved people sitting

---

8. Forest, *The Ladder of the Beatitudes* 48–49; Jordan, *The Sermon on the Mount*, 12–13.

9. For an account of Lewis's gentle strength, see Halberstam, *The Children*, 510–15.

down on country for as long as it took to have their claims for justice recognized. These cases provide striking evidence of what the meek inheriting the earth looks like. Frequently these activities by the meek have taken time and displayed immense perseverance and deep patience.[10] The sit-down by the Gurindji people, led by Vincent Lingiari on the Wave Hill pastoral lease, lasted for nearly a decade before they regained some of their land.[11] Less well known is the Pilbara Aboriginal Strike in Western Australia, which stretched over four years of protest from 1946–1949 before the local people were able to break the near-slavery conditions under which they had been employed in the pastoral industry. Anne Scrimgeour's account of the Pilbara strike, *On Red Earth Walking*, is a powerful and moving account of the power and the intelligence of the meek. The indigenous community used disciplined tactics that practitioners of nonviolence like James Lawson and Martin Luther King would have recognized without any difficulty.[12] The disciplined, patient resistance of those involved in the strikes illustrates the original meaning of meekness and demonstrates its relevance as a form of community engagement in the spirit of the Beatitudes.

Another area of activism where this combination of tenderness and strength is relevant is in campaigning on issues relating to climate change. The environmental campaigner and Quaker activist Alistair McIntosh has pointed to the importance of a spiritual grounding of nonviolence in the struggle for climate justice, calling for a spirituality of gentle, patient strength.[13]

Blessed are those who hunger and thirst for righteousness

"Blessed are those who hunger and thirst for righteousness, for they shall be satisfied." Hungering and thirsting for righteousness, a word whose meaning overlaps with that of justice, speaks to a desperate desire. We are looking here for the achievement of a social order functioning in a way that demonstrates shalom, completeness, well-being, peace, and flourishing. It should be clear why I have used the term "desperate" to indicate the depth of the desire for justice that the disciples and all those who were listening to Jesus are called to. Hunger and thirst are powerful drivers for the poor in the Middle East, the context in which this teaching was offered. Water was often not

---

10. For examples of meekness as nonviolent protest in bringing about social and political change, see Ackermann and Duvall, *A Force More Powerful*.
11. Hodgson, "From Little Things Big Things Grow."
12. Scrimgeour, *On Red Earth Walking*.
13. McIntosh, *Riders on the Storm*, 116–19.

easily available in hot and parched landscapes. For the vast majority of Jesus' listeners, hunger was a frequent experience, for many were tenant farmers living under harsh conditions. The longing for justice/righteousness is of such an intensity that it drives us to take action to achieve the goal we are seeking. If we are hungry and thirsty we will be driven to do something in a timely way to meet those human needs that go to our survival, our ability to keep on living. This image is a call for a passionate, energetic commitment to take action that works for human flourishing. We are called to seek for justice, even if it is on behalf of our enemies.

Jim Forest observes that a Christian "is obliged to see and respond to the real world with all its fear, pain and bloodstains . . . [and] to participate here and now in God's righteousness."[14] The fierceness and focus of this hunger is important for those for whom the action of seeking justice takes communal and institutional form. In directing our attention to the need for justice/righteousness the temptation to distort our activity to the imperative of institutional survival is put under severe question.

The outcome of hungering and thirsting for righteousness is that those who do so will have their hunger and thirsting quenched and they will witness the enactment of justice. But as we know, justice can never be achieved on a once-only basis. Accordingly, the need that brings us to hunger and thirst for justice/righteousness will continually recur. Supporting asylum seekers, for example acting to enable them to make their claim for justice, for a fair hearing, and just adjudication of their claim for protection, can require continuing action over many years and sometimes that hunger and thirst is slaked, and their safety and the possibility of flourishing is obtained. At that moment you can stop briefly and rejoice—but then the hunger will return when you consider the those whose claims are still being denied.

Blessed are the merciful

"Good on the merciful, for they shall receive mercy." Being merciful involves granting mercy to all who are in need of it. Here we emulate God by exercising compassion toward those who have failed in multiple ways, and by providing pardon to those who have done wrong to us or to our community. The Beatitude is addressed to those in a position to exercise this. The question comes back to us: do we wish to obtain mercy? Will we recognize mercy, and our own need for it, unless we have already learnt how to practice it towards others?

---

14. Forest, *The Ladder of the Beatitudes*, 69.

The church in Christendom was for the longest time associated with the exercise of judgment from a position of power and had been in a position to see that judgment enforced without recognizing its own need for mercy. In taking this stance it placed itself outside the scope of the Beatitudes. The church needs to recognize that it can no longer, and more importantly should no longer, remain in that space. Indeed, the church and its agencies are desperately in need of mercy for their manifold and grievous failures. The path towards receiving mercy involves learning how to become merciful. Institutions of any sort are rarely noted for the exercise of compassion, yet that is what we as the Christian church must attempt if we are in any way to receive mercy, to be the subjects of compassion. Being merciful is not only a matter of words but also a matter of action. If we are in any doubt what mercy and compassion require, we can always turn to the teaching of Jesus in the parables of the Prodigal Son and the Good Samaritan to inform our heart and mind.[15]

Mercy, empathy, and compassion are all closely related virtues. If we can begin to practice them within the life of the church, we may open the door for others who we have badly hurt to consider the possibility of extending mercy to the church. This is perilous and difficult territory, I know, because it can provide scope for institutions to manipulate those whose mercy they are seeking. Nevertheless, the invocation of the Beatitude is there, and the call to the practice of mercy may be the only way the door for the church to receive mercy can be opened.

Blessed are the pure in heart

"Good on the pure in heart, for they shall see God." The heart is the center of our willing, our being, and our doing. Being pure in heart is to be wholehearted in all that we do, not least in the way we approach living out the Beatitudes, in our seeking for justice and being merciful. This Beatitude then has to do with integrity of thought and action, a straightforwardness, a consistency between what we say and what we do. What we have here is an encouragement for consistency between our outward actions and our inner motivations. The call here is for action that displays integrity, transparency, and a necessary straightforwardness.

---

15. Marshall, *Compassionate Justice*, provides an extended discussion of the parables of the Good Samaritan and the Prodigal Son, and their relationship to law, crime, and restorative justice, that unpacks many of the complexities of the exercise of compassion, mercy, and forgiveness.

Epilogue: Lingering with the Beatitudes

This invocation can be read as being relevant to the character of institutions in their engagement with the community in service and advocacy. The need for straightforward dealing with the community arising from the institutional failings of churches and their agencies comes immediately to mind. This question of integrity in our institutions is intimidating when we remember recent failures brought about by their giving priority to institutional survival and reputation, not to the needs of those harmed by institutional abuse.

Bonhoeffer was thinking a good deal about purity of heart or integrity in reflecting on its importance for rebuilding institutions and relationships after the impending defeat of Germany. His observations and reflections apply very much to the situation of those who have experienced destructive institutions.

> We have been silent witnesses of evil deeds; we have been drenched by many storms; we have learnt the arts of equivocation and pretence; experience has made us suspicious of others and kept us from being truthful and open; intolerable conflicts have worn us down and even made us cynical. Are we still of any use? What we shall need is not geniuses, or cynics or misanthropes or clever tacticians, but plain honest, straightforward men. Will our inward power of resistance be strong enough, and or honesty with ourselves remorseless enough for us to find our way back to simplicity and straightforwardness?[16]

Integrity, this invocation suggests, is the key to seeing God. This is a hard and difficult saying, but it points to the need for coherence between who we are and our ability to see clearly. Jim Forest, drawing on the Orthodox theological tradition, points to the hope of not only seeing God, but also to finding joy in the radiance of uncreated light.[17] To see God is to take joy in the radiance of God. Forest points to Psalm 17:15: "As for me, I shall behold your face in righteousness; when I awake, I shall be satisfied, beholding your likeness."

Blessed are the peacemakers

"Good on the peacemakers, for they shall be called children of God." Peacemaking involves both a no and a yes. The no in peacemaking is the stance of rejecting violence, and the yes is of seeking reconciliation with those with

---

16. Bonhoeffer, *Letters and Papers from Prison*, 16–17.
17. Forest, *The Ladder of the Beatitudes*, 105.

whom you are in conflict. The goal is shalom, as peace that is a state of well-being and flourishing that takes in not only human life, but the whole of creation. To make peace is to engage actively in bringing God's redemption to bear on a broken society. It involves confronting conflict and working to bring about reconciliation and wholeness. This commitment to peacemaking requires patience, something I have mentioned in respect of other Beatitudes. It also involves taking ad hoc, rather than ideologically fixed, approaches to bring about change in pursuit of peace.

"Good on the peacemakers, for they shall be called children of God." They shall be recognized as the children of God, recognized as those who are furthering God's activity and purposes in the world. In one of those serendipitous moments, it turned out that I found myself working on this passage on the day celebrated as Martin Luther King Day in the United States. As someone who sought to bring change peacefully, King serves as a good example of peacemaking as a disturbing, disruptive activity. It is not simply an avoidance of conflict. It requires the willingness to take risks, and it requires a community to sustain that stance. If peacemaking is a characteristic of being a child of God, what does that tell us about God? Such a stance by the children aligns God with the activity of peacemaking and nudges us to rethink our image of God.

Blessed are those who are persecuted for righteousness' sake

"Good on those who are persecuted for righteousness' sake, for theirs is the kingdom of heaven."

Being persecuted for the sake of righteousness, for the sake of justice, is the question at issue in the last two Beatitudes. These two Beatitudes stand together as a way of emphasizing and reinforcing the importance of the message about persecution. Suffering for just causes, or for the achievement of justice, requires, as do several Beatitudes, patience and perseverance. Patience threads its way through almost every dimension of Jesus' teaching in the Beatitudes. These invocations require us to accept that we are not in control but are nevertheless called to be faithful even if it takes time and means we must endure suffering. Sitting behind this teaching is the assumption that the government and the powers that be will not always be just in their actions, and that we may have to live and suffer in leaning in against that injustice, being ready to suffer for resistance against government in our pursuit of justice. We are reminded that we stand here in the line of the Hebrew prophets, alongside Isaiah, Jeremiah, Ezekiel, Amos, and Micah.

I need to issue a caution here. Being persecuted and suffering for the sake of righteousness, in the struggle for justice, is not the same as "suffering" because we are self-righteous, and resentful about losing our privileges, a distinction that we need to keep in mind on our way out of Christendom. Having our residual Christendom privileges taken away is not the same as suffering persecution. Suffering for righteousness is not the same as having our social and political status challenged, another confusion that is proving common among church leaders and Christians in Australia in recent years.

Beatitudes and church-related agencies

Looking back at the accounts of community engagement in Part III, we can find in them traces of the practices of the Beatitudes as I have briefly discussed them here. The case studies of the practice of hospitality towards asylum seekers in chapter 10 lines up with the call to mercy and compassion. Presence with its correlative of patience, the theme of chapter 11, can also be understood as an expression of mourning, seeking mercy, and identifying with the poor in spirit. Hungering and thirsting for justice can empower us to take the form of efforts at advocacy that I discussed in chapter 9. The Salvation Army's work on Manus and Nauru that I discussed in chapter 8 saw their staff persecuted for their attempts to express mercy and obtain a modicum of justice for asylum seekers in the detention camps.

The Beatitudes provide a litmus test for assessing our priorities for community engagement after Christendom. Such engagement should be undertaken in a humble and patient spirit, yet passionate in its seeking for justice. In reflection on what that looks like I would point to its intrinsic connection with a practice of ad hoc, bottom-up approaches that work with people, not coming in over the top in a violent, controlling style. Such approaches cut against the grain of a culture in which in our debates about policy we compulsively talk about seeking "solutions" to "problems" with its implicit violation of the integrity of the people we are engaging with. That is a reflex and a language that we need to intentionally avoid if we are to remain in tune with the spirit of the Beatitudes.

In pointing us away from assuming that we should be "in control," the Beatitudes gesture towards a stance in which we are not tempted to reach for big solutions. The long-running TV series *Grand Designs* serves as a parable here. Every episode offers a cautionary narrative of an ambitious home building project that runs over budget, requires panicked redesign, rushed construction, and usually features windows that when they are eventually delivered don't actually fit. The program concludes with rueful reflections by the people attempting the project on crucial lessons learned, often and alas, too late. My takeaway message is that "modest" proposals that are humble, as opposed to grand designs, offer us the opportunity to learn as we go, ducking and weaving as we encounter a reality always more complex and shape-shifting than we anticipated. Such an approach keeps us open to a practice of engagement informed by the spirit of the Beatitudes.

A humble and patient approach to community engagement is supported by the documented failure in modernity of many large-scale, top-down attempts at social and economic transformation. We need to shift as a matter of habit to tactical responses that take account of conditions on the ground as an expression of "the art of the weak,"[18] the only real option for people and organizations who know they are not in control. We need to recognize that we can only proceed tactically, that is operating flexibly from the bottom up rather than assuming a top-down view.[19]

Humble community engagement will be skeptical, or at least highly cautious, about large-scale forms of social organization, with a consequent preference for decentralized bottom-up approaches informed by local knowledge. The French sociologist and theologian Jacques Ellul has emphasized community engagement through the creation of small groups and networks, advocacy in denouncing falsehood and oppression, and seeking generally to overturn top-down authority. Ellul has left us with an extensive theological and sociological legacy that is antithetical to the heritage of Christendom, with its assumption of top-down approaches, that are centered on government and the state.

> Christian social engagement should be ad hoc. Given that we live between the time of the inauguration and the consummation of the kingdom of God, there is no ideologically pure or utopian social arrangement for which we should strive. Any given social structure—no matter its strengths—is prone to fall under the sway of the powers of sin. Once one injustice is corrected with some new practice of equity, the new practice will, in turn, struggle with its own infidelities with regard to greed or pride or coercive force. Then a new corrective must be sought, and then again yet another.[20]

It is in the spaces generated by humble responsive actions that radical change may arise. The early Christians were modest in their community engagement. They did not attempt to take power within the Roman Empire,

---

18. De Certeau, *The Practice of Everyday Life*, 37.
19. De Certeau, *The Practice of Everyday Life*, 36–39.
20. Camp, *Scandalous Witness*, 164.

Epilogue: Lingering with the Beatitudes

though there was much in the empire of which they were critical. Yet the impact of their humble practices in the community over time was radical. They refused to wage war for Caesar because Jesus, whose authority overrode that of the emperor, had commanded them to love their enemies. Their response to infanticide was to exercise hospitality and take discarded babies into their own homes. This stance over time changed the way children were valued and brought into the culture an embodied commitment to the vulnerable that had not previously been there.

The approach I am sketching here leads us to a quiet opposition to political fundamentalism, a stance best understood as a specific set of beliefs leading to a political engagement that freezes at a particular moment in history a specific interpretation of authoritative texts, cultural understandings, and social judgments, and seeks enforcement of them as normative by the state. Such political views and practices as frozen are no longer subject to question and thus gather to themselves the aura of the sacred. A fundamentalist stance is characterized by marking out partisan boundaries, establishing who is in, who is out, who are friends and who are enemies. We are left here with a principle of exclusion, rather than an opportunity for dialogue.

A humble approach calls for a practice of respectful dialogue, listening for minority voices within and across traditions. Such an approach encourages us to pay attention to those with whom we differ, in engaging in some common project. To avoid fundamentalism, we need to work reflectively and critically with traditions, our own and others', recognizing that traditions are arguments extended through time. Fundamental agreements are defined and redefined both by those inside a tradition and in communication and dialogue with those outside of it. Dialogue will require us to acknowledge moral failings in our past practices, becoming conscious of intellectual and social limits to the process of change.

A practice of listening to the voice of others and critical conversation directed at discerning common goals and possible paths towards their achievement as the basis for approaching policy change has wide potential. Recent radical political organizing directed at discerning common goals, building community through processes of listening and finding a voice and shaping appropriate action, can be found in movements inspired by both Saul Alinsky and the civil rights movement in the United States. It also can be found in range of movements directed at specific policy areas and tangible goals such as fair trade, minimum wages, renewable energy—some of which have found a home in ecumenical activity as well as local congregations. Such listening and respectful dialogue enables coalitions to be built across groups with substantial differences.

Such an engagement involves resisting the compression of time arising from instantaneous communication and the demand for efficiency as rapidity of response, all of which works to subvert the democratic requirement that time be available for deliberation, discussion, and reconciliation of opposing viewpoints. The processes I am suggesting are time-consuming and demand a development of people capable of patient engagement. This approach can also be understood at a systemic level as keeping political activity open to pluralism of motivation and orientation of divergent ways of being in the world, a condition that can helpfully be termed the post-secular. By the "post-secular" I do not mean the return of religion, or a reenchantment, rather secularity in reflexive mode. The post-secular is a space in which people with motivations grounded in multiple specific traditions, cultures, or communities, engage in dialogue and common action in seeking to contribute to public well-being. I have avoided throughout this book providing a detailed plan or program for community engagement in the transition beyond Christendom. The dialogue I have just suggested is one more reason for not offering such programs with their temptation to lean on them as a source of assurance.

Discipleship in a time of uncertainty

I started this book by noting the disruptions (economic, environmental, and social) that been shaking up the world in the time it has taken me to write this book. Post-Christendom looks like a time of disruption and uncertainty dialed up to the nth degree. In a parting word of encouragement, let me draw your attention to the story in Luke 8:22–25. Here we have an episode where the disciples were reaching desperately for certainty in their understanding of who Jesus was. This passage in Luke seems appropriate in a time in which the church is in the midst of a perfect storm, in which all that is certain has been shaken loose.

> One day [Jesus] got into a boat with his disciples, and he said to them, "Let us go across to the other side of the lake." So, they put out, and while they were sailing, he fell asleep. A windstorm swept down on the lake, and the boat was filling with water, and they were in danger. They went to him and woke him up, shouting, "Master, Master, we are perishing!" And he woke up and rebuked the wind and the raging waves; they ceased, and there was a calm. He said to them, "Where is your faith?" They were afraid and amazed, and said to one another, "Who then is this,

Epilogue: Lingering with the Beatitudes

that he commands even the winds and the water, and they obey him?"

The disciples in the midst of the storm have their certainties disturbed. The world is out of control, their lives are at risk, and what they thought they knew about their teacher is radically being upended and perhaps extended in unsettling ways. The disciples ask "Who is this Jesus? Who is this person who stills the storm, who is in touch with the world of earth and wind and water?" The disciples, we should remember, are already on the way with Jesus. They have already committed themselves to follow him, but they are still grappling with the question: "Who is this Jesus that we are following?" They knew something of who he was, but now in a moment of existential crisis they find themselves asking even more questions about the one they are following.

Finding out who Jesus is not something that they can do once, and then move along the path of discipleship without needing to learn more. The disciples get to know who Jesus is through again and again taking the next step in following him, following him to Jerusalem, witnessing his confrontation with the powers of the empire and learning from the witness of the women of his resurrection. Later disciples found out even more of who Jesus is throughout the experience of the early church as they begin to bring about reconciliation across the boundaries of race and gender.

We too will find out who Jesus is by actually engaging in the ongoing practice of a discipleship and community engagement in lives that are informed and shaped by the Beatitudes. Stuart Murray helpfully picks up the theme of finding Jesus in following him and how this might be reflected in our community life, when he makes a disturbing proposal.

> We need to stop calling ourselves "Christians." Not only is the term compromised by its associations and debased by overuse, it is also rather presumptuous. Who are we to claim that we are like Christ? . . . Maybe we need a term that is both purposeful and restrained. Maybe we should claim no more (or less) than that we are "followers of Jesus." As followers we do not claim to have arrived at the destination, nor need we distinguish ourselves from others who are at different stages of the journey . . . Churches committed to following Jesus welcome fellow travelers unreservedly . . . Their ethos is one of following, learning, changing, growing, moving forward. Together, and as we reflect on the Gospels (and the rest of Scripture), we discover more of what it means to follow Jesus.[21]

---

21. Murray, *The Naked Anabaptist*, 61.

Community Engagement after Christendom

As I suggested at the beginning of this book, our challenge is to begin to reimagine what a discipleship of community engagement looks like. Whatever else it requires, we will need to let go of tightly held preconceptions as to the place of Christians and the church in our society. And we will need to let go of our desire for security and control in our time and place. After all, look where the path of reaching for security and control through Christendom has taken us. Following Jesus through community engagement in the forms of advocacy, hospitality, and presence with those who are on the margins is the path in front of us as we transition beyond Christendom.

Bibliography

Abbott, Tony. "Against the Prodigal State." *Policy* (Spring 2001) 37–39.
ABC. "No Advantage." *Four Corners*, April 29, 2013. https://www.abc.net.au/4corners/no-advantage/4660004.
Ackermann, Bruce, and Jack Duvall. *A Force More Powerful: A Century of Nonviolent Conflict*. New York: Palgrave, 2000.
Andrews, David. *Out and Out: Way-Out Community Work*. Preston, Victoria: Challenge, 2012.
———. *Plan Be: Be the Change You Want to See in the World*. Milton Keynes: Authentic, 2008.
Anglicare Australia. *Strategic Plan, 2014*. https://www.anglicare.asn.au/docs/default-source/default-document-library/aa_strategic-plan_fa.pdf?sfvrsn=4.
Anslow, Matt. "Prayer as a Weapon: Clasped Hands as Nonviolent Uprising." Tinsley Annual Lecture, Morling College, Sydney, 2015. https://www.morling.edu.au/module_resources/uploads/downloads/Tinsley%20Lecture/2015%20Annual%20Lecture%20Booklet.pdf.
———. "A Speech on Asylum Seekers and Love Makes a Way." *Life.remixed: the blog of Matt Anslow*, June 21, 2014. https://mattanslow.wordpress.com/tag/asylum-seekers/.
Asher, Allan. "Forgiving the Trespassers." *ABC*, May 28, 2014. https://www.abc.net.au/news/2014-05-28/asher-forgiving-the-trespassers/5483294.
Australia. *Commonwealth of Australia Constitution Act*. http://classic.austlii.edu.au/au/legis/cth/consol_act/coaca430/s116.html.
Australian Churches Refugee Taskforce. "Cathedrals and Churches around Australia Offer Sanctuary to Asylum Seekers Families Facing Deportation to Nauru". Press Release, February 4, 2016. http://www.vcc.org.au/news/item/87-cathedrals-and-churches-around-australia-offer-sanctuary-to-asylum-seeker-families-facing-deportation-to-nauru.
Australian Human Rights Commission. *The Forgotten Children: National Inquiry into Children in Immigration Detention, Review into Recent Allegations Relating to Conditions and Circumstances at the Nauru Regional Processing Centre: Final Report of an inquiry commissioned by the Minister for Immigration and Border Protection*. Sydney, NSW, 2014. https://humanrights.gov.au/our-work/asylum-seekers-and-refugees/publications/forgotten-children-national-inquiry-children.
Bailey, Megan. "An Economy Is Not a Society: Doveton Author Calls for Fair Go." *Herald Sun*. August 4, 2015. https://www.heraldsun.com.au/leader/south-east/

an-economy-is-not-a-society-doveton-author-calls-for-fair-go/news-story/ed70c5a5d9929b0a56edc557363fefd8.

———. "Doveton a 'Band One' Disadvantaged Suburb According to Jesuit Social Services and Catholic Social Services Australia." *Herald Sun,* August 4, 2015. https://www.heraldsun.com.au/leader/south-east/doveton-a-band-one-disadvantaged-suburb-according-to-jesuit-social-services-and-catholic-social-services-australia/news-story/e2c09c7098b2038c5645b61c2f8e446b.

Baptcare. *People Seeking Asylum.* Social Policy Paper 2017. https://www.baptcare.org.au/__data/assets/pdf_file/0015/20067/PEOPSEEKASYLUM-Social-Policy.pdf.

———. "Sanctuary Celebrates 10 Years with Community Dinner." December 2018. https://www.baptcare.org.au/why-baptcare/news/sanctuary-celebrates-10-years-with-community-dinner.

Barns, Ian. "Representing Jesus: Public Christianity in a Late Modern World." May 6, 2012, http://www.ethos.org.au/site/Ethos/filesystem/documents/in-depth/public%20policy/Barns%20-%20Representing%20Jesus%20(3).pdf.

Barrow, Simon. "How Easter Brings Regime Change." *Ekklesia,* April 2006. http://www.ekklesia.co.uk/content/barrow/article_060414easter.shtml.

———. "Redeeming Religion in the Public Sphere." Research Paper, *Ekklesia,* July 2006. http://www.ekklesia.co.uk/research/papers/0607barrow.

Bartley, Jonathan. *Faith and Politics after Christendom.* Milton Keynes: Paternoster, 2006.

Bastian, Lis. "Love Makes a Way." *The Lithgow Sprint,* March 2020. http://thelithgowsprint.org/organisations/love-makes-a-way/.

Beal, Timothy, K. *Esther.* Collegeville, MN: Liturgical, 1999.

Bedding, Chris, "Cranky Christians Against Asylum Seeker Cruelty." *ABC, The Drum,* May 20, 2014. https://www.abc.net.au/news/2014-05-20/bedding-love-makes-a-way/5465300.

Bell, Daniel M., Jr. "Jesus, the Jews, and the Politics of God's Justice." *Ex Auditu* 22 (2006) 87–112.

Berrigan, Daniel. *Daniel: Under the Siege of the Divine.* Farmington, NY: Plough, 1998.

———. *The Kings and Their Gods: The Pathology of Power.* Grand Rapids: Eerdmans, 2008.

Biesecker-Mast, Gerald. *Separation and the Sword in Anabaptist Persuasion: Radical Confessional Rhetoric from Schleitheim to Dordrecht.* Telford, PA: Cascadia, 2006.

Blough, Neil. *Christ in Our Midst: Incarnation, Church and Discipleship in the Theology of Pilgram Marpeck.* Kitchener, ON: Pandora, 2007.

———. "The Uncovering of the Babylonian Whore: Confessionalization and Politics seen from the Underside." *Mennonite Quarterly Review* 75 (2001) 37–55.

Bonhoeffer, Dietrich. *Letters and Papers from Prison.* New York: Simon & Schuster, 1997.

Boyd, Stephen R. "Anabaptism and Social Radicalism in Strasbourg, 1528–32: Pilgram Marpeck on Christian Social Responsibility." *Mennonite Quarterly Review* 63 (1989) 58–76.

———. *Pilgram Marpeck: His Life and Social Theology.* Durham, NC: Duke University Press, 1992.

Bradstock, Andrew. *Radical Religion in Cromwell's England: A Concise History from the English Civil War to the End of the Commonwealth.* New York: I. B. Tauris, 2011.

Bibliography

Bretherton, Luke. *Christ and the Common Life: Political Theology and the Case for Democracy*. Grand Rapids: Eerdmans, 2019.

Brett, Mark G. *Locations of God: Political Theology in the Hebrew Bible*. Oxford: Oxford University Press, 2019.

———. *Political Trauma and Healing: Biblical Ethics for a Postcolonial World*. Grand Rapids: Eerdmans, 2016.

Broughton, Geoff. "What Action should Christians Take?" August 15, 2014. (Pdf file available from author.)

Brueggemann, Walter. "Biblical Authority: A Personal Reflection." In *Telling Our Stories: Personal Accounts of Engagement with Scripture*, edited by Ray Gingerich and Earl Zimmerman, 259–69. Telford, PA: Cascadia, 2006.

———. *Cadences of Home: Preaching among Exiles*. Louisville: Westminster John Knox, 1997.

———. *A Commentary on Jeremiah: Exile and Homecoming*. Grand Rapids: Eerdmans, 1998.

———. "A Fourth-Generation Sellout." In *The Collected Sermons of Walter Brueggemann*, 164–67. Louisville: Westminster John Knox, 2011.

———. *Inscribing the Text: Sermons and Prayers of Walter Brueggemann*. Minneapolis: Fortress, 2011.

———. *Interpretation and Obedience*. Minneapolis: Augsburg Fortress, 1991.

———. *Out of Babylon*. Nashville: Abingdon, 2010.

———. *Redescribing Reality: What We Do When We Read the Bible*. London: SCM, 2009.

———. *The Theology of the Book of Jeremiah*. Cambridge: Cambridge University Press, 2007.

———. *The Word Militant: Preaching a Decentering Word*. Minneapolis: Fortress, 2007.

Brunswick Baptist Church. "BaptCare Sanctuary: Supported Accommodation for Asylum Seekers." http://brunswickbaptistchurch.org.au/in-brunswick/baptcare-sanctuary house/.

———. Ministries. http://brunswickbaptistchurch.org.au/.

Bryson, Lois, and Ian Winter. *Social Change, Suburban Lives: An Australian Newtown 1960s to 1990*. St Leonards, NSW: Allen and Unwin, 1999.

Budden, Chris. *Following Jesus in Invaded Space: Doing Theology on Aboriginal Land*. Eugene, OR: Pickwick, 2009.

Caddy, Joe, Fr. Interview with Douglas Hynd, April 11, 2014.

Calligeros, Marissa. "Anglican and Uniting churches offer sanctuary to asylum seekers after High Court ruling." *Age*, February 4, 2016. https://www.theage.com.au/national/victoria/melbourne-church-offers-sanctuary-to-asylum-seekers-after-high-court-ruling-20160204-gml603.html.

Camp, Lee C. *Scandalous Witness: A Little Political Manifesto for Christians*. Grand Raids: Eerdmans, 2020.

Campbell, Charles L., and Stanley P. Saunders. *The Word on the Street: Performing the Scriptures in the Urban Context*. Grand Rapids: Eerdmans, 2000.

Catholic Social Services Australia. *Annual Report, 2013–4*. https://cssa.org.au/wp-content/uploads/2019/04/CSSA-Annual-Report-2013-2014.pdf.

Cavanaugh, William. *Migrations of the Holy, God, State and the Political Meaning of the Church*. Grand Rapids: Eerdmans, 2011.

Bibliography

Chalmers, Max. "Christian Activists Tip They'll Win Asylum Seeker Debate." *New Matilda*, June 10, 2014. https://newmatilda.com/2014/06/10/christian-activists-tip-theyll-win-asylum-seeker-debate/.

Chappell, David L. *A Stone of Hope: Prophetic Religion and the Death of Jim Crow*. Chapel Hill, NC: University of North Carolina Press, 2004.

Chaves, Mark. "Denominations as Dual Structures: An Organizational Analysis." *Sociology of Religion* 54 (1993) 147–69.

Christoyannopoulos, Alexandre. *Christian Anarchism: A Political Commentary on the Gospel*. Abridged ed. Exeter: Imprint Academic, 2011.

Cleary, Ray, Rev. Interview with Douglas Hynd, December 5, 2013.

Considine, Mark. *Enterprising States: The Public Management of Welfare to Work*. Cambridge: Cambridge University Press, 2001.

Dancer, Anthony. *An Alien in a Strange Land: Theology in the Life of William Stringfellow*. Eugene, OR: Cascade, 2011.

Dastyari, Azadeh. "Let the Asylum Seekers Stay: Strengths and Weaknesses of Church Sanctuary as a Strategy for Law Reform." February 21, 2019. SSRN: https://ssrn.com/abstract=3339189.

Davidson, Helen. "Australia's Onshore Immigration Detention Unlike Any Other Liberal Democracy.'" *The Guardian*, June 17 2019. https://www.theguardian.com/australia-news/2019/jun/18/australias-onshore-immigration-detention-unlike-any-other-liberal-democracy.

Day, Linda M. *Esther: Abingdon Old Testament Commentary*. Nashville: Abingdon, 2005.

De Certeau, Michel. *The Practice of Everyday Life*. Berkeley, CA: University of California Press, 1984.

Doherty, Ben. "The Nauru Files: A Short History of Nauru, Australia's Dumping Ground for Refugees." *The Guardian*, August 9, 2016. https://www.theguardian.com/world/2016/aug/10/a-short-history-of-nauru-australias-dumping-ground-for-refugees.

Dow, Melissa. "The Politics of Exile: Jeremiah 29:1, 4–7." *Political Theology Network*, October 7, 2019. https://politicaltheology.com/category/the-politics-of-scripture/page/2/.

Du Mez, Kristin Kobes. *Jesus and John Wayne: How White Evangelicals Corrupted a Faith and Fractured a Nation*. New York: W. W. Norton, 2020.

Eagleton, Terry. *Reason, Faith and Revolution*. New Haven, CT: Yale University Press, 2010.

Edwards, Julie. "Visitors to Australia's Onshore Detention Centres Speak Out". *Crikey*, July 10, 2019. https://www.crikey.com.au/2019/07/10/visitors-onshore-detention-centres/.

Elisha, Omri. *Moral Ambition: Mobilization and Social Outreach in Evangelical Megachurches*. Berkeley, CA: University of California Press, 2011.

Ellul, Jacques. *The Politics of God and the Politics of Man*. Grand Rapid: Eerdmans, 1972.

———. *On Being Rich and Poor: Christianity in a Time of Economic Globalization*. Compiled, edited, and translated by William Vandenburg. Toronto: University of Toronto Press, 2014.

Epistle of Mathetes to Diognetus. Translated by Alexander Roberts and James Donaldson. http://www.earlychristianwritings.com/text/diognetus-roberts.html.

Bibliography

Farrell, Paul. "Churches Offer Sanctuary to Asylum Seekers Facing Deportation to Nauru." *The Guardian*, February 3, 2016. https://www.theguardian.com/australia-news/2016/feb/04/churches-offer-sanctuary-to-asylum-seekers-facing-deportation-to-nauru.

Forest, Jim. *The Ladder of the Beatitudes*. Maryknoll, NY: Orbis, 1999.

Fowkes, Lisa. "Perspectives: Rethinking Australia's Employment Services. History of Employment Service." *Jobs Australia*. https://www.ja.com.au/policy-advocacy/publications/history-employment-services.

Frame, Tom. *Church and State: Australia's Imaginary Wall*. Sydney: UNSW Press, 2006.

Freeman, Curtis. *Undomesticated Dissent: Democracy and the Public Virtue of Religious Nonconformity*. Waco, TX: Baylor University Press, 2017.

Friesen, Duane. *Artists, Citizens, Philosophers: Seeking the Peace of the City: An Anabaptist Theology of Culture*. Scottdale, PA: Herald, 2000.

Gallet, Wilma. "Christian Mission or an Unholy Alliance: The Changing Role of Church-Related Organisations in Contracted Service Delivery." PhD diss., University of Melbourne, 2016.

———. Interview with Douglas Hynd, January 22, 2014.

Gingerich, Ray. "Reading the Bible in Search of Jesus and the Way." In *Telling Our Stories: Personal Accounts of Engagement with Scripture*, edited by Ray Gingerich and Earl Zimmerman, 79–90. Telford, PA: Cascadia, 2006.

Gingerich, Ray, and Earl Zimmerman, eds. *Telling Our Stories: Personal Accounts of Engagement with Scripture*. Telford, PA: Cascadia, 2006.

Gleeson, Madeline. *Offshore: Behind the Wire on Manus and Nauru*. Sydney: NewSouth, 2016.

Goertz, Hans Jurgen. *The Anabaptists*. New York: Routledge, 1996.

Gornik, Mark R. *To Live in Peace: Biblical Faith and the Changing Inner City*. Grand Rapids: Eerdmans, 2002.

Goroncy, Jason. "Race and Christianity in Australia." *Post-Christendom Studies* 4 (2019–2020) 25–74.

Gorski, Philip S. *American Babylon: Christianity and Democracy Before and After Trump*. New York: Routledge, 2020.

Goza, Joel Edward. *America's Unholy Ghosts: The Racist Roots of Our Faith and Politics*. Eugene, OR: Cascade, 2019.

Greenman, Jeffrey P., et al. *Understanding Jacques Ellul*. Eugene, OR: Cascade, 2012.

Grossman, Jonathan. *Esther: The Outer Narrative and the Hidden Reading*. Winona Lake, IN: Eisenbrauns, 2011.

Haigh, Bruce. "The Salvation Army Is a Branch of Government." *Online Opinion*, May 16, 2013. http://www.onlineopinion.com.au/view.asp?article=15013.

———. "Salvos Lose Moral Compass On Way to Nauru." *Sydney Morning Herald*, December 12, 2012. http://www.smh.com.au/federal-politics/salvos-misplace-moral-compass-on-way-to-nauru-20121220-2bppy.html.

Halberstam, David. *The Children*. New York: New York Times, 1999.

Halse, Brad, Major. Interview with Douglas Hynd, March 12, 2014.

Hargaden, Kevin. *Theological Ethics in a Neoliberal Age*. Eugene, OR: Cascade, 2018.

Harink, Douglas. *1 & 2 Peter*. Brazos Theological Commentary on the Bible. Grand Rapids: Brazos, 2009.

Hart, David Bentley. *Atheist Delusions: The Christian Revolution and Its Fashionable Enemies*. New Haven, CT: Yale University Press, 2009.

Bibliography

Hatfield-Dodds, Lin. Interview with Douglas Hynd, February 6, 2014.

Heilke, Thomas. "Locating a Moral/Political Economy: Lessons from Sixteenth-Century Anabaptism." *Polity* 30 (Winter 1997) 199–229.

Hill, Christopher. *A Turbulent, Seditious and Factious People: John Bunyan and His Church 1628–1688*. Oxford: Oxford University Press, 1988.

———. *The World Turned Upside Down: Radical Ideas During the English Revolution*. Milton Keynes: Penguin, 2019.

Hill, Symon. "The Subversive Feast of Christ the King." *Ekklesia*. http://www.ekklesia.co.uk/node/13613.

Hodgson, Martin. "From Little Things Big Things Grow." *ABC*, August 26, 2011. https://www.abc.net.au/news/2011-08-26/hodgson-from-little-things-big-things-grow/2855942.

Hogan, Michael. "Worrying About Religion." *Australian Review of Public Affairs*, October 2006. http://www.australianreview.net/digest/2006/10/hogan.html.

Holland, Tom. *Dominion: The Making of the Western Mind*. London: Little, Brown, 2019.

Holt, Rebekah. "A Final Goodbye to Abdul, the Latest Man to Die in Australian Detention." *Crikey*, July 24, 2019. https://www.crikey.com.au/2019/07/24/abdul-aziz-death-australian-detention/.

Hudson, Michael. *. . . and forgive them their debts: Lending, Foreclosure and Redemption from Bronze Age Finance to the Jubilee Year*. Dresden: ISLET-Verlag, 2018.

Hurcombe, Tom. "Disestablishing the Kingdom." *Ekklesia*, December 8, 2008. http://www.ekklesia.co.uk/node/8138.

Hynd, Douglas. "The Impact of Neo-liberalism on Church-Related Agencies: Possibilities and Limits of Resistance." *Uniting Church Studies* 22 (2019) 35–50.

———. "On (Not) Becoming 'an Extension of the State' in 'Seeking the Flourishing of the City': A Theologically-Informed Inquiry into the Impact on 'Church-Related Agencies' of Contracting with Government to Provide Social Welfare and Human Services in Australia, 1996 to 2013." PhD diss., Australian Catholic University, 2017.

Isaacs, Mark. "Salvo Detention Workers Recruited through Facebook." *ABC PM*, June 14, 2014. http://www.abc.net.au/pm/content/2014/s4024225.htm.

———. "The Salvos on Nauru." *Pearls and Irritations: John Menadue's Public Policy Journal*, June 11, 2014. http://johnmenadue.com/blog/?p=1791.

———. *The Undesirables*. Melbourne: Hardie Grant, 2014.

Jack, Kristin. *Poetry and Prophecy*. Urban Neighbours of Hope, September 2011. https://issuu.com/servantsasia/docs/poetryprophecy.

Jenkins, David E. *The Contradiction of Christianity*. London: SCM, 1976.

Jesuit Refugee Services Australia. *Annual Report 2019*. https://aus.jrs.net/en/about-jrs-australia/our-impact/.

———. *Publications and Resources*. http://www.jrs.org.au/detention-issues/.

———. "Settlement and Community Building." https://jss.org.au/what-we-do/settlement-and-community-building/.

Jesuit Social Services. "The Harsh Reality of Onshore Immigration Detention in Australia." July 11, 2019. https://jss.org.au/the-harsh-reality-of-onshore-immigration-detention-in-australia/.

Jones, Chris, Rt. Rev. Interview with Douglas Hynd, February 11, 2014.

Jordan, Clarence. *The Sermon on the Mount*. Valley Forge, PA: Judson, 1970.

Bibliography

Kass, Leon. *The Beginning of Wisdom: Reading Genesis*. Chicago: University of Chicago Press, 2003.

Kaye, Bruce. *Colonial Religion: Conflict and Change in Church and State*. Hindmarsh: ATF, 2020.

Keesmaat, Sylvia, and Brian Walsh. *Romans Disarmed: Resisting Empire, Demanding Justice*. Grand Rapids: Brazos, 2019.

Klaassen, Walter. "The Anabaptist Critique of Constantinian Christendom." *Mennonite Quarterly Review* 55 (1981) 218–30.

———. "The Nature of the Anabaptist Protest." *Mennonite Quarterly Review* 45 (1971) 291–311.

Klaassen, Walter, et al., eds. *Later Writings by Pilgram Marpeck and his Circle*. Kitchener, ON: Pandora, 1999.

Klaassen, Walter, and William Klassen. *Marpeck: A Life of Dissent and Conformity*. Scottdale, PA: Herald, 2008.

Klassen, William. "The Limits of Political Authority as seen by Pilgram Marpeck." *Mennonite Quarterly Review* 56 (1982) 342–64.

———. "Pilgram Marpeck: Liberty Without Coercion." In *Profiles of Radical Reformers: Biographical Sketches from Thomas Muntzer to Paracelsus*, edited by Hans-Jorgen Goertz, 168–77. Scottdale, PA: Herald, 1982.

Klassen, William, and Walter Klaassen, eds. *The Writings of Pilgram Marpeck*. Scottdale, PA: Herald, 1978.

Koenig, John. *New Testament Hospitality: Partnership with Strangers as Promise and Mission*. Eugene, OR: Wipf and Stock, 2001.

Kreider, Alan. *The Patient Ferment of the Early Church: The Improbable Rise of Christianity in the Roman Empire*. Grand Rapids: Baker Academic, 2016.

Lash, Nicholas. *Theology on the Way to Emmaus*. London: SCM, 1986.

Laughland, Oliver, and Birdie Jabour. "Salvation Army Humanitarian Work on Manus and Nauru to End." *The Guardian*, December 12, 2013. http://www.theguardian.com/world/2013/dec/13/salvation-army-humanitarian-work-on-manus-and-nauru-to-end.

Lee, Gregory W. "Republics and Their Loves: Rereading the City of God 19." *Modern Theology* 27 (2011) 553–81.

Lewis, Simon. "Australian Churches Offer Sanctuary to Refugees Facing Return to Offshore Detention." *Time*, February 4, 2016. https://time.com/4207499/australian-churches-sanctuary-refugees/.

Lewellyn, Paul, Pastor. Interview with Douglas Hynd, January 22, 2014.

Long, Graham, Rev. Interview with Douglas Hynd, January 14, 2014.

———. *Love Over Hate: Finding Life by the Wayside*. Richmond, Victoria: Slattery, 2013.

———. *Stories from the Wayside*. St. Lucia, Queensland: University of Queensland Press, 2010.

———. *Wayside*. Sydney: NewSouth, 2016.

Love Makes a Way. Website. http://lovemakesaway.org.au/who-we-are/.

MacIntyre, Alasdair. "A Partial Response to My Critics." In *After MacIntyre: Critical Perspectives on the Work of Alasdair MacIntyre*, edited by John Horton and Susan Mendus, 283–304. Notre Dame, IN: University of Notre Dame Press, 1994.

Mahn, Jason A. *Becoming a Christian in Christendom: Radical Discipleship and the Way of the Cross in America's "Christian" Culture*. Minneapolis: Fortress, 2016.

Bibliography

Manne, Robert. "Australia's Uniquely Harsh Asylum Seeker Policy—How Did It Come About?" *ABC Religion and Ethics*, November 6, 2017. https://www.abc.net.au/religion/australias-uniquely-harsh-asylum-seeker-policy---how-did-it-come/10095226.

Marks, D. "Interview with J. Falzon, and L. Hatfield-Dodds: Govt's Welfare to Work Shunned." *ABC PM*, August 23, 2006. https://www.abc.net.au/pm/content/2006/s1722379.htm.

Markus, Robert. *Christianity and the Secular*. Notre Dame, IN: University of Notre Dame Press, 2006.

Marpeck, Pilgram. "An Epistle Concerning the Heritage and Service of Sin." In *The Writings of Pilgram Marpeck*, edited by William Klassen and Walter Klaassen, 412–17. Scottdale, PA: Herald, 1978.

———. "Explanation of the Testaments." In *The Writings of Pilgram Marpeck*, edited by William Klassen and Walter Klaassen, 555–67. Scottdale, PA: Herald, 1978.

———. "Exposé of the Babylonian Whore." In *Later Writings by Pilgram Marpeck and his Circle*, translated by Walter Klaassen, Werner Packull, and John Rempel, 21–48. Kitchener, ON: Pandora, 1999.

———. "Letter to the Strasbourg Council (1532)." In *The Writings of Pilgram Marpeck*, edited by William Klassen and Walter Klaassen, 306–8. Scottdale, PA: Herald, 1978.

———. "Pilgram Marpeck's Confession of 1532." In *The Writings of Pilgram Marpeck*, edited by William Klassen and Walter Klaassen, 107–57. Scottdale, PA: Herald, 1978.

———. "Response to Caspar Schwenckfeld's Judgement." In *Later Writings by Pilgram Marpeck and his Circle*, translated by Walter Klaassen, Werner Packull, and John Rempel, 67–157. Kitchener, ON: Pandora, 1999.

Marsh, Charles. *The Beloved Community: How Faith Shapes Social Justice, From the Civil Rights Movement to Today*. New York: Basic, 2005.

———. *God's Long Summer: Stories of Faith and Civil Rights*. Princeton, NJ: Princeton University Press, 1997.

Marsh, Charles, et al. *Lived Theology: New Perspectives on Method, Style and Pedagogy*. Oxford: Oxford University Press, 2017.

Marshall, Christopher. *Compassionate Justice: An Interdisciplinary Dialogue with Two Gospel Parables on Law, Crime, and Restorative Justice*. Eugene, OR: Cascade, 2012.

———. *Kingdom Come: The Kingdom of God in the Teaching of Jesus*. Eugene, OR: Wipf and Stock, 2015.

McAdam, Jane, and Fiona Chong. *Refugee Rights and Policy Wrongs: A Frank, Up-to-Date Guide by Experts*. Sydney: UNSW Press, 2019.

McCarraher, Eugene. *The Enchantments of Mammon: How Capitalism Became the Religion of Modernity*. Cambridge, MA: Harvard University Press, 2019.

McIntosh, Alistair. *Riders on the Storm: The Climate Crisis and the Survival of Being*. Edinburgh: Birlinn, 2020.

McLean, Olivia, Rev. Interview with Douglas Hynd, June 11, 2014.

McClendon, James Wm., Jr. *Biography as Theology: How Life Stories Can Remake Today's Theology*. Eugene, OR: Wipf and Stock, 2002.

McKenna, Jarrod. "Easter Made Me Do It! On Scapegoats, Asylum Seekers and Being Arrested." *ABC Religion and Ethics*, April 8, 2014. http://www.abc.net.au/religion/articles/2014/04/08/3981214.htm.

Bibliography

Mennonite Church USA. *Confession of Faith in a Mennonite Perspective*. https://www.mennoniteusa.org/who-are-mennonites/what-we-believe/confession-of-faith/.

Miles, Sara. *Jesus Freak: Feeding, Healing, Raising the Dead*. San Francisco: Jossey-Bass, 2010.

Monsma, Stephen V., and J. Christopher Soper. *The Challenge of Pluralism: Church and State in Five Democracies*. 2d ed. Lanham, MD: Rowman & Littlefield, 2009.

Morrison, Zoe. "Planting Hope." *The Monthly*, February 2020. https://www.themonthly.com.au/issue/2020/february/1580475600/zo-morrison/planting-hope#mtr.

Moulds, Paul, Major. Migration Legislation Amendment, Australian Parliament, Joint Committee on Human Rights. https://parlinfo.aph.gov.au/parlInfo/search/display/display.w3p;db=COMMITTEES;id=committees%2Fcommjnt%2F46787736-005b-46df-94f5-4a707fa02cdb%2F0008;query=Id%3A%22committees%2Fcommjnt%2F46787736-005b-46df-94f5-4a707fa02cdb%2F0000%22.

———. "No Sanction of Policy as Salvos Aid Asylum Seekers: The Salvation Army is Still Against Offshore Processing." *Sydney Morning Herald*, December 24, 2012. https://www.smh.com.au/politics/federal/no-sanction-of-policy-as-salvos-aid-asylum-seekers-20121223-2btec.html.

Murray, Les. *The Quality of Sprawl: Thoughts about Australia*. Sydney: Duffy & Snellgrove, 1999.

Murray, Phil. Interview with Douglas Hynd, January 24, 2014.

Murray, Stuart. *Biblical Interpretation in the Anabaptist Tradition*. Kitchener, ON: Pandora, 2000.

———. *The Naked Anabaptist: The Bare Essentials of a Radical Faith*. Scottdale, PA: Herald, 2010.

———. *Post-Christendom: Church and Mission in a Strange New World*. 2d ed. Eugene, OR: Cascade, 2018.

Murray-Williams, Stuart. "Post-Christendom and Post-Colonialism." *Anabaptism Today* 3, no. 1 (April 2021) 36–48.

Myers, Ched. *Binding the Strong Man. A Political Reading of Mark's Story of Jesus*. Maryknoll, NY: Orbis, 1988.

———. "'I Will Ask You a Question:' Interrogatory Theology." In *Theology Without Foundations: Religious Practice and the Future of Theological Truth*, edited by Stanley Hauerwas et al., 91–116. Nashville: Abingdon, 1994.

———. *Who Will Roll Away the Stone? Discipleship Queries for First World Christians*. Maryknoll: Orbis, 1994.

Neville, David J. "Dialectic as Method in Public Theology: Recalling Jacques Ellul." *International Journal of Public Theology* 2 (2008) 163–81.

New Matilda. "Nauru staff condemn cruel conditions." July 24, 2013. https://newmatilda.com/2013/07/24/nauru-staff-condemn-cruel-conditions/.

Newsom, Carol. *Daniel: A Commentary*. Louisville: Westminster John Knox, 2014.

Palmer, Parker. *A Company of Strangers: Christians and the Renewal of America's Public Life*. New York: Herder & Herder, 1983.

Pietersen, Lloyd. *Reading the Bible after Christendom*. Milton Keynes: Paternoster, 2011.

Quinlan, Frank. Interview with Douglas Hynd, November 18, 2013.

Refugee Council of Australia. "How Cuts to Support for People Seeking Asylum Will Affect People, States and Local Communities." January 26, 2019. https://www.refugeecouncil.org.au/srss-cuts-factsheet/.

BIBLIOGRAPHY

———. "Who is a Refugee? Who is an Asylum seeker?" https://www.refugeecouncil.org.au/who-is-a-refugee/.

Reynolds, Henry. *Truth-Telling: History, Sovereignty and the Uluru Statement.* NewSouth, 2021.

Ronalds, Paul. "Exclusive Interview: Paul Ronalds Save the Children CEO." *ABC Lateline*, October 30, 2015. http://www.abc.net.au/lateline/content/2015/s4342703.htm.

Rowland, Christopher. "Blake and the Bible: Bible Exegesis in the Work of William Blake." *International Journal of Systematic Theology* 7 (2005) 142–54.

———. "A Kingdom, but Not as We Know It." *Ekklesia*, November 20, 2008. http://www.ekklesia.co.uk/node/8020.

———. *Radical Prophet: The Mystics, Subversives and Visionaries who Strove for Heaven on Earth.* London: I. B. Taurus, 2017.

Rowland, Christopher, and Jonathan Roberts. *The Bible for Sinners: Interpretation in the Present Time.* Adelaide: ATF, 2008.

Royal Commission into Institutional Responses to Child Sexual Abuse. *Final Report.* Canberra, ACT, 2017. https://www.childabuseroyalcommission.gov.au/final-report.

Rudd, Kevin. "Faith in Politics." *The Monthly* (October 2006) 22–30.

St Vincent's Health Australia. "St Vincent's and Calvary Offer Medical Support to Asylum Seekers Applying for Church Sanctuary." February 2016. https://www.svha.org.au/newsroom/announcements/st-vincents-and-calvary-offer-medical-support-to-asylum-seekers-applying-for-church-sanctuary.

SBS News. "The Pastor Who Opened His Home to Former Criminals and Drug Addicts." *My Australia*, January 23, 2019. https://www.sbs.com.au/news/my-australia-the-pastor-who-opened-his-home-to-former-criminals-and-drug-addicts.

Scharnschlager, Leupold. "Leupold Scharnschlager's Farewell to the Strasbourg Council." *Mennonite Quarterly Review* 42 (1968) 211–18.

Scheittle, Christopher P. *Beyond the Congregation: The World of Christian Nonprofits.* Oxford: Oxford University Press, 2010.

Scott, James C. *Domination and the Arts of Resistance: Hidden Transcripts.* New Haven, CT: Yale University Press, 1990.

Scrimgeour, Anne. *On Red Earth Walking: The Pilbara Aboriginal Strike, Western Australia 1946–1949.* Clayton: Monash University Publishing, 2020.

Searle, Joshua T. *Theology after Christendom: Forming Prophets for a Post-Christendom World.* Eugene, OR: Cascade, 2018.

Sellwood, Peter. Interview with Douglas Hynd, May 12, 2014.

Shepherd, Andrew. "Facing, Naming and Engaging Violence: Reading Mark 5:1–20 in a Military-Digital Complex Age." *Zadok Papers* S249 (2020) 2–10.

Smith, Daniel L. "Jeremiah as a Prophet of Nonviolent Resistance." *Journal for the Study of the Old Testament* 43 (1989) 95–107.

———. *The Religion of the Landless: The Social Context of the Babylonian Exile.* Eugene, OR: Wipf and Stock, 2015.

Smith, James K. A. *How (Not) to Be Secular: Reading Charles Taylor.* Grand Rapids: Eerdmans, 2014.

———. *Imagining the Kingdom: How Worship Works.* Grand Rapids: Baker Academic, 2013.

Smith-Christopher, Daniel L. *A Biblical Theology of Exile.* Minneapolis: Fortress, 2002.

Bibliography

Snyder, C. Arnold. *Anabaptist History and Theology: An Introduction*. Kitchener, ON: Pandora, 1995.

———. "An Anabaptist Vision for Peace: Spirituality and Peace in Pilgram Marpeck." *Conrad Grebel Review* 10 (1992) 187–203.

Stephens, Ursula. "Mary McKillop: The Authenticity of Speaking Truth to Power." In *Serving Our Communities with Courage and Compassion*, edited by Gabrielle McMullen et al., 37–48. Cleveland, Queensland: ConnorCourt, 2020.

Stevens, Becca. "Living into the Prophetic Voice: Frank William Stringfellow's Greatest Witness." In *Can I Get a Witness? Thirteen Peacemakers, Community Builders, and Agitators for Faith and Justice*, edited by Charles Marsh et al., 177–96. Grand Rapids: Eerdmans, 2019.

Stewart, Melissa. "Meet the Wayside Chapel's New Pastor and CEO." *Insights*, April 5, 2018. https://www.insights.uca.org.au/meet-wayside-chapels-new-pastor-and-ceo/.

Stringfellow, William. *A Second Birthday: A Personal Confrontation with Illness, Pain, and Death*. Eugene, OR: Wipf and Stock, 2005.

———. *An Ethic for Christians and Other Aliens in a Strange Land*. Waco, TX: Word, 1973.

———. *Free in Obedience*. Eugene, OR: Wipf and Stock, 2006.

———. *Instead of Death*. Eugene, OR: Wipf and Stock, 2004.

———. *My People Is the Enemy: An Autobiographical Polemic*. Eugene, OR: Wipf and Stock, 2005.

———. *The Politics of Spirituality*. Eugene, OR: Wipf and Stock, 2006.

Sullivan, Francis. "Margin Call: The Risk of Integrity." In *Serving Our Communities with Courage and Compassion*, edited by Gabrielle McMullen et al., 23–33. Cleveland, Queensland: ConnorCourt, 2020.

Taylor, Charles. *A Secular Age*. Cambridge, MA: Harvard University Press, 2007.

Theophilus. "Asylum Seekers Praying for Change." *The Conversation*, May 14, 2014. http://theconversation.com/asylum-seekers-praying-for-change-26953.

Thomson, Jeremy. *Interpreting the Old Testament after Christendom*. Eugene, OR: Cascade, 2021.

Tomlinson, Matt, and Debra McDougall. *Christian Politics in Oceania*. New York: Bergbahn, 2013.

Treloar, Richard. *Esther and the End of "Final Solutions": Theodicy and Hebrew Biblical Narrative*. Adelaide: ATF, 2008.

Tyson, Paul. "Mr Morrison's ACC address: thoughts on our Pentecostal Prime Minister." *Engage Mail*, May 5, 2021. http://www.ethos.org.au/online-resources/Engage-Mail/mr-morrisons-acc-address.

The Uluru Statement from the Heart. https://ulurustatement.org/the-statement.

UnitingCare Australia. *UnitingCare Australia Mandate*. https://unitingcare.org.au/wp-content/uploads/2019/10/UA-Mandate-ASC-approved-10-Nov-2018.pdf.

Vanstone, Amanda. "Reforming Employment Assistance: Helping Australians into Real Jobs." Ministerial Statement by Senator the Honourable Amanda Vanstone, Minister for Employment, Education, Training and Youth Affairs. Education Employment, Training and Youth Affairs. Canberra, ACT: AGPS, 1996.

Vinson, Tony, et al. *Dropping Off the Edge: The Distribution of Disadvantage in Australia*. Jesuit Social Services, 2015. https://www.vinnies.org.au/icms_docs/222454_Dropping_off_the_edge_report.pdf.

Bibliography

Volf, Miroslav. *Exclusion and Embrace: A Theological Exploration of Identity, Otherness, and Reconciliation*. Nashville: Abingdon, 1996.

———. "Soft Difference: Theological Reflections on the Relation between Church and Culture in 1 Peter." *Ex Auditu* 10 (1994) 15–30.

Walsh, Brian J., and Sylvia C. Keesmaat. *Colossians Remixed: Subverting the Empire*. Downers Grove, IL: InterVarsity, 2004.

Wannenwetsch. *Political Worship*. Oxford: Oxford University Press, 2004.

Walzer, Michael. *In God's Shadow: Politics in the Hebrew Bible*. New Haven, CT: Yale University Press, 2012.

Warhurst, John. Interview with Douglas Hynd, November 7, 2013.

Wayside Chapel. Website. https://www.waysidechapel.org.au/.

———. "Inner Circle." https://www.waysidechapel.org.au/inner-circle/ .

———. "Programs." https://www.waysidechapel.org.au/programs/.

———. "Wayside Stories." https://www.waysidechapel.org.au/waysidestories/.

Weaver, Alain Epp. *States of Exile: Visions of Diaspora, Witness and Return*. Scottdale, PA: Herald, 2008.

Weaver, J. Denny. *Becoming Anabaptist: The Origin and Significance of Sixteenth-Century Anabaptism*. 2d ed. Scottdale, PA: Herald, 2005.

Wells, Samuel. *Power and Passion: Six Characters in Search of Resurrection*. Grand Rapids: Zondervan, 2007.

Whelan, Justin. "Why I prayed for asylum seekers in Scott Morrison's office." *The Guardian*, March 26, 2014. https://www.theguardian.com/commentisfree/2014/mar/27/scott-morrisons-office-asylum-protest.

Wildavsky, Aaron. *Assimilation versus Separation: Joseph the Administrator and the Politics of Religion in Biblical Israel*. New Brunswick, NJ: Transaction, 2009.

Wilson, Lindsay. *Joseph, Wise and Otherwise: The Intersection of Wisdom and Covenant in Genesis 37–50*. Carlisle: Paternoster, 2004.

Winter, Bruce W. *Seek the Welfare of the City: Christians as Benefactors and Citizens*. Grand Rapids: Eerdmans, 1994.

Winton, Tim. *Island Home: A Landscape Memoir*. Melbourne: Penguin Australia, 2015.

Wolterstorff, Nicholas. "Christian Political Reflection: Diognetian or Augustinian." *The Princeton Seminary Bulletin* 20 (1999) 150–68.

www.ingramcontent.com/pod-product-compliance
Lightning Source LLC
Chambersburg PA
CBHW022001220426
43663CB00007B/914